CLIFFS

P9-BJJ-978

California Basic Educational Skills Test

PREPARATION GUIDE

by

Jerry Bobrow, Ph.D.
Peter Z Orton, M.Ed.
William A. Covino, Ph.D.
Howard Horwitz, M.A.
Michael E. Carr, M.A.

Consultants

Harold Nathan, Ph.D.
Rich Michaels, M.A.
Merritt L. Weisinger, J.D.

Cliffs Notes
INCORPORATED

LINCOLN, NEBRASKA   68501

This book is dedicated to the memory of four close friends who devoted their lives to helping with the youth of Fontana, California:

Ron Jeffers
Ellis E. Robbins
Joe DeAugustine
John McGowan

Jerry Bobrow

ISBN 0-8220-2030-0

CONTENTS

Preface ix

Study Guide Checklist x

PART I: INTRODUCTION

FORMAT OF THE EXAMINATION 3

SCORING 3

GENERAL DESCRIPTION.. 3

QUESTIONS COMMONLY ASKED ABOUT THE NEW CBEST
    EXAMINATION 4

TAKING THE CBEST: TWO SUCCESSFUL OVERALL APPROACHES 7

PART II: ANALYSIS OF EXAM AREAS

INTRODUCTION TO THE READING COMPREHENSION SECTION 11
    • Ability Tested • Basic Skills Necessary •
       • Directions • Analysis of Directions •
          • Suggested Approach with Samples •
General Procedure for Answering Reading Comprehension
    Questions 15
The Five Key Questions for Understanding and Interpreting What
    You Read 15
    Main Idea.. 15
    Details 15
    Purpose... 15
    Style and Tone 16
    Difficult or Unusual Words.. 16
A Patterned Plan of Attack 16

INTRODUCTION TO THE MATHEMATICS SECTION 17
    • Ability Tested • Basic Skills Necessary •
       • Directions • Analysis of Directions •
          • Suggested Approach with Samples •

Mark Key Words 18
Pull out Information 20
Plug in Numbers 21
Work from the Answers 22
Approximate 23
Make Comparisons 24
Mark Diagrams 24
Draw Diagrams 28
Procedure Problems 31
Other Sources of Data—Graphs 32
Tips for Working Math Problems 37
A Patterned Plan of Attack 38

INTRODUCTION TO THE ESSAY SECTION 39
• Ability Tested • Basic Skills Necessary •
• Directions • Analysis of Directions •
• Suggested Approach with Samples •
• Some General Tips •
Sample A: Prewriting Methods and Essays 40
    Topic 40
    Clustering 41
    The "Story Formula" 42
    The Finished Essay 42
    Outlining 43
    Additional Finished Essays for Sample A 44
Sample B: Prewriting Methods and Essays 47
    Topic 47
    Clustering 47
    The Finished Essay 48
    The "Why" Essay 49
Poor Essays—What Not to Do 50
    Sample A 50
    Sample B 50
Important Terms Used in Essay Questions 51
    Examples 52
Practice Essay Topics 52
Essay Topic 1 Checklist 54
Essay Topic 2 Checklist 55
A Patterned Plan of Attack 56

PART III: ASSESSMENT MINI-TEST

ANSWER SHEET FOR THE MINI-TEST 59
MINI-TEST 61

Section I: Reading Comprehension 61
Section II: Mathematics 66
Section III: Essay Writing 69
Answer Key for the Mini-Test.. 70
Scoring Your CBEST Mini-Test.. 70
Analyzing Your Test Results.. 70
Mini-Test: Subject Area Analysis Sheet 71
Analysis—Tally Sheet for Questions Missed 71
Mini-Test Essay Checklist... 72

ANSWERS AND COMPLETE EXPLANATIONS FOR THE MINI-TEST 73
Section I: Reading Comprehension 73
Section II: Mathematics 75

PART IV: MATHEMATICS REVIEW

SYMBOLS, TERMINOLOGY, FORMULAS, AND GENERAL MATHEMATICAL
    INFORMATION.. 81
Common Math Symbols and Terms.. 81
Math Formulas 81
Important Equivalents 82
Measures.. 82
Math Words and Phrases 84
Mathematical Properties and Basic Statistics................................ 84
    Some Properties (Axioms) of Addition 84
    Some Properties (Axioms) of Multiplication 85
    A Property of Two Operations... 86
    Some Basic Terms in Statistics.. 86

ARITHMETIC 87
Arithmetic Diagnostic Test 87
    Questions... 87
    Answers... 88
Arithmetic Review 89
    Rounding Off 89
    Place Value 89
    Fractions 90
    Common Fractions and Improper Fractions 90
    Mixed Numbers... 90
    Reducing Fractions 91
    Adding Fractions 91
    Adding Mixed Numbers.. 91
    Subtracting Fractions 92
    Subtracting Mixed Numbers.. 92
    Multiplying Fractions 92

Multiplying Mixed Numbers.. 93
Dividing Fractions 93
Simplifying Fractions 93
Decimals.. 94
Adding and Subtracting Decimals 94
Multiplying Decimals 95
Dividing Decimals... 95
Changing Decimals to Percents... 96
Changing Percents to Decimals... 96
Changing Fractions to Percents... 96
Changing Percents to Fractions... 96
Changing Fractions to Decimals 96
Changing Decimals to Fractions 97
Finding Percent of a Number 97
Other Applications of Percent 97
Finding Percentage Increase or Percentage Decrease................... 98
Prime Numbers.. 98
Arithmetic Mean, or Average 98
Median 99
Mode 99
Squares and Square Roots.. 99
Square Root Rules... 100
Approximating Square Roots 101
Simplifying Square Roots... 101
Signed Numbers (Positive Numbers and Negative Numbers)..... 101
Addition of Signed Numbers.. 102
Subtraction of Signed Numbers... 102
Multiplying and Dividing Signed Numbers 102
Parentheses 103
Order of Operations.. 103

ALGEBRA 104
  Algebra Diagnostic Test 104
    Questions.. 104
    Answers... 104
  Algebra Review 105
    Equations 105
    Understood Multiplying 105
    Literal Equations 106
    Cross Multiplying 106
    Proportions... 106
    Evaluating Expressions 107
    Monomials and Polynomials... 107
    Adding and Subtracting Monomials 107

Multiplying and Dividing Monomials 107
Adding and Subtracting Polynomials 108
Multiplying Polynomials 108
Factoring 108
Inequalities 109

GEOMETRY 110
Geometry Diagnostic Test 110
Questions 110
Answers 114
Geometry Review 117
Lines 117
Angles 118
Types of Angles 119
Types of Lines 122
Polygons 122
Triangles 123
Facts about Triangles 123
Pythagorean Theorem 125
Quadrilaterals 127
Types of Quadrilaterals 127
Other Polygons 129
Facts about Polygons 129
Perimeter 129
Area 129
Circles 131
Parts of a Circle 132
Area and Circumference 133
Volume 134
Surface Area 134

PART IV: PRACTICE-REVIEW-ANALYZE-PRACTICE
Three Full-Length Practice Tests

PRACTICE TEST 1
Answer Sheet for Practice Test 1 141
Section I: Reading Comprehension 143
Section II: Mathematics 158
Section III: Essay Writing 169
Topic 1 169
Topic 2 170
Answer Key for Practice Test 1 171
Scoring Your CBEST Practice Test 1 171
Analyzing Your Test Results 171

Practice Test 1: Subject Area Analysis Sheet 172
Analysis—Tally Sheet for Questions Missed 172
Essay Topic 1 Checklist 173
Essay Topic 2 Checklist 174

ANSWERS AND COMPLETE EXPLANATIONS FOR PRACTICE TEST 1
Section I: Reading Comprehension 177
Section II: Mathematics 181

PRACTICE TEST 2
Answer Sheet for Practice Test 2 193
Section I: Reading Comprehension 195
Section II: Mathematics 213
Section III: Essay Writing 223
  Topic 1 223
  Topic 2 224
Answer Key for Practice Test 2 225
Scoring Your CBEST Practice Test 2 225
Analyzing Your Test Results 225
Practice Test 2: Subject Area Analysis Sheet 226
Analysis—Tally Sheet for Questions Missed 226
Essay Topic 1 Checklist 227
Essay Topic 2 Checklist 228

ANSWERS AND COMPLETE EXPLANATIONS FOR PRACTICE TEST 2
Section I: Reading Comprehension 231
Section II: Mathematics 236

PRACTICE TEST 3
Answer Sheet for Practice Test 3 247
Section I: Reading Comprehension 249
Section II: Mathematics 267
Section III: Essay Writing 277
  Topic 1 277
  Topic 2 278
Answer Key for Practice Test 3 279
Scoring Your CBEST Practice Test 3 279
Analyzing Your Test Results 279
Practice Test 3: Subject Area Analysis Sheet 280
Analysis—Tally Sheet for Questions Missed 280
Essay Topic 1 Checklist 281
Essay Topic 2 Checklist 282

ANSWERS AND COMPLETE EXPLANATIONS FOR PRACTICE TEST 3
Section I: Reading Comprehension 285
Section II: Mathematics 290

Final Preparation: "The Final Touches" 299

PREFACE

We know that getting a good score on the CBEST is important to you. Because the CBEST requires you to use some basic skills that you may not have used in many years, thorough preparation is the key to doing your best. This makes your study time more important than ever. Therefore it must be used most effectively.

Leading test preparation experts and instructors have developed this *Cliffs CBEST Preparation Guide*. It is thorough, direct, concise, and easy to use. The materials, techniques, and strategies presented here have been carefully researched, tested, and evaluated. They are presently used at CBEST preparation programs throughout California in colleges, universities, and teachers' associations.

This guide is divided into five parts:

PART I: Introduction—a general description of the exam, recent format, questions commonly asked, and basic overall strategies.

PART II: Analysis of Exam Areas—focuses on ability tested, basic skills necessary, directions, analysis, suggested approaches with samples, and additional tips.

PART III: Assessment Mini-Test—a short Mini-Test to familiarize you with the various tests and to assess your strengths and weaknesses.

PART IV: Mathematics Review—a short yet intensive review in basics of arithmetic, algebra, and intuitive geometry, with diagnostic tests in each area. Important terminology is also included.

PART V: Practice-Review-Analyze-Practice—three complete, full-length practice tests with answers and in-depth explanations.

The Mini-Test and each practice test are followed by analysis charts to assist you in evaluating your progress. This guide is not meant to substitute for comprehensive courses, but if you follow the Study Guide Checklist and study regularly, you'll get the best CBEST preparation possible.

STUDY GUIDE CHECKLIST

_____ 1. Read the CBEST information materials available at the Testing Office, Counseling Center, or Credentials Office at your undergraduate institution.

_____ 2. Become familiar with the Test Format, page 3.

_____ 3. Read the General Description and Questions Commonly Asked about the New CBEST, starting on page 3.

_____ 4. Learn the techniques of Two Successful Overall Approaches, page 7.

_____ 5. Carefully read Part II, Analysis of Exam Areas, starting on page 11.

_____ 6. Take the Mini-Test, starting on page 59.

_____ 7. Check your answers and analyze your results, starting on page 70.

_____ 8. Fill out the Tally Sheet for Questions Missed to pinpoint your mistakes, page 71.

_____ 9. Review Mathematical Terminology, starting on page 81.

_____ 10. Take the Arithmetic Diagnostic Test, starting on page 87, check your answers, and review the appropriate areas in the Arithmetic Review.

_____ 11. Take the Algebra Diagnostic Test, starting on page 104, check your answers, and review the appropriate areas in the Algebra Review.

_____ 12. Take the Geometry Diagnostic Test, starting on page 110, check your answers, and review the appropriate areas in the Geometry Review.

_____ 13. Strictly observing time allotments, take Practice Test 1, starting on page 141.

_____ 14. Check your answers and analyze your Practice Test 1 results, starting on page 171.

_____ 15. Fill out the Tally Sheet for Questions Missed to pinpoint your mistakes, page 172.

_____ 16. Study ALL the Answers and Complete Explanations to Practice Test 1, starting on page 177.

_____ 17. Have a friend or English instructor read and evaluate your essays using the Essay Checklists, pages 173 and 174.

_____ 18. Review weak areas as necessary.

_____ 19. Strictly observing time allotments, take Practice Test 2, starting on page 193.

_____ 20. Check your answers and analyze your Practice Test 2 results, starting on page 225.

_____ 21. Fill out the Tally Sheet for Questions Missed to pinpoint your mistakes, page 226.

_____ 22. Study ALL the Answers and Complete Explanations to Practice Test 2, starting on page 231.

_____ 23. Have a friend or English instructor read and evaluate your essays using the Essay Checklists, pages 227 and 228.

_____ 24. Review weak areas as necessary.

_____ 25. Strictly observing time allotments, take Practice Test 3, starting on page 247.

_____ 26. Check your answers and analyze your Practice Test 3 results, starting on page 279.

_____ 27. Fill out the Tally Sheet for Questions Missed to pinpoint your mistakes, page 280.

_____ 28. Study ALL the Answers and Complete Explanations to Practice Test 3, starting on page 285.

_____ 29. Have a friend or English instructor read and evaluate your essays using the Essay Checklists, pages 281 and 282.

_____ 30. Review weak areas as necessary.

_____ 31. Review Analysis of Exam Areas, starting on page 11.

_____ 32. Carefully read Final Preparation: "The Final Touches," page 299.

PART I: Introduction

CBEST
CALIFORNIA BASIC EDUCATIONAL SKILLS TEST

Format of the Examination

Reading Comprehension	65 Minutes	Approximately 50 Questions
Mathematics	70 Minutes	Approximately 50 Questions
	—Short Break—	
Essay Writing	60 Minutes	2 Topics

Scoring

All questions (except essays) are multiple choice—five answer choices. Scoring on each section is from 20 to 80, as follows:

61–80 Superior
42–60 Average
37–41 Marginal Performance
20–36 Needs Improvement

A total of 123 (all three sections combined) is necessary to pass, with a *minimum of 37* on each individual section.

NOTE: Since the test is new, format and scoring are subject to change.

GENERAL DESCRIPTION

The CBEST measures proficiencies in three general areas: reading, mathematics, and writing. The test is based upon the theory that teachers should be able to use those same skills that are taught to students and that are essential to students both in the classroom and outside school.

One score is provided for each of the three areas. Scores range from approximately 20 to 80 in each area.

QUESTIONS COMMONLY ASKED ABOUT THE NEW CBEST EXAMINATION

Q: WHO ADMINISTERS THE CBEST?

A: The CBEST is administered by Educational Testing Service (ETS) with guidelines drawn up by the California Superintendent of Public Instruction with the assistance of the Commission for Teacher Preparation and Licensing (CPTL) and an advisory board.

Q: WHO NEEDS TO PASS THE CBEST?

A: The CBEST is typically required for initial issuance of a credential. It may also be required for issuance of a permit, certificate, authorization, administrative credential, or renewal of emergency credential. You may need to take the exam if you have not been employed in teaching for more than thirty-nine months. IT IS IMPORTANT THAT YOU CHECK WITH YOUR STATE'S DEPARTMENT OF EDUCATION TO SEE IF YOU MUST TAKE THE TEST.

Q: DO I NEED THE CBEST FOR STUDENT TEACHING?

A: Some universities will require it. Check with the appropriate department or credentials office.

Q: WHEN AND WHERE IS THE CBEST GIVEN?

A: The CBEST is administered statewide six times each year. You can get dates and test locations by contacting Educational Testing Service (ETS) or CBEST Program, P.O. Box 1904, Berkeley, CA 94701—(415) 849-0950.

Q: DO I HAVE TO PAY AGAIN IF I REPEAT THE TEST?

A: You must pay the test fee each time you register to take the CBEST. In addition, if you register after the regular deadline but before the late registration deadline, an additional fee will be charged. Check with the registration center to be sure of current fees.

Q: WHAT MATERIALS SHOULD I TAKE TO THE TEST?

A: Be sure to take with you your admission ticket, some form of photo and signature identification, several Number 2 soft lead pencils with good erasers, a ballpoint pen for the essay section, and a watch to help pace yourself during the exam. No calculators, slide rules, or other aids will be permitted in the test center.

Q: WHAT IS ON THE CBEST?

A: The exam consists of three parts: 70 minutes of math multiple-choice questions; 65 minutes of reading comprehension multiple-choice questions; and 60 minutes to write two essays.

Q: WHAT IS A PASSING SCORE?

A: The total passing score, as established by the Superintendent of Public Instruction, is a total of 123 on all three sections combined and a minimum of 37 on each of the sections.

Q: WHEN WILL I GET MY SCORE REPORT?

A: Your test score will be mailed to you about four weeks after you take the CBEST. If you pass you will also receive a Permanent Verification Card and two transcript copies of this card to use as may be required. No additional transcripts will be provided to school districts or universities. You may, however, receive additional sets of transcript copies for a small fee.

Q: MAY I TAKE THE CBEST MORE THAN ONCE?

A: Yes. But remember, your plan is to pass on your *first* try.

Q: DO I NEED TO TAKE ALL THREE PARTS OF THE TEST?

A: You must *pass* all three parts of the test. However, if you previously have passed any part of the exam at one administration, you may then take only the sections you have not as yet passed. Thus you do not have to pass *all* sections in one examination; you can achieve a total passing score in separate administrations.

Q: SHOULD I GUESS ON THE TEST?

A: Yes! Since there is no penalty for guessing, GUESS if you have to. If possible, first try to eliminate some of the choices to increase your chances of choosing the right answer. But don't leave any of the answer spaces blank.

Q: SUPPOSE I DO TERRIBLY ON THE TEST. MAY I CANCEL MY CBEST SCORE?

A: Yes, you may cancel your CBEST score, but only if you notify the test supervisor *before* leaving the test center after you take the test. However, since no one will know your score except you, there is no reason to cancel, as no refund will be given.

Q: MAY I WRITE ON THE TEST?

A: Yes! As scratch paper will not be provided, you *must* do all of your work *in* the test booklet. Your answer sheet, however, must have no marks on it other than your personal information (name, registration number, etc.) and your answers.

Q: HOW SHOULD I PREPARE?

A: Understanding and practicing test-taking strategies will help a great deal. Subject matter review in arithmetic, simple algebra, and plane geometry is also invaluable. Some teachers' unions and universities offer preparation programs to assist you in attaining a passing score. Check with them for further information.

Q: WHAT IF I NEED TO CHANGE MY TEST DATE OR TEST CENTER?
A: Write or call CBEST Program, P.O. Box 1904, Berkeley, CA 94701— (415) 849-0950.

Q: HOW DO I REGISTER OR GET MORE INFORMATION?
A: Information is available from the Credential Preparation Office or from the CBEST Program, P.O. Box 1904, Berkeley, CA 94701—(415) 849-0950.

TAKING THE CBEST:
TWO SUCCESSFUL OVERALL APPROACHES

I. The "Plus-Minus" System

Many who take the CBEST don't get their best possible score because they spend too much time on difficult questions, leaving insufficient time to answer the easy questions. Don't let this happen to you. Since every question within each section is worth the same amount, use the following system.

1. Answer easy questions immediately.

2. When you come to a question that seems "impossible" to answer, mark a large minus sign ("−") next to it on your test booklet.

3. Then mark a "guess" answer on your answer sheet and move on to the next question.

4. When you come to a question that seems solvable but appears too time consuming, mark a large plus sign ("+") next to that question in your test booklet and register a guess answer on your answer sheet. Then move on to the next question.

Since your time allotment is just over one minute per question, a "time-consuming" question is a question that you estimate will take you more than several minutes to answer. But don't waste time deciding whether a question is a "+" or a "−." Act quickly, as the intent of this strategy is, in fact, to save you valuable time.

After working all the easy questions, your booklet should look something like this:

$$
\begin{array}{r}
1. \\
+\ 2. \\
3. \\
-\ 4. \\
+\ 5. \\
\text{etc.}
\end{array}
$$

5. After working all the problems you can do immediately in that section (the easy ones), go back and work your "+" problems. Change your "guess" on your answer sheet, if necessary, for those problems you are able to work.

6. If you finish working your "+" problems and still have time left, you can either

(A) attempt those "−" questions—the ones that you considered "impossible." Sometimes a problem later in that section will "trigger" your memory and you'll be able to go back and answer one of the earlier "impossible" problems.

or

(B) don't bother with those "impossible" questions. Rather, spend your time reviewing your work to be sure you didn't make any careless mistakes on the questions you thought were easy to answer.

REMEMBER: You do not have to erase the pluses and minuses you made on your *question booklet*. And be sure to fill in all your answer spaces—if necessary, with a guess. As there is no penalty for wrong answers, it makes no sense to leave an answer space blank. And, of course, remember that you may work only in one section of the test at a time.

II. The Elimination Strategy

Take advantage of being allowed to mark in your testing booklet. As you eliminate an answer choice from consideration, make sure to *mark it out in your question booklet* as follows:

(A)
?(B)
(C)
(D)
?(E)

Notice that some choices are marked with question marks, signifying that they may be possible answers. This technique will help you avoid reconsidering those choices you have already eliminated. It will also help you narrow down your possible answers.

Again, these marks you make on your testing booklet do not need to be erased.

PART II: Analysis of Exam Areas

This section is designed to introduce you to each area of the CBEST by carefully reviewing

1. Ability Tested
2. Basic Skills Necessary
3. Directions
4. Analysis of Directions
5. Suggested Approach with Samples

This section emphasizes important test-taking techniques and strategies and how to apply them to a variety of problem types. Sample essays are also included in this section as a guideline to assist students in evaluating their own essays and to point out some of the common errors in essay writing.

INTRODUCTION TO THE READING COMPREHENSION SECTION

The Reading Comprehension section is 65 minutes long and usually contains 50 questions (10 of which will be experimental, will not count toward your score, and may be scattered throughout the test). It consists of passages of approximately 200 words, shorter passages of approximately 100 words, short statements of one or more sentences, and graphic materials such as tables and charts. Each passage or statement is followed by questions based on its content.

Ability Tested

This section tests your ability to understand the content of the passages and any of the following: its main idea, supporting ideas, specific details, the author's purpose, the author's assumptions, the author's tone, strengths and weaknesses of the author's argument, inferences drawn from the passage, the relationship of the passage to its intended audience, supporting evidence in the passage, etc.

No outside knowledge is necessary; all questions can be answered on the basis of what is stated or implied in the passage.

Basic Skills Necessary

Understanding, interpreting, and analyzing passages are the important skills for this section. The technique of *actively* reading and marking a passage is also helpful.

Directions

A question or number of questions follow each of the statements or passages in this section. Using only the *stated* or *implied* information given in the statement or passage, answer the question or questions by choosing the *best* answer from among the five choices given.

Analysis of Directions

1. Answer all the questions for one passage before moving on to the next one. If you don't know the answer, take an educated guess or skip it.

2. Use only the information given or implied in a passage. Do not consider outside information, even if it seems more accurate than the given information.

Suggested Approach With Short Sample Passage

Two strategies that will improve your reading comprehension are *prereading the questions* and *marking the passage*. Readers who use these strategies tend to score much higher on reading tests than readers who don't.

Prereading the questions. Before reading the passage, read each question (but don't spend time reading all the multiple-choice answers) and circle the most important word or phrase. *Sample:*

The author's argument in favor of freedom of speech may be summarized in which of the following ways?
(A) If every speaker is not free, no speaker is.
(B) Speech keeps us free from the animal kingdom.
(C) As we think, so we speak.
(D) The Bill of Rights ensures free speech.
(E) Lunatic speeches are not free speeches.

The most *important* part is usually the most concrete and specific one. In this case, you might circle "freedom of speech." The question parts that you circle will be those you'll tend to remember when you read the passage. In this case, you would be likely to notice and pay close attention to "freedom of speech" when it occurs in the passage. Thus, prereading allows you to focus on the parts of the passage that contain the answers.

Marking the passage. After prereading the questions, read and mark the passage. *Always mark those spots that contain information relevant to the questions you've read. In addition, you should mark other important ideas and details.* More specific advice on marking, in reference to specific subareas of reading skills, follows. In general though, *remember not to overmark;* never make more than a few marks per paragraph in order to make those parts that you mark stand out.

Passage

*By the time a child starts school, he has mastered the major part of the rules of his grammar. He has managed to accomplish this remarkable feat in such a short time by experimenting with and generalizing the rules all by himself. Each child, in effect, rediscovers language in the first few years of his life.

*When it comes to vocabulary growth, it is a different story. Unlike grammar, the chief means through which vocabulary is learned is memorization.*And some people have a hard time learning and remembering new words.

*—Indicates portions of the passage which refer directly to a question you've skimmed. Also marked are main points and key terms.

1. A child has (mastered) many (rules of grammar by) about the age of
   (A) 3   (D) 10
   (B) 5   (E) 18
   (C) 8

The first sentence of the passage contains several words from this question, so it is likely to contain the correct answer. "By the time a child starts school" tells us that the answer is 5. Before choosing (B), you should look at all the answers and cross out those which seem incorrect.

2. Although vocabulary growth involves memorization and grammar learning doesn't, we may conclude that (both vocabulary and grammar make use of)
   (A) memorization   (D) children
   (B) study skills   (E) teachers
   (C) words

The question asks you to simply use your common sense. (A) is incorrect; it contradicts both the passage and the question itself. (D) and (E) make no sense. (B) is a possibility, but (C) is better, because grammar learning in young children does not necessarily involve study ideas, but does involve words.

3. The (last sentence) in the passage implies that
   (A) some people have no trouble learning and remembering new words
   (B) some people have a hard time remembering new words
   (C) grammar does not involve remembering words
   (D) old words are not often remembered
   (E) learning and remembering are kinds of growth

Implies tells us that the answer is something suggested, but not explicitly stated in the passage. (B) is explicitly stated in the passage, so it may be eliminated. But (B) implies the opposite: if *some* people have a hard time, then it must be true that *some* people don't. (A) is therefore the correct choice. (C), (D), and (E) are altogether apart from the meaning of the last sentence.

Another Short Sample Passage

St. Augustine was a contemporary of Jerome. After an early life of pleasure, he became interested in a philosophical religion called Manichaeism, a derivative of a Persian religion, in which the (forces of good) constantly struggle with those of (evil.) Augustine was eventually converted to Christianity by St. Ambrose of Milan. His (*Confessions*) was an autobiography that served as an inspiration to countless of thousands who believed that virtue would ultimately win.

1. St. Augustine's conversion to Christianity was probably influenced by
    (A) his confessional leanings
    (B) his contemporaries
    (C) the inadequacy of a Persian religion to address Western moral problems
    (D) his earlier interest in the dilemma of retaining virtue
    (E) the ravages of a life of pleasure

Having skimmed this question, you should have marked the portion of the passage which mentions Augustine's conversion and paid attention to the events (influences) leading to it. (A) requires speculating beyond the facts in the paragraph; there is also no evidence in the passage to support (C) or (E). (B) is too vague and general to be the best answer. (D) points toward Augustine's earlier interest in Manichaeism, and the last sentence suggests that Augustine's interest in retaining virtue continued through his Christian doctrine. Well supported as it is, (D) is the best answer.

2. From the information in the passage, we must conclude that Augustine was a
    (A) fair-weather optimist   (D) failed optimist
    (B) cockeyed optimist   (E) glib optimist
    (C) hardworking optimist

Skimming *this* question is not very helpful; it does not point specifically to any information in the passage. Questions of this sort usually assess your overall understanding of the meaning, style, tone, or point of view of the passage. In this case, you should recognize that Augustine is a serious person; therefore, more lighthearted terms like *fair-weather* (A), *cock-eyed* (B), and *glib* (E) are probably inappropriate. (D) contradicts Augustine's success as an "inspiration to countless thousands." (C) corresponds with his ongoing, hopeful struggle to retain virtue in the world; it is the best answer.

3. Judging from the reaction of thousands to Augustine's *Confessions,* we may conclude that much of his world at that time was in a state of
    (A) opulence   (D) reformation
    (B) misery   (E) sanctification
    (C) heresy

Having skimmed this question, you should have marked the last sentence of the passage as the place to look for the answer. That Augustine's readers were inspired implies that they *required inspiration,* that they were in some sort of uninspiring, or *negative* situation. (A) and (E) must therefore be eliminated because they are positive terms. (D) is not necessarily a negative term, and so is probably not the best answer. (C), although a negative term, does not describe a state of being which thirsts for inspiration. (B) does, and (B) therefore is the best choice.

GENERAL PROCEDURE FOR ANSWERING READING COMPREHENSION QUESTIONS

1. *Skim the questions,* circling the word or phrase that stands out in each question. *Don't* read the answer choices.

2. *Read and mark the passage,* paying special attention to information relevant to the questions you've skimmed.

3. *Answer the questions.* Base your answers *only on the material given in the passage.* Assume that the information in each passage is accurate. The questions test your understanding of the passage alone; they do *not* test the historical background of the passage, the biography of the author, or previous familiarity with the work from which the passage is taken.

THE FIVE KEY QUESTIONS FOR UNDERSTANDING AND INTERPRETING WHAT YOU READ

Main Idea

What is the main idea of the passage? After reading any passage, try summarizing it in a brief sentence. To practice this very important skill, read the editorials in your local paper each day and *write* a brief sentence summarizing each one.

Details

What details support the main idea? Usually such details are facts, statistics, experiences, etc., that strengthen your understanding of and agreement with the main idea.

Purpose

What is the purpose of the passage? Ask yourself what the author is trying to accomplish. The four general purposes are (1) to narrate (tell a story), (2) to describe, (3) to inform, and (4) to persuade.

Style and Tone

Are the style and tone of the passage objective or subjective? In other words, is the author presenting things *factually* or from a *personal point of view?* If an author is subjective, you might want to pin down the nature of the subjectivity. Ask yourself, is the author optimistic? pessimistic? angry? humorous? serious?

Difficult or Unusual Words

What are the difficult or unusual words in the passage? Readers who do not *mark* words that are difficult or used in an unusual way in a passage often forget that the words occurred at all and have difficulty locating them if this becomes necessary. By calling your attention to difficult or unusual words you increase your chances of defining them by understanding their meaning in context.

A PATTERNED PLAN OF ATTACK

Reading Comprehension

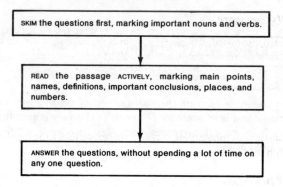

INTRODUCTION TO THE MATHEMATICS SECTION

The mathematics section of the test is 70 minutes long and usually contains 50 questions (10 of which will be experimental, will not count toward your score, and may be scattered throughout the test). The questions are selected from different areas of mathematics (for instance: measurement, ratio, percent, diagram reading, and interpreting formulas). Complex computation is not required, and most of the terms used are general, commonly encountered mathematical expressions (for instance: area, perimeter, integer, and prime number).

Ability Tested

This part of the exam tests your ability to use your cumulative knowledge of mathematics and your reasoning ability. Computation is minimal; you are not required to have memorized many specific formulas or equations. A general working understanding of math concepts that *any* teacher may need is most important—averaging grades, reading charts and graphs, understanding diagrams that could appear in class, interpreting test results, etc.

Basic Skills Necessary

A cumulative knowledge of mathematics is necessary for this section of the CBEST—from elementary grades through at least one year in high school, and possibly one year in college. Thus, no single course specifically prepares examinees for this part of the test.

Directions

In the questions or incomplete statements below, select the one *best* answer or completion of the five choices given.

Analysis of Directions

You have 70 minutes to do 50 problems. This averages to just over one minute per problem. Keep that in mind as you attack each problem. Even if you know you can work a problem but that it will take you far, far longer than one minute, you should skip it and return to it later if you have time. Remember, you want to do all the easy, quick problems first, before spending valuable time on the others.

There is no penalty for guessing, so you should not leave any blanks. If you do not know the answer to a problem but you can size it up to get a general range for your answer, you may be able to eliminate one or more of the answer choices. This will increase your odds of guessing the correct answer. But even if you cannot eliminate any of the possible choices, take a guess because there is no penalty for wrong answers.

Above all, be sure that your answers on your answer sheet correspond to the proper numbers on your question sheet. Placing one answer in the incorrect number on the answer sheet could possibly shift *all* your answers to the incorrect spots. Be careful of this!

SUGGESTED APPROACH WITH SAMPLES

Here are a number of different approaches which can be helpful in attacking many types of mathematics problems. Of course, these strategies will not work on *all* the problems, but if you become familiar with them, you'll find they'll be helpful in answering quite a few questions.

Mark Key Words

Circling and/or underlining key words in each question is an effective test-taking technique. Many times you may be misled because you may overlook a key word in a problem. By circling or underlining these key words, you'll help yourself focus on what you are being asked to find. Remember, you are allowed to mark and write on your testing booklet. Take advantage of this opportunity. *For example:*

1. In the following number, which digit is in the thousandths place?

6574.12398

(A) 2   (B) 3   (C) 5   (D) 7   (E) 9

The key words here is *thousandths*. By circling it you will be paying closer attention to it. This is the kind of question which, under time pressure and testing pressure, may often be misread. It may be easily misread as *thousands* place. Hopefully your circling the important words will minimize the possibility of misreading. Your completed question may look like this after you mark the important words or terms:

1. Which (digit) is in the (thousandths) place?

6574.12(3)98

(A) 2   (B) 3   (C) 5   (D) 7   (E) 9

Here's another example:

2. If 3 yards of ribbon cost $2.97, what is the price per foot?
   (A) $.33   (B) $.99   (C) $2.94   (D) $3.00   (E) $8.91

The key word here is *foot*. Dividing $2.97 by 3 will tell you only the price per *yard*. Notice that $.99 is one of the choices, (B). You must still divide by 3 (since there are 3 feet per yard) to find the cost per foot, $.99 divided by 3 is $.33, which is choice (A). Therefore it would be very helpful to circle the words *price per foot* in the problem.

And another example:

3. If $3x + 1 = 16$, what is the value of $x - 4$?
   (A) 19   (B) 16   (C) 5   (D) 1   (E) -1

The key here is *find the value of x − 4*. Therefore circle $x - 4$. Note that solving the original equation will tell only the value of x:

$$3x + 1 = 16$$
$$3x = 15$$
$$x = 5$$

Here again notice that 5 is one of the choices, (C). But the question asks for the value of $x - 4$, not just x. To continue, replace x with 5 and solve:

$$x - 4 =$$
$$5 - 4 = 1$$

The correct answer choice is (D).

And one more example:

4. Together a bat and ball cost $1.25. The bat costs $.25 more than the ball. What is the cost of the bat?
   (A) $.25   (B) $.50   (C) $.75   (D) $1.00   (E) $1.25

The key words here are *cost of the bat*, so circle those words. If we solve this algebraically:

x = ball
x + .25 = bat (cost $.25 more than the ball)
Together they cost $1.25

$$(x + .25) + x = 1.25$$
$$2x + .25 = 1.25$$
$$2x = 1.00$$
$$x = .50$$

But this is the cost of the *ball*. Notice that $.50 is one of the choices, (B). Since x = .50, then x + .25 = .75. Therefore, the bat costs $.75, which is choice (C). *Always answer the question that is being asked.* Circling the key word or words will help you do that.

Pull out Information

Pulling information out of the wording of a word problem can make the problem more workable for you. Pull out the given facts and identify which of those facts will help you to work the problem. Not all facts will always be needed to work out the problem. *For example:*

1. Bill is 10 years older than his sister. If Bill was 25 years of age in 1983, in what year could he have been born?
    (A) 1948   (B) 1953   (C) 1958   (D) 1963   (E) 1968

The key words here are *in what year* and *could he have been born*. Thus the solution is simple: 1983 − 25 = 1958, answer (C). Notice that you pulled out the information *25 years of age* and *in 1983*. The fact about Bill's age in comparison to his sister's age was not needed, however, and was not pulled out.

Another example:

2. John is 18 years old. He works for his father for ¾ of the year, and he works for his brother for the rest of the year. What is the ratio of the time John spends working for his brother to the time he spends working for his father per year?
    (A) ¼   (B) ⅓   (C) ¾   (D) 4/3   (E) 4/1

The key word *rest* points to the answer:

$1 - \frac{3}{4} =$

$\frac{4}{4} - \frac{3}{4} = \frac{1}{4}$ (the part of the year John works for his brother)

Also, a key idea is the way in which the ratio is to be written. The problem becomes that of finding the ratio of ¼ to ¾.

$$\frac{\frac{1}{4}}{\frac{3}{4}} = \frac{1}{4} \div \frac{3}{4} = \frac{1}{\cancel{4}} \times \frac{\cancel{4}^{1}}{3} = \frac{1}{3}$$

Therefore the answer is choice (B). Note that here John's age is not needed to solve the problem.

Sometimes you may not have sufficient information to solve the problem. *For instance:*

3. A woman purchased several skirts at $15 each plus one more for $12.
   What was the average price of each skirt?
   (A) $12   (D) $15
   (B) $13   (E) not enough information
   (C) $14

To calculate an average, you must have the total amount and then divide by
the number of items. The difficulty here, however, is that *several skirts at
$15* does not specify exactly *how many* skirts were purchased at $15 each.
Does *several* mean two? Or does it mean three? *Several* is not a precise
mathematical term. Therefore there is not enough information to pull out to
calculate an average. The answer is (E).

Plug in Numbers

When a problem involving variables (unknowns, or letters) seems difficult
and confusing, simply replace those variables with numbers. Simple numbers
will make the arithmetic easier for you to do. Usually problems using
numbers are easier to understand. Be sure to make logical substitutions. Use
a positive number, a negative number, or zero when applicable to get the full
picture. *For example:*

1. If x is a positive integer in the equation 2x = y, then y must be
   (A) a positive even integer
   (B) a negative even integer
   (C) zero
   (D) a positive odd integer
   (E) a negative odd integer

At first glance this problem appears quite complex. But let's plug in some
numbers and see what happens. For instance, first plug in 1 (the simplest
positive integer) for x:

$$2x = y$$
$$2(1) = y$$
$$2 = y$$

Now try 2:

$$2x = y$$
$$2(2) = y$$
$$4 = y$$

Try it again. No matter what positive integer is plugged in for x, y will always
be positive and even. Therefore the answer is (A).

Another example:

2. If a, b, and c are all positive whole numbers greater than 1 such that a <
   b < c, which of the following is the largest quantity?
   (A) a(b + c)   (D) they are all equal
   (B) ab + c   (E) cannot be determined
   (C) ac + b

Substitute 2, 3, and 4 for a, b, and c, respectively.

a(b + c) =	ab + c =	ac + b =
2(3 + 4) =	2(3) + 4 =	2(4) + 3 =
2(7) = 14	6 + 4 = 10	8 + 3 = 11

Since 2, 3, and 4 meet the conditions stated in the problem and choice (A)
produces the largest numerical value, it will consistently be the largest
quantity. Therefore, a(b + c) is the correct answer, (A).

Work from the Answers

At times the solution to a problem will be obvious to you. At other times it
may be helpful to work from the answers. If a direct approach is not obvious
to you, try working from the answers. This technique is even more efficient
when some of the answer choices are easily eliminated. *For example:*

1. Barney can mow the lawn in 5 hours, and Fred can mow the lawn in 4
   hours. How long will it take them to mow the lawn together?
   (A) 8 hours   (D) 4 hours
   (B) 5 hours   (E) 2⅖ hours
   (C) 4½ hours

You may never have worked a problem like this, or perhaps you have worked
one but do not remember the procedure required to find the answer. If this is
the case, try working from the answers. Since Fred can now mow the lawn in
4 hours by himself, it will take less than 4 hours if Barney helps him.
Therefore choices (A), (B), (C), and (D) are ridiculous. Thus the correct
answer—by working from the answers and eliminating the incorrect ones—is
(E).

Another example:

2. Find the counting number that is less than 15 and when divided by 3 has a
   remainder of 1, but when divided by 4 has a remainder of 2.
   (A) 5   (B) 8   (C) 10   (D) 12   (E) 13

By working from the answers, you can eliminate wrong answer choices. For instance, (B) and (D) can be immediately eliminated because they are divisible by 4, leaving no remainder. Choices (A) and (E) can also be eliminated because they leave a remainder of 1 when divided by 4. Therefore the correct answer is (C): 10 leaves a remainder of 1 when divided by 3 and a remainder of 2 when divided by 4.

Approximate

If a problem involves calculations with numbers that seem tedious and time consuming, round off or approximate those numbers. Replace those numbers with whole numbers that are easier to work with. Find the answer choice that is closest to your approximated answer. *For example:*

1. The value for $(.889 \times 55)/9.97$ to the nearest tenth is
   (A) 49.1   (B) 17.7   (C) 4.9   (D) 4.63   (E) .5

Before starting any computations, take a glance at the answers to see how far apart they are. Notice that the only close answers are (C) and (D), but (D) is not a possible choice, since it is to the nearest hundredth, not tenth. Now making some quick approximations, $.889 \approx 1$ and $9.97 \approx 10$, leaving the problem in this form:

$$\frac{1 \times 55}{10} = \frac{55}{10} = 5.5$$

The closet answer is (C); therefore it is the correct answer. Notice that choices (A) and (E) are not reasonable.

Or:

2. The value of $\sqrt{7194/187}$ is approximately
   (A) 6   (B) 9   (C) 18   (D) 35   (E) 72

Round off both numbers to the hundreds place. The problem then becomes:

$$\sqrt{\frac{7200}{200}}$$

This is much easier to work. By dividing, the problem now becomes:

$$\sqrt{36} =$$

$$= 6$$

The closest answer choice is the exact value of choice (A).

Make Comparisons

At times, questions will require you to compare the sizes of several decimals, or of several fractions. If decimals are being compared, make sure that the numbers being compared have the same number of digits. (Remember: Zeros to the far right of a decimal point can be inserted or eliminated without changing the value of the number.)

For example:

1. Put these in order from smallest to largest: .6, .16, .66⅔, .58
   - (A) .6, .16, .66⅔, .58
   - (B) .58, .16, .6, .66⅔
   - (C) .16, .58, .6, .66⅔
   - (D) .66⅔, .6, .58, .16
   - (E) .58, .6, .66⅔, .16

Rewrite .6 as .60; therefore all of the decimals now have the same number of digits: .60, .16, .66⅔, .58. Treating these as though the decimal point were not there (this can be done only when all the numbers have the same number of digits to the right of the decimal), the order is as follows: .16, .58, .60, .66⅔. The correct answer is (C). Remember to circle *smallest to largest* in the question.

2. Put these in order from smallest to largest: ⅝, ¾, ⅔
   - (A) ⅔, ¾, ⅝
   - (B) ⅔, ⅝, ¾
   - (C) ⅝, ⅔, ¾
   - (D) ¾, ⅝, ⅔
   - (E) ¾, ⅔, ⅝

Using common denominators, we find: $⅝ = {}^{15}/_{24}$, $¾ = {}^{18}/_{24}$, and $⅔ = {}^{16}/_{24}$.

Therefore the order becomes: ⅝, ⅔, ¾.

Using decimal equivalents: $5/8 = .625$
$$3/4 = .75 \text{ or } .750$$
$$2/3 = .66⅔ \text{ or } .666⅔$$

The order again becomes: ⅝, ⅔, ¾. The answer is (C).

Mark Diagrams

When a figure is included with the problem, mark the given facts on the diagram. This will help you visualize all the facts that have been given. *For example:*

1. If each square in the figure
   has a side of length 1,
   what is the perimeter?
   (A) 8
   (B) 12
   (C) 14
   (D) 16
   (E) 20

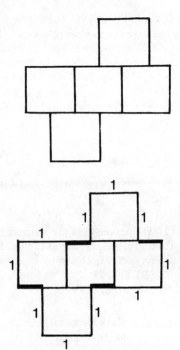

Mark the known facts:

We now have a calculation for the perimeter: 10 *plus* the darkened parts.
Now look carefully at the top two darkened parts. They will add up to 1.
(Notice how the top square may slide over to illustrate that fact.)

These together total 1

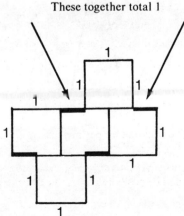

The same is true for the bottom
darkened parts. They will add to 1.
Thus, the total perimeter is 10 + 2,
or 12, choice (B).

$\triangle$ ABC is isosceles

$\overline{AB} = \overline{AC}$

2. The perimeter of the isosceles triangle is 42″. The two equal sides are each three times as long as the third side. What are the lengths of each side?

(A) 21, 21, 21   (D) 18, 18, 6

(B) 6, 6, 18   (E) 4, 19, 19

(C) 18, 21, 3

Mark the equal sides on the diagram:

$\overline{AB}$ and $\overline{AC}$ are each three times as long as $\overline{BC}$:

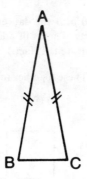

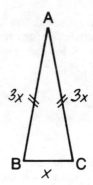

The equation for perimeter is:

$$3x + 3x + x = 42$$
$$7x = 42$$
$$x = 6$$

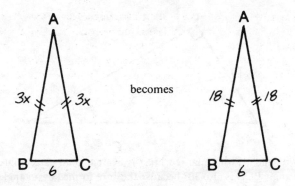

becomes

The answer is (D). NOTE: This problem could have been solved by working from the answers given.

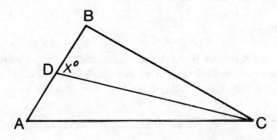

3. In the triangle above, CD is an angle bisector, angle ACD is 30°, and angle ABC is a right angle. What is the measurement of angle x in degrees?

(A) 30°   (D) 75°
(B) 45°   (E) 180°
(C) 60°

You should have read the problem and marked as follows:

In the triangle above, CD is an angle bisector (STOP AND MARK IN THE DRAWING), angle ACD is 30° (STOP AND MARK IN THE DRAWING), and angle ABC is a right angle (STOP AND MARK IN THE DRAWING). What is the measurement of angle x in degrees? (STOP AND MARK IN OR CIRCLE WHAT YOU ARE LOOKING FOR IN THE DRAWING.)

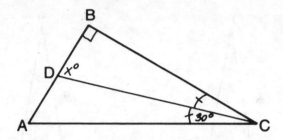

Now with the drawing marked in, it is evident that, since angle ACD is 30°, then angle BCD is also 30° because they are formed by an angle bisector (divides an angle into two equal parts). Since angle ABC is 90° (right angle) and BCD is 30°, then angle x is 60° because there are 180° in a triangle. $180 - (90 + 30) = 60$. The correct answer is (C). ALWAYS MARK IN DIAGRAMS AS YOU READ DESCRIPTIONS AND INFORMATION ABOUT THEM. THIS INCLUDES WHAT YOU ARE LOOKING FOR.

Draw Diagrams

Drawing diagrams to meet the conditions set by the word problem can often make the problem easier for you to work. Being able to "see" the facts is more helpful than just reading the words. *For example:*

1. If all sides of a square are doubled, the area of that square is
   (A) doubled
   (B) tripled
   (C) multiplied by 4
   (D) remains the same
   (E) not enough information to tell

One way to solve this problem is to draw a square and then double all its sides. Then compare the two areas:

your first diagram

doubling every side

Notice that the total area of the new square will now be four times the original square. The correct answer is (C).

2. A hiking team begins at camp and hikes 5 miles north, then 8 miles west, then 6 miles south, then 9 miles east. In what direction must they now travel in order to return to camp?
   (A) north
   (B) northeast
   (C) northwest
   (D) west
   (E) They already are at camp.

For this question, your diagram would look something like this:

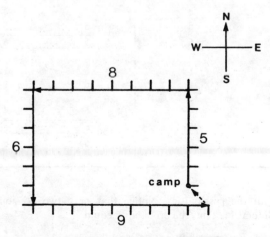

Thus they must travel northwest (C) to return to camp. Note that in this case it is important to draw your diagram very accurately.

3. What is the probability of throwing two dice in one toss so that they total 11?

(A) 1/6   (B) 1/11   (C) 1/18   (D) 1/20   (E) 1/36

Following are listed, for your information, the total possibilities. But you would NOT want to construct a chart of this length to answer a question because it is too time consuming. You could, instead, simply list all the possible combinations resulting in 11 (5 + 6 and 6 + 5) and realize that the total possibilities are 36 (6 × 6).

TOTAL POSSIBILITIES

First Die	Second Die	First Die	Second Die
1	1	4	1
1	2	4	2
1	3	4	3
1	4	4	4
1	5	4	5
1	6	4	6
2	1	5	1
2	2	5	2
2	3	5	3
2	4	5	4
2	5	5	5
2	6	(5	6)
3	1	6	1
3	2	6	2
3	3	6	3
3	4	6	4
3	5	(6	5)
3	6	6	6

These are all the possibilities. Notice that only two possibilities (those circled) will total 11. Thus the probability equals

$$\frac{\text{possibilities totaling 11}}{\text{total possibilities}} = \frac{2}{36} = \frac{1}{18}$$

Answer (C) is correct.

Procedure Problems

Some problems may not ask you to solve and find a correct numerical answer. Rather, you may be asked *how to work* the problem. *For instance:*

1. To find the area of the following figure, a student would use which formula?

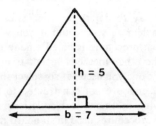

    I. area = base times height
   II. area = ½ times base times height
  III. area = one side squared

  (A) I   (B) II   (C) III   (D) I and II   (E) I and III

Notice that it is not necessary to use any of the numerical values given in the diagram. You are to simply answer how the problem is to be worked. In such cases don't bother working the problem; it is merely a waste of time. The correct answer is (B) II.

Or:

2. 51 × 6 could be quickly mentally calculated by
   (A) 50 × 6 + 1
   (B) 51 + 51 + 51 + 51 + 51 + 51
   (C) (50 × 6) + (1 × 6)
   (D) (50 × 6) + 1/6
   (E) adding fifty-one sixes

Answer (C) is correct. The quickest method of calculating 51 × 6 is to first multiply 50 × 6 (resulting in 300), then multiplying 1 × 6 (resulting in 6), and adding them together (300 + 6 = 306). Answer choices (B) and (E) will give the correct answer as well (306) but neither is the best way to *quickly* calculate the answer.

Sometimes, however, actually working the problem can be helpful. *For instance:*

3. The fastest method to solve $7/48 \times 6/7 =$ would be to
   (A) invert the second fraction and then multiply
   (B) multiply each column across and then reduce to lowest terms
   (C) find the common denominator and then multiply across
   (D) divide 7 into numerator and denominator, divide 6 into numerator and denominator, and then multiply across
   (E) reduce the first fraction to lowest terms and then multiply across

In this problem, the way to determine the fastest procedure may be to actually work the problem as you would if you were working toward an answer. Then see if that procedure is listed among the choices. You should then compare it to the other methods listed. Is one of the other *correct* methods faster than the one you used? If so, select the fastest.

These types of problems are not constructed to test your knowledge of *obscure* tricks in solving mathematical equations. Rather they test your knowledge of common procedures used in standard mathematical equations. Thus the fastest way to solve this problem would be to first divide 7 into the numerator and denominator:

$$\frac{\cancel{7}^{1}}{48} \times \frac{6}{\cancel{7}_{1}} =$$

Then divide 6 into the numerator and denominator:

$$\frac{\cancel{7}^{1}}{\cancel{48}_{8}} \times \frac{\cancel{6}^{1}}{\cancel{7}_{1}} =$$

Then multiply across:

$$\frac{\cancel{7}^{1}}{\cancel{48}_{8}} \times \frac{\cancel{6}^{1}}{\cancel{7}_{1}} = \frac{1}{8}$$

The correct answer is (D).

Other Sources of Data—Graphs

Certain problems will be based on graphs that are included in the test. You will need to be able to read and interpret the data on each graph as well as do some arithmetic with this data.

In working with graphs, spend a few moments to understand the title of each graph, as well as what the numbers on the graph are representing.

- Ask yourself if you can (1) read numbers and facts given on the graph and (2) understand what amount those numbers represent.

- There are three main types of graphs. They are (1) circle graphs, (2) bar graphs, and (3) line graphs.

- The amounts in decimal or fractional form on a circle graph will always total one whole. The amounts in percentage form on a circle graph will always total 100%.

- The amounts written as money, or in numerical form, on a circle graph will always add up to the total amount being referred to.

- Be sure to thoroughly read the paragraph under a graph if there is one and to interpret a legend if one is included.

- On bar or line graphs it is sometimes helpful to use the edge of your answer sheet as a straightedge. This will help you line up points on the graph with their numerical value on the graph scale. Also, look for trends such as increases, decreases, sudden low points, or sudden high points.

Questions 1, 2, and 3 refer to the following circle graph (pie chart).

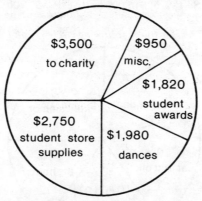

**How the Kettle School Distributed
Its Fund-Raising Earnings in 1979
(1979 fund-raising earnings totaled $11,000)**

1. The amount of money given to charity in 1979 was approximately what percent of the total amount earned?
   (A) 18%   (B) 34%   (C) 45%   (D) 50%   (E) 82%

2. Last year, 1978, the Kettle School spent 40% of its earnings on student store supplies. This percent exceeds the 1979 figure by how much?
   (A) 0%   (B) 10%   (C) 15%   (D) 30%   (E) 85%

3. If the Kettle School spends the same percentage on dances every year, how much will they spend in 1980 if their earnings are $15,000?
   (A) $270   (B) $2,700   (C) $4,000   (D) $11,000
   (E) $15,000

Answers to questions 1, 2, and 3

1. The answer is (B). Set up a simple ratio:

$$\frac{\text{money to charity}}{\text{total}} = \frac{\$3,500}{\$11,000} \simeq \frac{1}{3} = 33\frac{1}{3}\%$$

2. The answer is (C).

$$\frac{\text{student store supplies in 1979}}{\text{total}} = \frac{\$2,750}{\$11,000} = 25\% \qquad 40\% - 25\% = 15\%$$

3. The answer is (B).

$$\text{This year } \frac{\$1,980}{\$11,000} = 18\%$$

So 18% of \$15,000 next year = \$2,700

Questions 4, 5, and 6 refer to the following circle graph (pie chart).

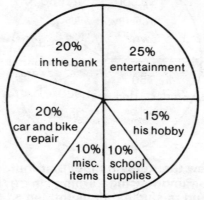

How John Spends His Monthly Paycheck

4. If John receives \$100 per paycheck, how much money does he put in the bank?
    (A) \$2   (B) \$20   (C) \$35   (D) \$80   (E) \$100

5. John spends more than twice as much on _____ as he does on school supplies.
    (A) car and bike repair   (D) miscellaneous items
    (B) his hobby   (E) cannot be determined
    (C) entertainment

6. The ratio of the amount of money John spends on his hobby to the amount he puts in the bank is
   (A) ½   (B) ⅔   (C) ¾   (D) ⅝   (E) ⅙

Answers to questions 4, 5, and 6

4. The answer is (B). 20% of $100 = .2(100) = $20.00.

5. The answer is (C). School supplies are 10%. The only amount more than twice 10% (or 20%) is 25% (entertainment).

6. The answer is (C). Set up the ratio:

$$\frac{\text{amount to hobby}}{\text{amount to bank}} = \frac{15}{20} = \frac{3}{4}$$

Questions 7, 8, and 9 refer to the following bar graph.

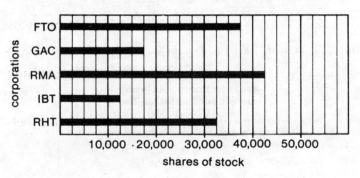

Shares of Stock X Owned by Five Major Corporations

7. The number of shares owned by RHT exceeds the number of shares owned by GAC by
   (A) 10,000   (D) 20,000
   (B) 15,000   (E) 32,500
   (C) 17,500

8. The number of shares of stock owned by IBT is approximately what percent of that owned by FTO?
   (A) 18%   (B) 25%   (C) 33%   (D) 42%   (E) 50%

9. The number of shares of stock owned by RMA exceeds which other corporations' by more than 20,000?
   (A) GAC and IBT   (D) IBT and FTO
   (B) FTO and RHT   (E) IBT and RHT
   (C) GAC and FTO

Answers to questions 7, 8, and 9

7. The answer is **(B)**.

$$\begin{array}{r} 32{,}500 \text{ RHT} \\ -\ 17{,}500 \text{ GAC} \\ \hline 15{,}000 \end{array}$$

8. The answer is **(C)**. 12,500 is what percent of 37,500?

$$\frac{12{,}500}{37{,}500} = \frac{1}{3} \approx 33\%$$

9. The answer is **(A)**.

$$\begin{array}{r} 42{,}500 \text{ RMA} \\ -\ 17{,}500 \text{ GAC} \\ \hline 25{,}000 \end{array} \qquad \begin{array}{r} 42{,}500 \text{ RMA} \\ -\ 12{,}500 \text{ IBT} \\ \hline 30{,}000 \end{array}$$

Questions 10, 11, and 12 are based on the following graph.

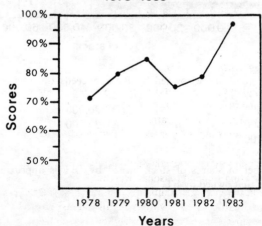

**Average Score (Statewide)
On Student Aptitude Test
1978–1983**

10. Between which two years was the greatest rise in average test scores?
    (A) 1978 and 1979   (D) 1981 and 1982
    (B) 1979 and 1980   (E) 1982 and 1983
    (C) 1980 and 1981

11. In which year was the average score approximately 85%?
    (A) 1978   (B) 1979   (C) 1980   (D) 1981   (E) 1982

12. Approximately what was the highest score achieved statewide on the test?
    (A) 80%   (D) 97%
    (B) 85%   (E) cannot be determined
    (C) 90%

Answers to questions 10, 11, and 12

10. (E) The most efficient way to compute greatest rise is to locate the *steepest* upward slope on the chart. Note that the steepest climb is between 1982 and 1983. Therefore choice (E) indicates the greatest rise in average test scores.

11. (C) According to the graph, the average test score was approximately 85% in 1980 (C). In such cases when you must read the graph for a precise measurement, it may be helpful to use your answer sheet as a straightedge to more accurately compare points with the grid marks along the side.

12. (E) The first thing you should do when confronted with a graph or chart is read its title to understand what the graph is telling you. In this case the graph is relating information about *average scores*. It tells you nothing about the *highest* score achieved. Thus (E) is the correct answer.

Tips for Working Math Problems

1. Read the question carefully, circling what you are looking for.
2. Pull out important information.
3. Draw, sketch, or mark in diagrams.
4. If you know a simple method, or formula, work the problem out as simply and quickly as possible.
5. If you do not know a simple method, or formula,
    (a) try eliminating some unreasonable choices.
    (b) work from the answers or substitute in numbers if appropriate.
    (c) try approximating to clarify thinking and simplify work.
6. Always make sure that your answer is reasonable.

A PATTERNED PLAN OF ATTACK

Mathematics

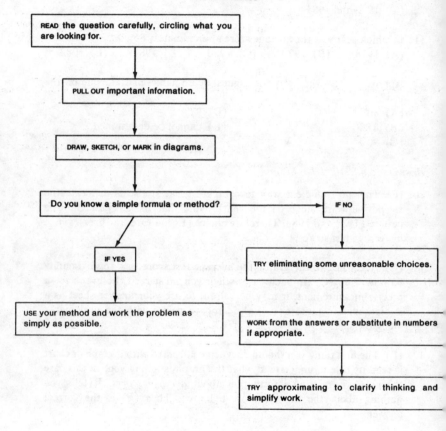

READ the question carefully, circling what you are looking for.

PULL OUT important information.

DRAW, SKETCH, or MARK in diagrams.

Do you know a simple formula or method?

IF NO

IF YES

TRY eliminating some unreasonable choices.

USE your method and work the problem as simply as possible.

WORK from the answers or substitute in numbers if appropriate.

TRY approximating to clarify thinking and simplify work.

ALWAYS MAKE SURE YOUR ANSWER IS REASONABLE.

INTRODUCTION TO THE ESSAY SECTION

The writing section of the CBEST is 60 minutes in length and contains two essay questions. You are asked to draw upon your personal experience and observations for information, examples, and generalizations to be used in your writing.

The total of the two essay questions generates a raw score that ranges from 4 to 16 (scaled score of approximately 20 to 80).

Ability Tested

The writing section of this exam tests your ability to read a topic carefully, to organize your ideas before you write, and to write with clarity and precision.

Basic Skills Necessary

This section requires a basic college level writing background. Papers are scored on the writer's ability to perform the following: development and organization of ideas with supporting evidence or specific examples; understanding of the essay's intended audience (for example, a speech urging members of the Board of Education to vote a certain way); comprehension of the assigned task; skillful use of language; and correctness of mechanics, usage, and paragraphing.

Directions

In this section, you will have 60 minutes to plan and write two essays, one for each topic given. You may use the bottom of this page to organize and plan your essay before you begin writing. You should plan your time wisely. Read each topic carefully to make sure that you are properly addressing the issue or situation. YOU MUST WRITE ON THE SPECIFIED TOPIC. AN ESSAY ON ANOTHER TOPIC WILL NOT BE ACCEPTABLE.

The two essay questions included in this section are designed to give you an opportunity to write clearly and effectively. Use specific examples whenever appropriate to aid in supporting your ideas. Keep in mind that the quality of your writing is much more important than the quantity.

Your essays are to be written on the special answer sheets provided. No other paper may be used. Your writing should be neat and legible. Because you have only a limited amount of space in which to write, please do NOT skip lines, do NOT write excessively large, and do NOT leave wide margins.

Remember, use the bottom of this page for any organizational notes you may wish to make.

Analysis of Directions

On the written essay portion of the CBEST you will have 60 minutes to write on two assigned topics. (Note that the exact allocation of time may change on future tests—at present *you* must divide the 60 minutes between the two essays. Check to ensure your understanding of the time allotment before you begin to organize your thoughts.)

You will have space for prewriting. It is recommended that you use this space to organize your thoughts. Double-check to determine how much space you have in which to write your essay. At present, the test provides two blank sides of lined 8½" by 11" paper per essay.

Some General Tips

1. Read the topic twice—three times if necessary—before writing. Circle key words. This will help you focus on the assigned task.
2. Use a form of "prewriting" *before* you begin writing your actual essay. Prewriting may consist of outlining, brainstorming, clustering, etc.
3. Spend about five minutes organizing your thoughts before you begin writing. A poorly written essay is often the result of inadequate planning.
4. Don't let spelling slow down your writing. That is, keep the flow of your writing going; then come back later to correct spelling errors.
5. If possible, leave several minutes at the end to reread and edit/correct your essay. Don't make extensive changes when you reread; just correct spelling errors and other minor flaws.
6. Don't use excessively large writing, don't leave wide margins, and don't skip any lines.
7. Double-check your time allotment and the amount of space you have in which to write each essay.

SAMPLE A: PREWRITING METHODS AND ESSAYS

Topic

Some students can look back on their years in school and pinpoint one particular course or one particular teacher most instrumental in shaping their lives.

Reflect on your own school years and focus on one such instructor or course. Describe the conditions or qualities that made that particular experience or teacher special.

Clustering

Use prewriting (clustering) as a way of organizing your thoughts before you write. After you choose a topic, write it down on the prewriting area and draw a circle around that topic:

For a few moments, think of all the elements of that topic and connect them to the central topic cluster:

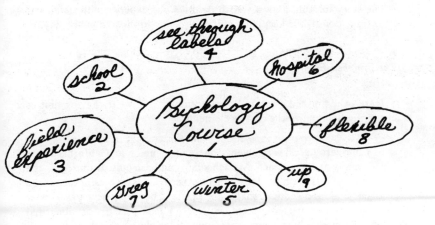

You can then number the parts of the cluster to give an order to your thoughts. You do not have to use all of the elements of your cluster. Clustering provides a way to put all of your thoughts down on paper before you write so you can quickly see the structure of the whole paper.

The "Story Formula"

One good way to approach a question that asks you to describe one experience is through the use of the "story formula." The story formula consists of

A. Setting—where the story took place
B. Main characters—who were the people in the story
C. Plot—the problem in the story or the crisis to be overcome
D. Climax—the turning point in the story
E. Resolution—the ending or how you are now as a result of the experience

So, in the sample essay—

Paragraph 1—introduce the setting and the main characters in the story
Paragraph 2—introduce the plot
Paragraph 3—introduce the climax } number of paragraphs may vary
Final paragraph—introduce the resolution

The story formula allows you to describe one experience in detail using clear transitions while keeping a unifying theme throughout your essay.

The Finished Essay

Here's the finished essay in "story formula," the writer having first used clustering to organize the essay's elements.

Ten years ago, I was twenty-one and a junior at California State University at Long Beach. My schooling had been quite traditional, and because of this I regarded my college experience as a necessary means to an end and rarely educational. Shortly after I began my second semester in the Education Department, however, I took a course in abnormal psychology that became most instrumental in shaping my life.

On a cold blustery winter day, as I drove to my part-time job at the neuropsychiatric hospital, I had a nagging feeling that the psychology class I enrolled in was slowly changing my point of view. As I drove onto the damp parking lot and walked in the doorway to the children's unit, my professor's words haunted me: "The challenge of the new psychology is to look beyond the 'labels' given to people and to see for oneself the human being that is there." I mulled over in my mind whether this day would bring me any closer to that goal.

That day a new patient arrived. He was a four-year-old, child pinned tightly with the label of "autistic." His name was Gregory, and in him I saw immediately all that I had previously only read about. He had all of the usual behaviors of a child who was autistic. He would not respond to touch or affection, engaged in constant finger flicking and hand gazing, and seemed to withdraw into his own world.

In the days that passed I spent much time with Gregory, involving him in whatever I was doing, always maintaining some physical contact with him. It was not until the fourteenth day that I dropped my ever-so-precious label.

Gregory and I frequently engaged in games, but his favorite game was entitled "Up." In this game I was to lift Gregory into the air as he gleefully shouted out, "up, up!" After several times my arms grew weary, and instead of putting him down, I held Gregory in my arms. There we stood in an embrace of trust—an opening to a place beyond his label. Tears flowed freely from my eyes as he calmly touched each one with his fingers, smiling as their wetness served to cement our relationship. Somehow, in that moment, all of what I had read mattered little compared to what I now knew. As my professor had warned us in class, "The labels only serve to make things easy—it is up to you to discover the truth."

Each day I went to the neuropsychiatric institute filled with a joy I had never known, yet in one sharp moment it was all shattered. One December 26, 1972, Gregory was transferred to a state mental institution. Over the advice of the staff and the doctors, Gregory was taken to a place where he would wear his label forever.

The next few weeks at the hospital seemed empty to me. A challenge by a professor to see through the labels and the willingness and trust of a four-year-old child enabled me to learn a lesson that I shall never forget. For the first time a college course provided me with a real learning experience; all of the coursework that I had taken never touched me as deeply as this one course.

Outlining

Another way of prewriting is outlining. A simple outline for Sample A could go something like this:

Course: Music 101—Introduction to Mozart

I. Caused me to change my major
   A. Hated economics but never knew it
   B. Music raised my spirits—new outlook on life
II. Broadened my life
   A. Began attending concerts—became more social
   B. Got out of the house
   C. Appreciation for a new art form—now more open about other things as well
III. Developed new skills
   A. Learned how to listen better
   B. Began learning to play French horn
      1. Made new friends in Community Orchestra
      2. Met my present husband who played first-chair French horn in Community Orchestra

Organizing an outline like the one above (it need not be this formal) will help you write a well-structured, well-planned essay. You can readily see that constructing a good essay from the outline above would be a fairly simple task.

Whatever way you prewrite—cluster, outline, etc.—the important thing is that you think and plan before you actually begin writing your essay.

Additional Finished Essays for Sample A

Following are two more attempts for Sample A. Both essays are evaluated in detail (comments run alongside each paragraph). Analyze each essay's strengths or weaknesses.

ESSAY 1

1. Orienting the reader to the writer's background and experience.

2. Designating the points which he or she will discuss; focusing the essay.

3. Restricting the discussion appropriately.

By the time I was a junior in college, I had developed criteria for good teaching and bad teaching, criteria based on my experiences during those first two college years. The good teachers were always (1) models of enthusiasm and curiosity about their subject, (2) interested in students' fulfilling their own potential and not trying to please the instructor, and (3) friendly as well as scholarly. Of the few good teachers I enjoyed, Bob Lincoln (a professor of English) was the best.

4. Vivid portrait of bad teacher and the effects of bad teaching.

Four times a week, sluggish and yawning from listening to my classics professor drone endlessly in a muffled monotone about Zeus and the Olympians, I slumped into Dr. Lincoln's class on the Victorian novel. And always he would lift my spirits with his own spirited approach; his was a remarkable talent for making connections between the experiences of Jane Eyre, Becky Sharp, and Adam Bede, and very modern problems of repression, alienation, and greed. He showed that good teachers make their subjects part of their own life and time and that literature can help us understand ourselves.

5. Balanced, contrasting sentence addressing point (1) from first paragraph. Able to control syntax, reference to specific details, orderly phrasing.

6. Thesis sentence, highlighting the significance of this paragraph.

But Dr. Lincoln never imposed his viewpoints on us. The importance of the literature was ours to decide. We kept journals in which we wrote about how instances in the novels were like those in our own experience, and by sharing those responses in class we learned how many different viewpoints a novel can provoke and learned to respect each other's differences. All this came about because Dr. Lincoln was more interested in what the subject meant to us than what it meant to him.

7. Effective transition (*but*), reference to point (2).

8. Clear, brief sentence; interesting contrast with longer ones.

9. Specific supporting details, logical parallel structure.

10. Summary sentence, reinforcing the overall point of the paragraph.

11. Reference to point (3) of the opening paragraph.

His attention to our learning didn't stop at the end of a class meeting. Always willing to make himself available for further discussion, Dr. Lincoln even invited us to his home at times. These uncommon occasions, sharing the professor's "natural habitat," helped us to learn that teachers are people, too, and that the best teachers are those who transform their students into a community, not just a bunch of anonymous paper pushers.

12. Specific supporting detail.

13. Additional information, fluency, and humor; clearly states the significance of the experience and its relationship to the general topic.

14. Ties the past into the present gracefully.

15. Summary conclusion that does more than simply restate what has already been said.

Each day of my own training in education and practice in teaching, I try to remember what Dr. Lincoln taught me. Good teaching takes energy, commitment, and good humor; it is a product of people, not merely of books and papers.

ESSAY 2

1. Fragment sentence, which states information irrelevant to the topic and already known to the audience.

2. Faulty parallelism, subject-verb disagreement, missing verb, vague sentence structure and diction.

3. Seemingly irrelevant point. Paragraph as a whole lacks focus and clarity.

4. Faulty logic.

5. Example of unclear relevance, ungrammatical verb, adjective-adverb confusion

6. Vague pronoun reference, vague sentence in general. Paragraph lacks a clear thesis.

7. Run-on sentences, full of vague cliches, missing verb preceding *in,* spelling error; in general a crazy quilt of undeveloped ideas.

8. Faulty logic, missing question mark, misspelling.

9. Vague sentence.

As a person who would like to be a full-time teacher and who is right now student teaching until I pass my courses and this test, so that I can apply for promising positions. I can say that my best teachers throughout elementary, secondary school and higher was always on my side and very much a sense of humor. As long as we had the assignment read, he would discuss it with us.

Good teaching makes you want to know more, especially for tests since they are how we learn. I remember one day I have studied extremely complete, and then the test was not what I expected. This is what I mean by good teaching.

And then another time I enjoyed the class so much that when it came time to "show what you know" I was ready, willing and able, with so many of the lectures in an interesting fashion, to show me that if the teacher likes his job, than there is nothing to worry about.

How many times have you looked for the teacher and he doesn't answer the phone or even make an effort to be their. Giving of yourself is when you take extra time to make sure that students know how they got the answers.

10. Restatement of part of the question, disguised attempt to focus the conclusion, inappropriate verb (*doing*).

11. Vague pronoun reference.

The conditions or qualities that made the particular experience special, in conclusion, were what I find myself doing whenever I think about teaching and try to do something out of the ordinary. And it works.

In general, the response is disunified, lacks relevant and specific details, does not address only *one* instructor or experience, lacks planning and organization, and displays a number of mechanical errors.

SAMPLE B: PREWRITING METHODS AND ESSAYS

Topic

A recent movement in education has been called "Back to Basics." Its proponents argue that the curriculum should concentrate only on reading, writing, and mathematics skills and completely ignore such courses as sociology, art appreciation, and drama.

Imagine that you are a school principal faced with the task of making policy for your school. Present your argument(s) either for or against "Back to Basics."

Clustering

Using the clustering technique for prewriting, this is what the cluster for Sample B might look like.

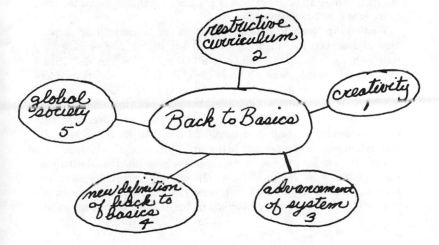

The Finished Essay

As principal of your school, I have seen many educational movements come and go. Some are worthy of the attention given to them, and others should be ignored because of their devastating effect on the educational system. One such movement that falls into the latter category is the "Back to Basics" movement. Its proponents argue that education should concentrate on reading, writing, and mathematics skills and completely ignore such courses as drama, art appreciation, and sociology. I am against the "Back to Basics" movement because it inhibits creativity, fails to recognize the importance of the arts, and restricts the curriculum.

The enhancement of creative thinking is primal to the advancement of any educational system. To create, to invent, or to discover, one needs not only to have freedom of thought but the exposure and application of that creativity to all areas of the curriculum. To concentrate on only reading, writing, and mathematics would restrict thinking to a narrow focus. The future needs thinkers who can create in the widest spectrum so as to be able to meet the challenge of a global society.

The "Back to Basics" proponents also fail to see that a restrictive curriculum of only mathematics, reading, and writing fails to support the many great advancements made in our culture by those whose first exposures to art, drama, or sociology took place in the schools. The great artists who have changed the way people see; the great dramatists who have told their stories worldwide; and the great sociologists who have helped us to understand social relations, organizations, and changes in our culture have all been products of an education that included the arts as basic to a well-rounded education.

Finally, the "Back to Basics" supporters fail to see in their narrow view of education that the basics *include* art, drama, and sociology as well as music, dance, and computer literacy. "Basics," by definition, means that knowledge which is needed by children in our society in order to compete and simply survive in that society. The "Back to Basics" movement is an attempt to take education back to a time that has long since passed. The narrow focus of the movement also overlooks the integrative value of reading, writing, and mathematics throughout all curriculum areas and especially in the arts.

The "Back to Basics" issue is a sad attempt to restrict the information that children need for their future. It will stifle creativity in those knowledge areas upon which our society is dependent. So, as your principal, I hope that you on the school board continue to support an education for the future—an education that defines the "basics" as those curriculum areas beyond the courses of reading, writing, and mathematics. We must meet the future with an education that *includes* art, drama, and sociology.

The "Why" Essay

One good way to approach a question which asks you to explain, analyze, or evaluate is to use a "why" essay format. A "why" essay is built around a thesis sentence. The thesis sentence begins with your opinion, followed by the word *because* and then a list of the most important reasons why the opinion is valid, reasonable, or well founded. For example, in the Sample B essay the thesis statement is:

I am against the "Back to Basics" movement because it inhibits creativity, fails to recognize the importance of the arts, and restricts the curriculum.

The thesis statement comes at the end of the introductory paragraph followed by paragraphs that explain each of your reasons. Finally the paper ends with a summary of the reasons and a restatement of the thesis sentence.

The "why essay" format could look like this in outline form:

Paragraph	"Why Essay" Format	Sample B Examples by Paragraph
1	Introduction—Thesis Sentence	Paragraph 1
2	Reason 1	Paragraph 2
3	Reason 2	Paragraph 3
4	Reason 3	Paragraph 4
5	Conclusion	Paragraph 5

Each paragraph should contain approximately three to five sentences. The introduction invites the reader to read on. Your reasons (three are often sufficient) that follow should give examples or evidence to support each reason. Your concluding paragraph summarizes your reasons and restates the thesis statement.

POOR ESSAYS—WHAT NOT TO DO

Sample A

One course I had in college which was instrumental in shaping my life was a college speech course. I was not a talkative person. During classroom discussions, my teacher made me participate and that was something I had not done in a long time.

This particular subject was a coed class and I had to discuss the current issues of today. There were only three females in a class of forty men.

After the semester was over, I was quite a different person than before the speech class.

I am now employed by the Over the Rainbow School District as a kindorgotten teacher in an area where people don't speak good. I feel happy to see the children grow up with the kind of experiences I can give them.

Analysis

This Sample A essay contains major faults in the writing. The essay lacks unity, focus, and a clear description of one experience.

The paper has only a brief description that gives the reader a hint of the setting and early experiences.

The paper rushes to the conclusion (resolution) without giving the reader an experience that caused a change. Simply enrolling in a class does not cause one to change. The writer left out a description of any experience that caused this change.

The paper lacks a unified, clear focus without a described experience and fails to go beyond a general discussion. The final sentence doesn't seem to fit because we still don't know why this course was special and how it helped this person in his or her job as a teacher.

The paper also contains many flaws in grammar and usage.

Sample B

Back to Basics is wrong for the schools. I don't like it. For one thing what are we going to do with all of the extra teachers when they fire all of the others. I will probably lose my job cause I have only been teaching for four years.

People get bored with the same thing day after day and the children will come to hate school and that is not good. I love to teach art and drama in my classroom. I have not taught sociology yet though. I know the children in my class could not stand to have only reading, writing, and mathematics. All the time without ever a break. Behavior problems would increase because the children would be so board that I would have to be very strict to have any control. Those people in the back to basics movement probably have never taught and are just mad at schools because they have to pay taxes to the schools and they are mad. Being a teacher I don't like the back to basics movement and don't want to see it.

Analysis

This Sample B essay has major flaws in its organization, development, and grammar. It does not have a clear beginning, middle, and end. Nowhere in the paper is there a clear thesis statement; reasons are merely scattered throughout the paper.

In this paper the author fails to choose the two or three most important reasons and develop them fully, giving examples or evidence. The sentence beginning "Behavior problems ..." hints at a possible example; yet this thought is not well developed with examples or evidence.

The paper contains many basic grammar and usage errors.

IMPORTANT TERMS USED IN ESSAY QUESTIONS

Pay close attention to how the essay question is phrased. Are you asked to compare and contrast? Or simply to describe? It is very important to focus on the exact assigned task; if you don't answer the question asked, you will receive little credit for your work. Some terms to look for:

Describe: Requires the use of adjectives, adverbs, and descriptive type phrases. You are trying to "paint a mental picture" for your reader.

Compare: Requires analyzing similarities and differences between two or more items.

Explain: Requires reasons substantiating an opinion or strengthening an argument. Answers the question "why?"

Contrast: Requires setting up a comparison between items, usually focusing on their differences.

Discuss: Usually allows a more open-ended approach, enabling the writer a broader range of possibilities of approach.

Argue (or Present a Point of View): Requires the writer to take only one point of view (either pro or con) and substantiate the position. Don't be concerned about taking the "right" or "wrong" position. That doesn't matter. What matters is, whichever position you take, that it be soundly and clearly supported.

Examples

In most essay questions, regardless of "type" ("compare" or "describe" or "explain"), you will need to use *examples* to support your thoughts. Thinking in terms of examples will also be helpful in planning your writing.

Compare and Contrast

Compare a time in your life when a teacher helped you and a time when a teacher hindered you. Explain *which* teacher you learned the most from as a result of these experiences.

When writing an essay on a question that asks you to compare or contrast two things, you can use this framework as a basic outline for your paper:

Paragraph 1: Introduction
1. Introduce reader to topic.
2. Restate question and tell opinion and reasons. (thesis)

Paragraph 2
1. Describe one teacher and his or her attributes.
2. Tell how the teacher helped you.
3. Include your feelings about the experience.

Paragraph 3
1. Describe second teacher and his or her attributes.
2. Tell how this teacher hindered you.
3. Include your feelings about the experience.

Paragraph 4: Conclusion
1. Tell how and why one teacher was the better one for you.
2. Restate thesis.

PRACTICE ESSAY TOPICS

Following are topics you may use for practice. Allow 30 minutes to plan and write each essay. Give yourself about a half-page to organize your notes and two sides of lined 8½" x 11" paper to write the actual essay. Then, upon completion of each essay, evaluate, or have a friend evaluate, your writing using the checklist provided.

Topic 1

Should there be any restriction on how many years a teacher may teach the same subject or the same grade level? Explain your answer and, if possible, use personal experiences.

Topic 2

Describe a particular time in your life when you had difficulty making an important decision.

Topic 3

Every year more and more computers are finding their way into the classroom. Discuss and explain your opinions on the growing use of computer-assisted instruction in the classroom.

Topic 4

Some have argued that imagination is not as important as perspiration. Take one side of the argument and present your own personal feelings on the matter.

Topic 5

We meet many people in the course of our lifetimes. Choose one particular person you would call the most unforgettable and describe why he or she is so unforgettable.

Topic 6

Many recent high school graduates discover that, despite possessing a high school diploma, they have no specific skills to enable them to obtain employment. Explain your feelings about introducing a "vocational skills program" as an alternative choice to the academic high school curriculum.

Topic 7

Recent educational experiments have included ungraded classrooms which consist of students grouped by level of achievement rather than by age. Imagine that such an "ungraded classroom" system is suggested for your school. Write a strong argument (either pro or con) to be read at the next meeting of the Board of Education.

Topic 8

Our lives have high points and low points. Choose one particular high point or low point and describe why it had such impact on you.

Topic 9

Some educators maintain that an all-male or all-female environment is beneficial to learning. Compare and contrast the advantages of such an academic environment to those of a coeducational atmosphere.

ESSAY TOPIC 1 CHECKLIST

Diagnosis/Prescription for Timed Writing Exercise

A good essay will:

_____ address the assignment
     be well focused
_____ be well organized
     smooth transition between paragraphs
     coherent, unified
_____ be well developed
     contain specific examples to support points
_____ be grammatically sound (only minor flaws)
     correct sentence structure
     correct punctuation
     use of standard written English
_____ use language skillfully
     variety of sentence types
     variety of words
_____ be legible
     clear handwriting
     neat

ESSAY TOPIC 2 CHECKLIST

Diagnosis/Prescription for Timed Writing Exercise

A good essay will:

_____ address the assignment
                   be well focused
_____ be well organized
                   smooth transition between paragraphs
                   coherent, unified
_____ be well developed
                   contain specific examples to support points
_____ be grammatically sound (only minor flaws)
                   correct sentence structure
                   correct punctuation
                   use of standard written English
_____ use language skillfully
                   variety of sentence types
                   variety of words
_____ be legible
                   clear handwriting
                   neat

A PATTERNED PLAN OF ATTACK

Essay Writing

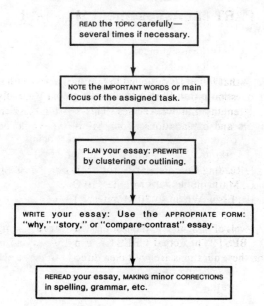

READ the TOPIC carefully—
several times if necessary.

NOTE the IMPORTANT WORDS or main
focus of the assigned task.

PLAN your essay: PREWRITE
by clustering or outlining.

WRITE your essay: Use the APPROPRIATE FORM:
"why," "story," or "compare-contrast" essay.

REREAD your essay, MAKING minor CORRECTIONS
in spelling, grammar, etc.

PART III: Assessment Mini-Test

The Mini-Test that follows is designed to familiarize you with some of the basic CBEST question types. It should also assist you in briefly assessing some of your strengths and weaknesses. This short assessment includes complete answers and explanations. Your Mini-Test should be timed as follows:

Section I: Reading Comprehension—12 Minutes; 10 Questions
Section II: Mathematics—13 Minutes; 10 Questions
Section III: Essay Writing—30 Minutes; 1 Essay

The format, levels of difficulty, and question structures are similar to those on the actual CBEST. The actual CBEST is copyrighted and may not be duplicated, and these questions are not taken directly from the actual tests.

SECTION I: READING COMPREHENSION

1 Ⓐ Ⓑ Ⓒ Ⓓ Ⓔ
2 Ⓐ Ⓑ Ⓒ Ⓓ Ⓔ
3 Ⓐ Ⓑ Ⓒ Ⓓ Ⓔ
4 Ⓐ Ⓑ Ⓒ Ⓓ Ⓔ
5 Ⓐ Ⓑ Ⓒ Ⓓ Ⓔ

6 Ⓐ Ⓑ Ⓒ Ⓓ Ⓔ
7 Ⓐ Ⓑ Ⓒ Ⓓ Ⓔ
8 Ⓐ Ⓑ Ⓒ Ⓓ Ⓔ
9 Ⓐ Ⓑ Ⓒ Ⓓ Ⓔ
10 Ⓐ Ⓑ Ⓒ Ⓓ Ⓔ

SECTION II: MATHEMATICS

1 Ⓐ Ⓑ Ⓒ Ⓓ Ⓔ
2 Ⓐ Ⓑ Ⓒ Ⓓ Ⓔ
3 Ⓐ Ⓑ Ⓒ Ⓓ Ⓔ
4 Ⓐ Ⓑ Ⓒ Ⓓ Ⓔ
5 Ⓐ Ⓑ Ⓒ Ⓓ Ⓔ

6 Ⓐ Ⓑ Ⓒ Ⓓ Ⓔ
7 Ⓐ Ⓑ Ⓒ Ⓓ Ⓔ
8 Ⓐ Ⓑ Ⓒ Ⓓ Ⓔ
9 Ⓐ Ⓑ Ⓒ Ⓓ Ⓔ
10 Ⓐ Ⓑ Ⓒ Ⓓ Ⓔ

MINI-TEST

SECTION I: READING COMPREHENSION

Time: 12 Minutes
10 Questions

DIRECTIONS

A question or number of questions follow each of the statements or passages in this section. Using only the *stated* or *implied* information given in the statement or passage, answer the question or questions by choosing the *best* answer from among the five choices given.

Questions 1 and 2 refer to the following passage.

The new vehicle inspection program is needed to protect the quality of the state's air, for us and for our children. Auto exhausts are a leading contributor to coughing, wheezing, choking, and pollution. The state's long-term interests in the health of its citizens and in this area as a place to live, work, and conduct business depend on clean air.

1. Which of the following is an unstated assumption made by the author?
   (A) Working and conducting business may be different activities.
   (B) The state has been interested in the health of its citizens even before this inspection program was proposed.
   (C) Exhaust emissions contribute to pollution.
   (D) The new inspection program will be effective.
   (E) Our ancestors did not suffer from air pollution.

2. Which of the following, if true, would most seriously weaken the argument above?
   (A) Since smog devices were made mandatory automotive equipment by the existing inspection program three years ago, pollution has decreased dramatically and continues to decrease.
   (B) Pollution problems are increasing in other states as well as in this one.
   (C) Sometimes coughing, wheezing, and choking are caused by phenomena other than pollution.
   (D) Vehicle inspectors are not always careful.
   (E) The state should not impose its interests upon the citizenry but should instead allow public health to be regulated by private enterprise.

Recent studies indicate that more violent crimes are committed during hot weather than during cold weather. Thus, if we could control the weather, the violent crime rate would drop.

3. The argument above makes which of the following assumptions?

I. The relationship between weather conditions and crime rate is merely coincidental.

II. The relationship between weather conditions and crime rate is causal.

III. The relationship between weather conditions and crime rate is controllable.

(A) I and II
(B) II and III
(C) I, II, and III

(D) I only
(E) II only

Deliberations of our governing bodies are held in public in order to allow public scrutiny of each body's actions and take to task those actions which citizens feel are not, for whatever reason, in their best interests.

4. With which of the following statements would the author of the above passage probably agree?

(A) Deliberations of our governing bodies should be held in public.

(B) Public scrutiny usually results in the criticism of our governing bodies.

(C) The best interests of the public usually do not coincide with the motives of our governing bodies.

(D) No government decisions ought to be kept from the public.

(E) Citizens in other countries are not cared for by the government.

Questions 5, 6, and 7 refer to the following passage.

Today the study of language in our schools is somewhat confused. It is the most traditional of scholastic subjects being taught in a time when many of our traditions no longer fit our needs. You to whom these pages are addressed speak English and are therefore in a worse case than any other literate people.

People pondering the origin of language for the first time usually arrive at the conclusion that it developed gradually as a system of conventionalized grunts, hisses, and cries and must have been a very simple affair in the beginning. But when we observe the language behavior of what we regard as primitive cultures, we find it strikingly elaborate and complicated. Stefansson, the explorer, said that "In order to get along reasonably well an Eskimo must have at the tip of his tongue a vocabulary of more than 10,000 words, much larger than the active vocabulary of an average businessman who speaks English. Moreover these Eskimo words are far more highly inflected than those of any of the well-known European languages, for a single noun can be spoken or written in several hundred different forms, each having a precise meaning different from that of any other. The forms of the verbs are even more numerous. The Eskimo language is, therefore, one of the most difficult in the world to learn, with the result that almost no traders or explorers have even tried to learn it. Consequently there has grown up, in intercourse between Eskimos and whites, a jargon similar to the pidgin English used in China, with a vocabulary of from 300 to 600 uninflected words, most of them derived from Eskimo but some derived from English, Danish, Spanish, Hawaiian and other languages. It is this jargon which is usually referred to by travellers as 'the Eskimo language.' "[1]

[1] *The Encyclopaedia Britannica,* Fourteenth Edition, Vol. 8, p. 709.

5. The size of the Eskimo language spoken by most whites is
   (A) spoken in England, Denmark, Spain, and Hawaii
   (B) less than the size of the language spoken by Eskimos
   (C) highly inflected
   (D) inestimable
   (E) irrelevant

6. Some of the evidence about language in the passage is taken from the observations of
   (A) linguists   (D) an explorer
   (B) Eskimos   (E) primitive cultures
   (C) businessmen

7. The passage implies that a "traditional" course in today's schools would be
   (A) Advances in Biology: The Creation of Artificial Life
   (B) Social Revolution in America
   (C) The History of the English Language
   (D) Television and Its Impact
   (E) Disco Dancing as Psychotherapy

We doubt that the latest government report will scare Americans away from ham, bacon, sausages, hot dogs, bologna, and salami or that it will empty out the bars or cause a run on natural food supplies. If a diet were to be mandated from Washington, Americans probably would order the exact *opposite* course. Therefore, the diet that does make sense is to eat a balanced and varied diet composed of foods from *all* food groups and containing a reasonable caloric intake.

8. Which of the following is (are) specifically implied by the passage?

    I. Vitamins are necessary to combat disease.
   II. A recent report warned of the risks of meat and alcoholic beverages.
  III. Unorthodox suggestions for a more nutritional diet were recently made by the government.

    (A) I only   (D) I and II
    (B) II only   (E) II and III
    (C) III only

Questions 9 and 10 refer to the following passage.

Beginning this fall, Latino and Asian students will not be allowed to transfer out of bilingual classes (that is, a program in which courses are given in a student's native language) until they pass strict competency tests in math, reading, and writing—as well as spoken English. The board and its supporters say this will protect children from being pushed out of bilingual programs before they are ready. They have hailed this as a victory for bilingual education.

9. Which of the following, if true, is the strongest criticism of the position of the board?
    (A) A foreign student may be quite competent in math without being competent in English.
    (B) Some native students already in English-speaking classes are unable to pass the competency tests.
    (C) Most foreign students require many months of practice and instruction before mastering English skills.
    (D) Many students prefer to transfer out of bilingual classes before they have achieved competency in English.
    (E) Holding back students will double the number of students in bilingual classes—twice as many Latino and Asian children isolated from the English-speaking mainstream.

10. The argument above would be most strengthened if the author were to explain
    (A) how efficient the bilingual program is
    (B) how well staffed the bilingual program is
    (C) whether the community supports the bilingual program
    (D) whether any board members do not support the bilingual program
    (E) how the students feel about the bilingual program

STOP. IF YOU FINISH BEFORE TIME IS CALLED, CHECK YOUR WORK ON THIS SECTION ONLY. DO NOT WORK ON ANY OTHER SECTION IN THE TEST.

SECTION II: MATHEMATICS

Time: 13 Minutes
10 Questions

DIRECTIONS

In the questions or incomplete statements below, select the one *best* answer or completion of the five choices given.

1. $1\frac{7}{9}$ is between
   (A) $1\frac{7}{9}$ and $1\frac{9}{9}$
   (B) $1\frac{1}{9}$ and $1\frac{5}{9}$
   (C) $\frac{7}{9}$ and $1\frac{1}{9}$
   (D) $\frac{5}{3}$ and $\frac{7}{3}$
   (E) $\frac{5}{6}$ and $\frac{7}{6}$

2. Which of the items is the most expensive per unit?
   (A) 4 for \$5
   (B) 5 for \$6
   (C) 6 for \$7
   (D) 8 for \$9
   (E) \$1 each

3. The best way to quickly approximate the answer to the problem 8.232 × 2.96 = is to
   (A) multiply, then round off the answer
   (B) round 8.232 to 8, then multiply
   (C) round 2.96 to 3, then multiply
   (D) round 8.232 to 8, and 2.96 to 3, then multiply
   (E) count decimal places

4. Area = base times height (A = bh) is the formula for which of the following figures?

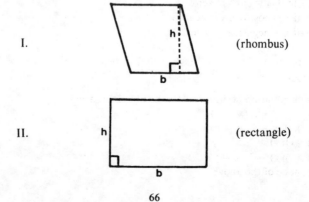

I.   (rhombus)

II.   (rectangle)

66

III.

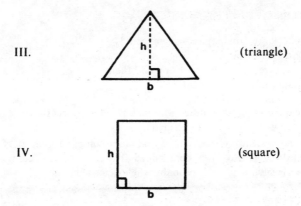

(triangle)

IV.

(square)

(A) I and II
(B) I and III
(C) II and IV
(D) III
(E) I, II, and IV

5. What is the sales tax on $132.95 if the tax rate is 7%?
   (A) $.93
   (B) $9.30
   (C) $9.31
   (D) $63.06
   (E) $93.07

6. In the equation x + y = 8, which of the following *must* be true?
   (A) x = 4, and y = 4
   (B) x and y are both positive
   (C) neither x nor y is zero
   (D) if x is positive, y is negative
   (E) if x is negative, y is positive

7. The product of two numbers is equal to twice the difference of the two numbers.

   Which equation best represents the above situation?
   (A) x + y = 2 (x − y)
   (B) x + y = 2 (x ÷ y)
   (C) (x)(y) = 2 (x ÷ y)
   (D) (x)(y) = 2 (x − y)
   (E) none of the above

8. $\sqrt{26} \approx 5.1$

To check the problem above, you could
(A) divide 27 by 5.1
(B) square 5 and square .1 and add them
(C) multiply 5.1 times 5.1
(D) count decimal places
(E) none of the above

9. During a steady winter snow, a student compiled a chart of snowfall readings. If it was later determined that one of the readings was not correct, which reading is probably the inaccurate one?

AMOUNT OF SNOWFALL

TIME	READING IN INCHES
1:00	.88
1:10	.93
1:20	.98
1:30	1.03
1:40	1.12
1:50	1.13
2:00	1.18

(A) .93   (D) 1.12
(B) .98   (E) 1.13
(C) 1.03

10. How many pounds of tea worth 93¢ per pound must be mixed with tea worth 75¢ per pound to produce 10 pounds of tea worth 85¢ per pound?
(A) 2⅔   (B) 3½   (C) 4⅘   (D) 5⅝   (E) 9½

STOP. IF YOU FINISH BEFORE TIME IS CALLED, CHECK YOUR WORK ON THIS SECTION ONLY. DO NOT WORK ON ANY OTHER SECTION IN THE TEST.

SECTION III: ESSAY WRITING

Time: 30 Minutes
1 Essay

DIRECTIONS

In this section, you will have 30 minutes to plan and write an essay for the topic given. You may use the bottom of this page to organize and plan your essay before you begin writing. You should plan your time wisely. Read the topic carefully to make sure that you are properly addressing the issue or situation. YOU MUST WRITE ON THE SPECIFIED TOPIC. AN ESSAY ON ANOTHER TOPIC WILL NOT BE ACCEPTABLE.

The essay question included in this section is designed to give you an opportunity to write clearly and effectively. Use specific examples whenever appropriate to aid in supporting your ideas. Keep in mind that the quality of your writing is much more important than the quantity.

Your essays are to be written on the special answer sheets provided. No other paper may be used. Your writing should be neat and legible. Because you have only a limited amount of space in which to write, please do NOT skip lines, do NOT write excessively large, and do NOT leave wide margins.

Remember, use the bottom of this page for any organizational notes you may wish to make.

Topic

Sports are viewed by some to be an integral part of the learning experience. Others, however, feel that sports are not essential to the learning experience and, in fact, should be eliminated, as they waste valuable educational funding. Present one side of this argument and substantiate your views with supporting evidence or reasons.

FOR YOUR ESSAY, USE TWO SIDES OF AN 8½" BY 11" LINED SHEET OF PAPER.

ANSWER KEY FOR THE MINI-TEST

SECTION I READING COMPREHENSION	SECTION II MATHEMATICS
1. D	1. D
2. A	2. A
3. E	3. D
4. A	4. E
5. B	5. C
6. D	6. E
7. C	7. D
8. B	8. C
9. E	9. D
10. A	10. D

SCORING YOUR CBEST MINI-TEST

To score your CBEST Mini-Test, total the number of correct responses for each section of the test separately. Do not subtract any points for questions attempted but missed, as there is no penalty for guessing. The score for each section is then scaled from 20 to 80. (About 70% right is a passing score.)

ANALYZING YOUR TEST RESULTS

The charts on the following page should be used to carefully analyze your results and spot your strengths and weaknesses. The complete process of analyzing each subject area and each individual question should be completed for this Mini-Test and for each Practice Test. These results should be reexamined for trends in types of error (repeated errors) or poor results in specific subject areas. THIS REEXAMINATION AND ANALYSIS IS OF TREMENDOUS IMPORTANCE FOR EFFECTIVE TEST PREPARATION.

MINI-TEST: SUBJECT AREA ANALYSIS SHEET

	Possible	Completed	Right	Wrong
Reading Comprehension	10			
Mathematics	10			
TOTAL	20			

ANALYSIS—TALLY SHEET FOR QUESTIONS MISSED

One of the most important parts of test preparation is analyzing WHY you missed a question so that you can reduce the number of mistakes. Now that you have taken the Mini-Test and corrected your answers, carefully tally your mistakes by marking them in the proper column.

	REASON FOR MISTAKE			
	Total Missed	Simple Mistake	Misread Problem	Lack of Knowledge
Reading Comprehension				
Mathematics				
TOTAL				

Reviewing the above data should help you determine WHY you are missing certain questions. Now that you have pinpointed the type of error, when you take Practice Test 1, focus on avoiding your most common type.

MINI-TEST ESSAY CHECKLIST

Diagnosis/Prescription for Timed Writing Exercise

A good essay will:

_____ address the assignment
     be well focused
_____ be well organized
     smooth transitions between paragraphs
     coherent, unified
_____ be well developed
     contain specific examples to support points
_____ be grammatically sound (only minor flaws)
     correct sentence structure
     correct punctuation
     use of standard written English
_____ use language skillfully
     variety of sentence types
     variety of words
_____ be legible
     clear handwriting
     neat

ANSWERS AND COMPLETE EXPLANATIONS FOR THE MINI-TEST

SECTION I: READING COMPREHENSION

1. (D) In order to argue for a new inspection program, the author must assume that that particular program, if enacted, will be effective. (C), the only other choice related to the points of the argument, expresses stated information rather than an unstated assumption.

2. (A) The argument for further supervision of vehicle use is most weakened by the statement that present safeguards are already doing the job. (C) and (D) slightly weaken the argument but do not address the overall position of the author.

3. (E) The only correct choice is II; it is argued that hot weather *causes* crime. This is not mere coincidence, and the statement does not state that we *can* control the weather.

4. (A) By describing in very positive terms the effects of public deliberations, the author suggests the opinion that such deliberations *should* be public.

5. (B) Only answers (B), (D), and (E) could refer to *size*. (B) summarizes the information of paragraph 2, which tells us that an Eskimo's vocabulary is over 10,000 words, whereas the conversation between Eskimos and whites is made up of 300 to 600 words—less than one-tenth of the real Eskimo vocabulary.

6. (D) "Stefansson, the explorer," makes an observation about the Eskimo language in the second paragraph.

7. (C) The passage says that language "is the most traditional of scholastic subjects." The only choice directly involving language is (C). And all of the other choices are very untraditional.

8. (B) Since the author doubts that Americans will stop eating meats or visiting bars, one must conclude that the author is referring to the latest government report warning of the risks of meat and alcoholic beverages. Statement I concerning vitamins may be true but is not *specifically* implied other than in a very general sense (nutrition). Statement III is not true; there is nothing to suggest that the government report made "unorthodox" suggestions.

9. (E) Choices (A) and (B) are irrelevant to the argument, and (D) is an illogical criticism. (E) is a logical conclusion that poses a significant problem.

10. (A) All of the other choices are much less relevant than the issue of how efficiently and effectively the program helps students to achieve competency.

SECTION II: MATHEMATICS

1. (D) $1\frac{7}{9}$ can be expressed as $\frac{16}{9}$ (an improper fraction). Note that expressing the term as ninths will eliminate choices (A), (B), and (C) as possible answers. Changing choice (D) to fractions expressed in ninths gives

$$\frac{5}{3} = \frac{15}{9}$$
$$\frac{7}{3} = \frac{21}{9}$$

   Thus, $\frac{16}{9}$ falls between the fractions listed in choice (D).

2. (A) The cost per unit breaks down as follows:

   (A) $5/4 = \$1.25$
   (B) $6/5 = \$1.20$
   (C) $7/6 =$ approximately $\$1.17$
   (D) $8/7 =$ approximately $\$1.14$
   (E) $\$1.00$

   Thus answer (A) is the most expensive.

3. (D) To best approximate the answer to the problem, round off each number to a whole number. This will make multiplication very simple: $8 \times 3 = 24$. Though answer choice (A) will also yield a rounded-off answer of 24, it is not the best way to approximate.

4. (E) Area = base times height ($A = bh$) is the formula for the area of a quadrilateral (four-sided figure). The height is measured as the perpendicular drawn to the base from the highest point on the opposite side. Thus, $A = bh$ pertains to the rhombus, rectangle, and square (I, II, and IV).

5. (C) To find the tax at 7% on \$132.95, simply round off and multiply (the rule for rounding off is "5 or above rounds up"): 7% times \$133.

$$.07 \times \$133 = \$9.31$$

6. (E) Choices (A), (B), (C), and (D) may all possibly be true but don't necessarily have to be true. Note the important word *must* in the question. Only choice (E) *must* be true: If x is a negative number, y *must* be a positive number so that their sum will equal (positive) 8.

75

7. (D) You should have a working knowledge of these expressions:

> *sum*—the result of addition
> *difference*—the result of subtraction
> *product*—the result of multiplication
> *quotient*—the result of division

Therefore, the *product of two numbers* may be represented as (x)(y). The *difference of the two numbers* may be either x − y or y − x. The term *twice* indicates that the expression is to be multiplied by 2. Thus, the entire expression breaks down as follows:

The product of two numbers is equal to twice the difference of the two numbers.
           (x) (y)   =   2   (x − y)

Therefore, (x) (y) = 2 (x − y)

8. (C) The problem reads, "The square root of 26 approximately equals 5.1"; the way to check it is to verify that 5.1 squared (multiplied by itself) approximately equals 26. Thus, you should multiply 5.1 times 5.1.

9. (D) The chart indicates that, except for the reading at 1:40, there was a steady accumulation of snowfall of approximately .05 inches every 10 minutes. Thus, if the reading at 1:40 were incorrect—if it were actually 1.08 instead of 1.12 as recorded—then the steady rise of .05 inches each 10 minutes could be maintained.

$$
\begin{array}{r}
.88 \\
+.05 \\
.93 \\
+.05 \\
.98 \\
+.05 \\
1.03 \\
+.09 \\
1.12 \\
+.01 \\
1.13 \\
+.05 \\
1.18
\end{array}
$$

10. **(D)** The only reasonable answer is 5⅗, since 85¢ per pound is slightly closer to 93¢ per pound than it is to 75¢ per pound. Then slightly more than half of the 10 pounds must be 93¢ per pound.

$$
\begin{array}{ll}
93¢ & \\
& \quad 8¢ \text{ away} \\
85¢ & \\
& \quad 10¢ \text{ away} \\
75¢ &
\end{array}
$$

Using the elimination strategy (marking out the obviously incorrect answer choices) is the best way to answer this question.

PART IV: Mathematics Review

The following pages are designed to give you an intensive review of the basic skills used on the CBEST Mathematics section. Arithmetic, algebra, geometry, axioms, properties of numbers, terms, and simple statistics are covered. Before you begin the diagnostic review tests, it would be wise to become familiar with basic mathematics terminology, formulas, and general mathematical information, a review of which begins on the following page. Then proceed to the arithmetic diagnostic test, which you should take to spot your weak areas. Then use the arithmetic review that follows to strengthen those areas.

After reviewing the arithmetic, take the algebra diagnostic test and once again use the review that follows to strengthen your weak areas. Next, take the geometry diagnostic test and carefully read the complete geometry review.

Even if you are strong in arithmetic, algebra, and geometry, you may wish to skim the topic headings in each area to refresh your memory of important concepts. If you are weak in math, you should read through the complete review. *Note, however, that recent CBESTs have emphasized arithmetic more than they have algebra and geometry. Therefore, you should spend the major portion of your review time on sharpening your arithmetic skills and knowledge of terms and concepts.*

SYMBOLS, TERMINOLOGY, FORMULAS, AND GENERAL MATHEMATICAL INFORMATION

COMMON MATH SYMBOLS AND TERMS

Symbol References:

$=$ is equal to	$\geq$ is greater than or equal to
$\neq$ is not equal to	$\leq$ is less than or equal to
$>$ is greater than	$\parallel$ is parallel to
$<$ is less than	$\perp$ is perpendicular to

Natural numbers—the counting numbers: 1, 2, 3, . . .

Whole numbers—the counting numbers beginning with zero: 0, 1, 2, 3, . . .

Integers—positive and negative whole numbers and zero: . . . $-3, -2, -1,$ 0, 1, 2, . . .

Odd numbers—numbers not divisible by 2: 1, 3, 5, 7, . . .

Even numbers—numbers divisible by 2: 0, 2, 4, 6, . . .

Prime number—number divisible by only 1 and itself: 2, 3, 5, 7, 11, 13, . . .

Composite number—number divisible by more than just 1 and itself: 4, 6, 8, 9, 10, 12, 14, 15, . . .

Squares—the result when numbers are multiplied by themselves, ($2 \cdot 2 = 4$) ($3 \cdot 3 = 9$): 1, 4, 9, 16, 25, 36, . . .

Cubes—the result when numbers are multiplied by themselves twice, ($2 \cdot 2 \cdot 2 = 8$), ($3 \cdot 3 \cdot 3 = 27$): 1, 8, 27, . . .

MATH FORMULAS

Triangle	Perimeter $= s_1 + s_2 + s_3$
	Area $= \frac{1}{2}bh$
Square	Perimeter $= 4s$
	Area $= s \cdot s$, or s^2
Rectangle	Perimeter $= 2(b + h)$, or $2b + 2h$
	Area $= bh$, or lw
Parallelogram	Perimeter $= 2(l + w)$, or $2l + 2w$
	Area $= bh$
Trapezoid	Perimeter $= b_1 + b_2 + s_1 + s_2$
	Area $= \frac{1}{2}h(b_1 + b_2)$, or $h\left(\dfrac{b_1 + b_2}{2}\right)$
Circle	Circumference $= 2\pi r$, or πd
	Area $= \pi r^2$

Pythagorean theorem (for right triangles) $a^2 + b^2 = c^2$

The sum of the squares of the legs of a right triangle equals the square of the hypotenuse.

Cube   Volume $= s \cdot s \cdot s = s^3$

                         Surface area $= s \cdot s \cdot 6$

Rectangular Prism   Volume $= l \cdot w \cdot h$

                         Surface area $= 2(lw) + 2(lh) + 2(wh)$

IMPORTANT EQUIVALENTS

$\frac{1}{100} = .01 = 1\%$	$\frac{1}{3} = .33\frac{1}{3} = 33\frac{1}{3}\%$
$\frac{1}{10} = .1 = 10\%$	$\frac{2}{3} = .66\frac{2}{3} = 66\frac{2}{3}\%$
$\frac{1}{5} = \frac{2}{10} = .2 = .20 = 20\%$	$\frac{1}{8} = .125 = .12\frac{1}{2} = 12\frac{1}{2}\%$
$\frac{3}{10} = .3 = .30 = 30\%$	$\frac{3}{8} = .375 = .37\frac{1}{2} = 37\frac{1}{2}\%$
$\frac{2}{5} = \frac{4}{10} = .4 = .40 = 40\%$	$\frac{5}{8} = .625 = .62\frac{1}{2} = 62\frac{1}{2}\%$
$\frac{1}{2} = \frac{5}{10} = .5 = .50 = 50\%$	$\frac{7}{8} = .875 = .87\frac{1}{2} = 87\frac{1}{2}\%$
$\frac{3}{5} = \frac{6}{10} = .6 = .60 = 60\%$	$\frac{1}{6} = .16\frac{2}{3} = 16\frac{2}{3}\%$
$\frac{7}{10} = .7 = .70 = 70\%$	$\frac{5}{6} = .83\frac{1}{3} = 83\frac{1}{3}\%$
$\frac{4}{5} = \frac{8}{10} = .8 = .80 = 80\%$	$1 = 1.00 = 100\%$
$\frac{9}{10} = .9 = .90 = 90\%$	$2 = 2.00 = 200\%$
$\frac{1}{4} = \frac{25}{100} = .25 = 25\%$	$3\frac{1}{2} = 3.5 = 3.50 = 350\%$
$\frac{3}{4} = \frac{75}{100} = .75 = 75\%$	

MEASURES

Customary System, or English System

Length
    12 inches (in) = 1 foot (ft)
    3 feet = 1 yard (yd)
    36 inches = 1 yard
    1,760 yards = 1 mile (mi)
    5,280 feet = 1 mile

Area
    144 square inches (sq in) = 1 square foot (sq ft)
    9 square feet = 1 square yard (sq yd)

Weight
    16 ounces (oz) = 1 pound (lb)
    2000 pounds = 1 ton (T)

Capacity
  2 cups = 1 pint (pt)
  2 pints = 1 quart (qt)
  4 quarts = 1 gallon (gal)
  4 pecks = 1 bushel

Time
  365 days = 1 year
  52 weeks = 1 year
  10 years = 1 decade
  100 years = 1 century

Metric System, or The International System of Units
(SI, Le Système International d'Unités)

Length—meter
  Kilometer (km) = 1000 meters (m)
  Hectometer (hm) = 100 meters
  Dekameter (dam) = 10 meters

    Meter
  10 decimeters (dm) = 1 meter
  100 centimeters (cm) = 1 meter
  1000 millimeters (mm) = 1 meter

Volume—liter
  Common measures
  1000 milliliters (ml, or mL) = 1 liter (l, or L)
  1000 liters = 1 kiloliter (kl, or kL)

Mass—gram
  Common measures
    1000 milligrams (mg) = 1 gram (g)
    1000 grams = 1 kilogram (kg)
    1000 kilograms = 1 metric ton (t)

Some Approximations
  Meter is a little more than a yard
  Kilometer is about .6 mile
  Kilogram is about 2.2 pounds
  Liter is slightly more than a quart

MATH WORDS AND PHRASES

Words that signal an operation:

ADDITION
- Sum
- Total
- Plus
- Increase
- More than
- Greater than

MULTIPLICATION
- Of
- Product
- Times
- At (Sometimes)
- Total (Sometimes)

SUBTRACTION
- Difference
- Less
- Decreased
- Reduced
- Fewer
- Have left

DIVISION
- Quotient
- Divisor
- Dividend
- Ratio
- Parts

MATHEMATICAL PROPERTIES AND BASIC STATISTICS

Some Properties (Axioms) of Addition

- *Commutative* means that the *order* does not make any difference.

$$2 + 3 = 3 + 2$$
$$a + b = b + a$$

NOTE: Commutative does *not* hold for subtraction.

$$3 - 1 \neq 1 - 3$$
$$a - b \neq b - a$$

- *Associative* means that the *grouping* does not make any difference.

$$(2 + 3) + 4 = 2 + (3 + 4)$$
$$(a + b) + c = a + (b + c)$$

The grouping has changed (parentheses moved), but the sides are still equal.

NOTE: Associative does *not* hold for subtraction.

$$4 - (3 - 1) \neq (4 - 3) - 1$$
$$a - (b - c) \neq (a - b) - c$$

- The *identity element* for addition is 0. Any number added to 0 gives the original number.

$$3 + 0 = 3$$
$$a + 0 = a$$

- The *additive inverse* is the opposite (negative) of the number. Any number plus its additive inverse equals 0 (the identity).

$$3 + (-3) = 0; \text{ therefore } 3 \text{ and } -3 \text{ are inverses}$$
$$-2 + 2 = 0; \text{ therefore } -2 \text{ and } 2 \text{ are inverses}$$
$$a + (-a) = 0; \text{ therefore } a \text{ and } -a \text{ are inverses}$$

Some Properties (Axioms) of Multiplication

- *Commutative* means that the *order* does not make any difference.

$$2 \times 3 = 3 \times 2$$
$$a \times b = b \times a$$

NOTE: Commutative does *not* hold for division.

$$2 \div 4 \neq 4 \div 2$$

- *Associative* means that the *grouping* does not make any difference.

$$(2 \times 3) \times 4 = 2 \times (3 \times 4)$$
$$(a \times b) \times c = a \times (b \times c)$$

The grouping has changed (parentheses moved), but the sides are still equal.

NOTE: Associative does *not* hold for division.

$$(8 \div 4) \div 2 \neq 8 \div (4 \div 2)$$

- The *identity element* for multiplication is 1. Any number multiplied by 1 gives the original number.

$$3 \times 1 = 3$$
$$a \times 1 = a$$

- The *multiplicative inverse* is the reciprocal of the number. Any number multiplied by its reciprocal equals 1.

$$2 \times \frac{1}{2} = 1; \text{ therefore } 2 \text{ and } \frac{1}{2} \text{ are inverses}$$
$$a \times 1/a = 1; \text{ therefore } a \text{ and } 1/a \text{ are inverses}$$

A Property of Two Operations

- The *distributive property* is the process of distributing the number on the outside of the parentheses to each number on the inside.

$$2(3 + 4) = 2(3) + 2(4)$$
$$a(b + c) = a(b) + a(c)$$

NOTE: You cannot use the distributive property with only one operation.

$$3(4 \times 5 \times 6) \neq 3(4) \times 3(5) \times 3(6)$$
$$a(bcd) \neq a(b) \times a(c) \times a(d) \text{ or } (ab)(ac)(ad)$$

Some Basic Terms in Statistics

- To find the arithmetic *mean,* or average, simply total the numbers and divide by the number of numbers.

Find the arithmetic mean of 3, 5, 6, 7, and 9. The total is: $3 + 5 + 6 + 7 + 9 = 30$. Then divide 30 by 5, giving a mean, or average, of 6.

- To find the *mode,* look for the most frequently occurring score or measure.

Find the mode of these scores: 3, 5, 5, 5, 6, 7. The mode is 5, since it appears most. If there are two modes, distribution of scores is called *bimodal.*

- To find the *median,* arrange the scores or numbers in order by size. Then find the middle score or number.

Find the median of these scores: 2, 5, 7, 3, 6. First arrange them in order by size: 7, 6, 5, 3, 2. The middle score is 5; therefore the median is 5. If the number of scores is even, take the average of the two middle scores. Find the median of these scores: 2, 5, 7, 4, 3, 6. First arrange them in order by size: 7, 6, 5, 4, 3, 2. The two middle numbers are 4 and 5; therefore the median is $4\frac{1}{2}$.

- The *range* of a group of scores or numbers is calculated by subtracting the smallest from the largest.

Find the range of the scores 3, 2, 7, 9, 12. The range is $12 - 2 = 10$.

ARITHMETIC

ARITHMETIC DIAGNOSTIC TEST

Questions

1. $6 = ?/4$
2. Change $5\frac{3}{4}$ to an improper fraction.
3. Change $\frac{32}{6}$ to a whole number or mixed number in lowest terms.
4. $\frac{2}{5} + \frac{3}{5} =$
5. $\frac{1}{3} + \frac{1}{4} + \frac{1}{2} =$
6. $1\frac{3}{8} + 2\frac{5}{6} =$
7. $\frac{7}{9} - \frac{5}{9} =$
8. $11 - \frac{2}{3} =$
9. $6\frac{1}{4} - 3\frac{3}{4} =$
10. $\frac{1}{6} \times \frac{1}{6} =$
11. $2\frac{3}{8} \times 1\frac{5}{6} =$
12. $\frac{1}{4} \div \frac{3}{2} =$
13. $2\frac{3}{7} \div 1\frac{1}{4} =$
14. $.07 + 1.2 + .471 =$
15. $.45 - .003 =$
16. $\$78.24 - \$31.68 =$
17. $.5 \times .5 =$
18. $8.001 \times 2.3 =$
19. $.7\overline{)\ .147}$
20. $.002\overline{)\ 12}$
21. $\frac{1}{3}$ of $\$7.20 =$
22. Circle the larger number: 7.9 or 4.35
23. 39 out of 100 means:

24. Change 4% to a decimal.

25. 46% of 58 =

26. Change .009 to a percent.

27. Change 12.5% to a fraction.

28. Change ⅜ to a percent.

29. Is 93 prime?

30. What is the percent increase of a rise in temperature from 80° to 100°?

31. Average 0, 8, and 10

32. 8^2 =

33. Approximate $\sqrt{30}$

Answers

1. 24

2. ²³⁄₄

3. 5²⁄₆ or 5⅓

4. ⁵⁄₅ or 1

5. ¹³⁄₁₂ or 1¹⁄₁₂

6. 4⁵⁄₂₄

7. ²⁄₉

8. 10⅓

9. 2²⁄₄ or 2½

10. ¹⁄₃₆

11. ²⁰⁹⁄₄₈ or 4¹⁷⁄₄₈

12. ⅙

13. ⁶⁸⁄₃₅ or 1³³⁄₃₅

14. 1.741

15. .447

16. $46.56

17. .25

18. 18.4023

19. .21

20. 6,000

21. $2.40

22. 7.9

23. 39% or ³⁹⁄₁₀₀

24. .04

25. 26.68

26. .9% or ⁹⁄₁₀%

27. ¹²⁵⁄₁₀₀₀ or ⅛

28. 37.5% or 37½%

29. No

30. 25%

31. 6

32. 64

33. 5.5 or 5½

ARITHMETIC REVIEW

Rounding Off

To round off any number:

1. Underline the place value to which you're rounding off.
2. Look to the immediate right (one place) of your underlined place value.
3. Identify the number (the one to the right). If it is 5 or higher, round your underlined place value up 1. If the number (the one to the right) is 4 or less, leave your underlined place value as it is and change all the other numbers to its right to zeros. *For example:*

Round to the nearest thousands:

$$345,\underline{6}78 \quad \text{becomes } 346,000$$
$$92\underline{8},499 \quad \text{becomes } 928,000$$

This works with decimals as well. Round to the nearest hundredth:

$$3.4\underline{6}78 \quad \text{becomes } 3.47$$
$$298,435.0\underline{8}3 \quad \text{becomes } 298,435.08$$

Place Value

Each position in any number has *place value*. For instance, in the number 485, 4 is in the hundreds place, 8 is in the tens place, and 5 is in the ones place. Thus, place value is as follows:

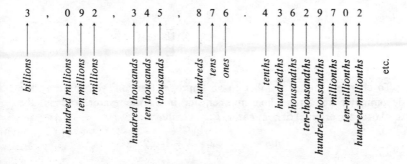

89

Fractions

Fractions consist of two numbers: a *numerator* (which is above the line) and a *denominator* (which is below the line).

$$\frac{1}{2} \frac{\text{numerator}}{\text{denominator}} \qquad \text{or} \qquad \text{numerator } \frac{1}{2} \text{ denominator}$$

The denominator lets us know the number of equal parts into which something is divided. The numerator tells us how many of these equal parts are contained in the fraction. Thus, if the fraction is ⅗ of a pie, then the denominator 5 tells us that the pie has been divided into 5 equal parts, of which 3 (numerator) are in the fraction.

Sometimes it helps to think of the dividing line (in the middle of a fraction) as meaning "out of." In other words, ⅗ would also mean 3 "out of" 5 equal pieces from the whole pie.

Common Fractions and Improper Fractions

A fraction like ⅗, where the numerator is smaller than the denominator, is less than one. This kind of fraction is called a *common fraction*.

But sometimes a fraction may be more than one. This is when the numerator is larger than the denominator. Thus, ¹²/₇ is more than one. This is called an *improper fraction*.

Mixed Numbers

When a term contains both a whole number (such as 3, 8, 25, etc.) and a fraction (such as ½, ¼, ¾, etc.), it is called a *mixed number*. For instance, 5¼ and 290¾ are both mixed numbers.

To change an improper fraction to a mixed number, you divide the denominator into the numerator. *For example:*

$$\frac{18}{5} = 3\tfrac{3}{5} \qquad \begin{array}{r} 3 \\ 5\overline{)18} \\ \underline{15} \\ 3 \end{array}$$

To change a mixed number to an improper fraction, you multiply the denominator times the whole number, add in the numerator, and put the total over the original denominator. *For example:*

$$4\tfrac{1}{2} = \tfrac{9}{2} \qquad 2 \times 4 + 1 = 9$$

Reducing Fractions

A fraction must be reduced to *lowest terms*. This is done by dividing both the numerator and denominator by the largest number that will divide evenly into both. For example, $^{14}/_{16}$ is reduced by dividing both terms by 2, thus giving us $^7/_8$. Likewise, $^{20}/_{25}$ is reduced to $^4/_5$ by dividing both numerator and denominator by 5.

Adding Fractions

To add fractions, you must first change all denominators to their *lowest common denominator* (LCD)—the lowest number that can be divided evenly by all the denominators in the problem. When you have all the denominators the same, you may add fractions by simply adding the numerators (the denominator remains the same). *For example:*

$$\frac{3}{8} = \frac{3}{8}$$
$$+\ \frac{1}{2} = \frac{4}{8} \longleftarrow \begin{cases}\text{one-half is}\\ \text{changed to}\\ \text{four-eighths}\end{cases}$$
$$\frac{7}{8}$$

$$\frac{1}{4} = \frac{3}{12}$$
$$+\ \frac{1}{3} = \frac{4}{12} \ \begin{cases}\text{change both}\\ \text{fractions to}\\ \text{LCD of 12}\end{cases}$$
$$\frac{7}{12}$$

In the first example, we changed the $^1/_2$ to $^4/_8$ because 8 is the lowest common denominator, and then we added the numerators 3 and 4 to get $^7/_8$.

In the second example, we had to change both fractions to get the lowest common denominator of 12, and then we added the numerators to get $^7/_{12}$. Of course, if the denominators are already the same, just add the numerators. *For example:*

$$^6/_{11} + {}^3/_{11} = {}^9/_{11}$$

Adding Mixed Numbers

To add mixed numbers, the same rule (find the LCD) applies, but make sure that you always add the whole numbers to get your final answer. *For example:*

$$2^1/_2 = 2^2/_4 \longleftarrow \begin{cases}\text{one-half is changed}\\ \text{to two-fourths}\end{cases}$$
$$+\ 3^1/_4 = 3^1/_4$$
$$5^3/_4 \begin{cases}\text{remember to add the}\\ \text{whole numbers}\end{cases}$$

Subtracting Fractions

To subtract fractions, the same rule (find the LCD) applies, except that you subtract the numerators. *For example:*

$$\begin{array}{r} \frac{7}{8} = \frac{7}{8} \\ - \frac{1}{4} = \frac{2}{8} \\ \hline \frac{5}{8} \end{array} \qquad \begin{array}{r} \frac{3}{4} = \frac{9}{12} \\ - \frac{1}{3} = \frac{4}{12} \\ \hline \frac{5}{12} \end{array}$$

Subtracting Mixed Numbers

When you subtract mixed numbers, sometimes you may have to "borrow" from the whole number, just like you sometimes borrow from the next column when subtracting ordinary numbers. *For example:*

$$\begin{array}{r} \overset{4\ \ 11}{6\cancel{5}1} \\ - 129 \\ \hline 522 \end{array} \qquad \begin{array}{r} \overset{3\frac{7}{6}}{\cancel{4}\frac{1}{6}} \\ - 2\frac{5}{6} \\ \hline 1\frac{2}{6} = 1\frac{1}{3} \end{array}$$

you borrowed 1 from the 10's column

you borrowed one in the form % from the 1's column

To subtract a mixed number from a whole number, you have to "borrow" from the whole number. *For example:*

$$\begin{array}{r} 6\ \ \ = 5\frac{5}{5} \longleftarrow \\ - 3\frac{1}{5} = 3\frac{1}{5} \\ \hline 2\frac{4}{5} \end{array}$$

borrow one in the form of ⅗ from the 6

remember to subtract the remaining whole numbers

Multiplying Fractions

Simply multiply the numerators, then multiply the denominators. Reduce to lowest terms if necessary. *For example:*

$$\frac{2}{3} \times \frac{5}{12} = \frac{10}{36} \qquad \text{reduce } \frac{10}{36} \text{ to } \frac{5}{18}$$

This answer had to be reduced as it wasn't in lowest terms.

Canceling when multiplying fractions: You could first have "canceled." That would have eliminated the need to reduce your answer. To cancel, find a number that divides evenly into one numerator and one denominator. In this case, 2 will divide evenly into 2 in the numerator (it goes in one time) and 12 in the denominator (it goes in 6 times). *Thus:*

$$\frac{\overset{1}{\cancel{2}}}{3} \times \frac{5}{\cancel{12}} =$$
$$_{6}$$

Now that you've canceled, you can multiply out as you did before.

$$\frac{\overset{1}{\cancel{2}}}{3} \times \frac{5}{\underset{6}{\cancel{12}}} = \frac{5}{18}$$

Remember, you may cancel only when *multiplying* fractions.

Multiplying Mixed Numbers

To multiply mixed numbers, first change any mixed number to an improper fraction. Then multiply as previously shown. To change mixed numbers to improper fractions:

1. multiply the whole number by the denominator of the fraction
2. add this to the numerator of the fraction
3. this is now your numerator
4. the denominator remains the same

$$3\tfrac{1}{3} \times 2\tfrac{1}{4} = {}^{10}\!/_3 \times {}^9\!/_4 = {}^{90}\!/_{12} = 7{}^6\!/_{12} = 7\tfrac{1}{2}$$

Then change the answer, if in improper fraction form, back to a mixed number and reduce if necessary.

Dividing Fractions

To divide fractions, invert (turn upside down) the second fraction and multiply. Then reduce if necessary. *For example:*

$$\frac{1}{6} \div \frac{1}{5} = \frac{1}{6} \times \frac{5}{1} = \frac{5}{6} \qquad \frac{1}{6} \div \frac{1}{3} = \frac{1}{6} \times \frac{3}{1} = \frac{3}{6} = \frac{1}{2}$$

Simplifying Fractions

If either numerator or denominator consists of several numbers, these numbers must be combined into one number. Then reduce if necessary. *For example:*

$$\frac{28 + 14}{26 + 17} = \frac{42}{43} \quad \text{or}$$

$$\frac{\frac{1}{4} + \frac{1}{2}}{\frac{1}{3} + \frac{1}{4}} = \frac{\frac{1}{4} + \frac{2}{4}}{\frac{4}{12} + \frac{3}{12}} = \frac{\frac{3}{4}}{\frac{7}{12}} = \frac{3}{4} \times \frac{12}{7} = \frac{36}{28} = \frac{9}{7} = 1\frac{2}{7}$$

Decimals

Fractions may also be written in decimal form by using a symbol called a *decimal point*. All numbers to the left of the decimal point are whole numbers. All numbers to the right of the decimal point are fractions with denominators of only 10, 100, 1,000, 10,000, etc., as follows:

$$.6 = \frac{6}{10} = \frac{3}{5}$$

$$.7 = \frac{7}{10}$$

$$.07 = \frac{7}{100}$$

$$.007 = \frac{7}{1000}$$

$$.0007 = \frac{7}{10,000}$$

$$.00007 = \frac{7}{100,000}$$

$$.25 = \frac{25}{100} = \frac{1}{4}$$

Adding and Subtracting Decimals

To add or subtract decimals, just line up the decimal points and then add or subtract in the same manner you would add or subtract regular numbers. *For example:*

$$23.6 + 1.75 + 300.002 = \begin{array}{r} 23.6 \\ 1.75 \\ 300.002 \\ \hline 325.352 \end{array}$$

Adding in zeros can make the problem easier to work:

$$\begin{array}{r} 23.600 \\ 1.750 \\ 300.002 \\ \hline 325.352 \end{array}$$

and
$$54.26 - 1.1 = \begin{array}{r} 54.26 \\ - 1.10 \\ \hline 53.16 \end{array}$$

and
$$78.9 - 37.43 = \begin{array}{r} 8 \\ 78.\cancel{9}^{1}0 \\ - 37.4\ 3 \\ \hline 41.4\ 7 \end{array}$$

Whole numbers can have decimal points to their right. *For example:*

$$17 - 8.43 - \begin{array}{r} 6\ 9 \\ 1\cancel{7}.\cancel{0}^{1}0 \\ - 8.4\ 3 \\ \hline 8.5\ 7 \end{array}$$

Multiplying Decimals

To multiply decimals, just multiply as usual. Then count the total number of digits above the line which are to the right of all decimal points. Place your decimal point in your answer so there is the same number of digits to the right of it as there was above the line. *For example:*

$$\begin{array}{r} 40.012 \leftarrow 3 \text{ digits} \\ \times\quad 3.1 \leftarrow 1 \text{ digit} \\ \hline 40012 \\ 120036 \\ \hline 124.0372 \leftarrow 4 \text{ digits} \end{array}$$

total of 4 digits above the line that are to the right of the decimal point

decimal point placed so there is same number of digits to the right of the decimal point

Dividing Decimals

Dividing decimals is the same as dividing other numbers, except that if the divisor (the number you're dividing by) has a decimal, move it to the right as many places as necessary until it is a whole number. Then move the decimal point in the dividend (the number being divided into) the same number of places. Sometimes you may have to add zeros to the dividend (the number inside the division sign).

$$1.25\overline{)5.} = 125\overline{)500.}\ \ \overset{4.}{}$$

or

$$0.002\overline{)26.} = 2\overline{)26000.}\ \ \overset{13000.}{}$$

Changing Decimals to Percents

To change decimals to percents:

1. move the decimal point two places to the right and
2. insert a percent sign

$$.75 = 75\% \qquad .05 = 5\%$$

Changing Percents to Decimals

To change percents to decimals:

1. eliminate the percent sign and
2. move the decimal point two places to the left (sometimes adding zeros will be necessary)

$$75\% = .75 \qquad 5\% = .05$$
$$23\% = .23 \qquad .2\% = .002$$

Changing Fractions to Percents

To change a fraction to a percent:

1. multiply by 100 and
2. insert a percent sign

$$1/2 = 1/2 \times 100 = 100/2 = 50\%$$
$$2/5 = 2/5 \times 100 = 200/5 = 40\%$$

Changing Percents to Fractions

To change percents to fractions:

1. divide the percent by 100,
2. eliminate the percent sign, and
3. reduce if necessary

$$60\% = 60/100 = 3/5 \qquad 13\% = 13/100$$

Changing Fractions to Decimals

To change a fraction to a decimal simply do what the operation says. In other words, $^{13}/_{20}$ means 13 divided by 20. So do just that (insert decimal points and zeros accordingly):

$$20\overline{)13.00} = .65 \qquad 5/8 = 8\overline{)5.000} = .625$$

Changing Decimals to Fractions

To change a decimal to a fraction:

1. move the decimal point two places to the right,
2. put that number over 100, and
3. reduce if necessary

$.65 = 65/100 = 13/20$
$.05 = 5/100 = 1/20$
$.75 = 75/100 = 3/4$

Read it: .8
Write it: 8/10
Reduce it: 4/5

Finding Percent of a Number

To determine percent of a number, change the percent to a fraction or decimal (whichever is easier for you) and multiply. Remember, the word "of" means multiply.

What is 20% of 80?

$20/100 \times 80 = 1600/100 = 16$ or $.20 \times 80 = 16.00 = 16$

What is 12% of 50?

$12/100 \times 50 = 600/100 = 6$ or $.12 \times 50 = 6.00 = 6$

What is 1/2% of 18?

$\frac{1/2}{100} \times 18 = 1/200 \times 18 = 18/200 = 9/100$ or $.005 \times 18 = .09$

Other Applications of Percent

Turn the question word-for-word into an equation. For "what" substitute the letter x; for "is" substitute an *equal sign*; for "of" substitute a *multiplication sign*. Change percents to decimals or fractions, whichever you find easier. Then solve the equation.

18 is what percent of 90?

$$18 = x(90)$$
$$18/90 = x$$
$$1/5 = x$$
$$20\% = x$$

10 is 50% of what number?

$$10 = .50(x)$$
$$10/.50 = x$$
$$20 = x$$

What is 15% of 60?

$$x = 15/100 \times 60 = 90/10 = 9$$
$$\text{or} \quad .15(60) = 9$$

Finding Percentage Increase or Percentage Decrease

To find the *percentage change* (increase or decrease), use this formula:

$$\frac{\text{change}}{\text{starting point}} \times 100 = \text{percentage change}$$

For example:

What is the percentage decrease of a $500 item on sale for $400?

Change: $500 - 400 = 100$

$$\frac{\text{change}}{\text{starting point}} \times 100 = \frac{100}{500} \times 100 = \frac{1}{5} \times 100 = 20\% \text{ decrease}$$

What is the percentage increase of Jon's salary if it went from $150 a month to $200 a month?

Change: $200 - 150 = 50$

$$\frac{\text{change}}{\text{starting point}} \times 100 = \frac{50}{150} \times 100 = \frac{1}{3} \times 100 = 33\frac{1}{3}\% \text{ increase}$$

Prime Numbers

A *prime number* is a number that can be evenly divided by only itself and one. For example, 19 is a prime number because it can be evenly divided only by 19 and 1, but 21 is not a prime number because 21 can be evenly divided by other numbers (3 and 7).

The only even prime number is 2; thereafter any even number may be divided evenly by 2. Zero and one are *not* prime numbers. The first ten prime numbers are 2, 3, 5, 7, 11, 13, 17, 19, 23, and 29.

Arithmetic Mean, or Average

To find the *average* of a group of numbers:

1. add them up and
2. divide by the number of items you added

For example:

What is the average of 10, 20, 35, 40, and 45?

$$10 + 20 + 35 + 40 + 45 = 150$$
$$150 \div 5 = 30$$
The average is 30

What is the average of 0, 12, 18, 20, 31, and 45?

$$0 + 12 + 18 + 20 + 31 + 45 = 126$$
$$126 \div 6 = 21$$
The average is 21

What is the average of 25, 27, 27, and 27?

$$25 + 27 + 27 + 27 = 106$$
$$106 \div 4 = 26\frac{1}{2}$$
The average is $26\frac{1}{2}$

Median

A *median* is simply the middle number of a list of numbers after it has been written in order. (If the list contains an even number of items, average the two middle numbers to get the median.) For example, in the following list—3, 4, 6, 9, 21, 24, 56—the number 9 is the median.

Mode

The *mode* is simply the number most frequently listed in a group of numbers. For example, in the following group —5, 9, 7, 3, 9, 4, 6, 9, 7, 9, 2—the mode is 9 because it appears more often than any other number.

Squares and Square Roots

To *square* a number just multiply it by itself. For example, 6 squared (written 6^2) is 6 x 6 or 36. 36 is called a perfect square (the square of a whole number). Any exponent means multiply by itself that many times. *For example:*

$$5^3 = 5 \times 5 \times 5 = 125$$
$$8^2 = 8 \times 8 = 64$$

Remember, $x^1 = x$ and $x^0 = 1$ when x is any number (other than 0).

Following is a list of perfect squares:

$$0^2 = 0 \qquad 5^2 = 25 \qquad 9^2 = 81$$
$$1^2 = 1 \qquad 6^2 = 36 \qquad 10^2 = 100$$
$$2^2 = 4 \qquad 7^2 = 49 \qquad 11^2 = 121$$
$$3^2 = 9 \qquad 8^2 = 64 \qquad 12^2 = 144 \quad \text{etc.}$$
$$4^2 = 16$$

Square roots of nonperfect squares can be approximated. Two approximations you may wish to remember are:

$$\sqrt{2} \simeq 1.4$$
$$\sqrt{3} \simeq 1.7$$

To find the *square root* of a number, you want to find some number that when multiplied by itself gives you the original number. In other words, to find the square root of 25 you want to find the number that when multiplied by itself gives you 25. The square root of 25, then, is 5. The symbol for square root is $\sqrt{}$. Following is a list of perfect (whole number) square roots:

$$\sqrt{0} = 0 \qquad \sqrt{16} = 4 \qquad \sqrt{64} = 8$$
$$\sqrt{1} = 1 \qquad \sqrt{25} = 5 \qquad \sqrt{81} = 9$$
$$\sqrt{4} = 2 \qquad \sqrt{36} = 6 \qquad \sqrt{100} = 10 \quad \text{etc.}$$
$$\sqrt{9} = 3 \qquad \sqrt{49} = 7$$

Square Root Rules

Two numbers multiplied under a radical (square root) sign equal the product of the two square roots. *For example:*

$$\sqrt{(4)(25)} = \sqrt{4} \times \sqrt{25} = 2 \times 5 = 10 \text{ or } \sqrt{100} = 10$$

and likewise with division:

$$\sqrt{\frac{64}{4}} = \frac{\sqrt{64}}{\sqrt{4}} = \frac{8}{2} = 4 \text{ or } \sqrt{16} = 4$$

Addition and subtraction, however, are different. The numbers must be combined under the radical before any computation of square roots may be done. *For example:*

$$\sqrt{10 + 6} = \sqrt{16} = 4 \qquad (\sqrt{10 + 6} \text{ does } not \text{ equal } [\neq] \ \sqrt{10} + \sqrt{6})$$

or $\quad \sqrt{93 - 12} = \sqrt{81} = 9$

Approximating Square Roots

To find a square root which will not be a whole number, you should approximate. *For example:*

Approximate $\sqrt{57}$

Because $\sqrt{57}$ is between $\sqrt{49}$ and $\sqrt{64}$, it will fall somewhere between 7 and 8. And because 57 is just about halfway between 49 and 64, $\sqrt{57}$ is therefore approximately $7\frac{1}{2}$.

Approximate $\sqrt{83}$

$$\sqrt{81} < \sqrt{83} < \sqrt{100}$$
$$9 10$$

Since $\sqrt{83}$ is slightly more than $\sqrt{81}$ (whose square root is 9), then $\sqrt{83}$ is a little more than 9. Since 83 is only two steps up from the nearest perfect square (81) and 17 steps to the next perfect square (100), then 83 is $\frac{2}{19}$ of the way to 100.

$$\frac{2}{19} \approx \frac{2}{20} = \frac{1}{10} = .1$$

Therefore: $$\sqrt{83} \approx 9.1$$

Simplifying Square Roots

To simplify numbers under a radical (square root sign):

1. factor the number to two numbers, one (or more) of which is a perfect square,
2. then take the square root of the perfect square(s), and
3. leave the others under the $\sqrt{}$

Simplify $\sqrt{75}$

$$\sqrt{75} = \sqrt{25 \times 3} = \sqrt{25} \times \sqrt{3} = 5\sqrt{3}$$

Simplify $\sqrt{200}$

$$\sqrt{200} = \sqrt{100 \times 2} = \sqrt{100} \times \sqrt{2} = 10\sqrt{2}$$

Simplify $\sqrt{900}$

$$\sqrt{900} = \sqrt{100 \times 9} = \sqrt{100} \times \sqrt{9} = 10 \times 3 = 30$$

Signed Numbers (Positive Numbers and Negative Numbers)

On a number line, numbers to the right of 0 are positive. Numbers to the left of 0 are negative, as follows:

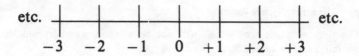

Given any two numbers on a number line, the one on the right is always larger, regardless of its sign (positive or negative).

Addition of Signed Numbers

When adding two numbers with the same sign (either both positive or both negative), add the numbers and keep the same sign. *For example:*

$$\begin{array}{r} +5 \\ +\ +7 \\ \hline +12 \end{array} \qquad \begin{array}{r} -8 \\ +\ -3 \\ \hline -11 \end{array}$$

When adding two numbers with different signs (one positive and one negative), subtract the numbers and keep the sign from the larger one. *For example:*

$$\begin{array}{r} +5 \\ +\ -7 \\ \hline -2 \end{array} \qquad \begin{array}{r} -59 \\ +\ +72 \\ \hline +13 \end{array}$$

Subtraction of Signed Numbers

To subtract positive and/or negative numbers, just change the sign of the number being subtracted and then add. *For example:*

$$\begin{array}{r} +12 \\ -\ +4 \\ \hline \end{array} \quad \begin{array}{r} +12 \\ +\ -4 \\ \hline +8 \end{array} \qquad \begin{array}{r} -19 \\ -\ +6 \\ \hline \end{array} \quad \begin{array}{r} -19 \\ +\ -6 \\ \hline -25 \end{array}$$

$$\begin{array}{r} -14 \\ -\ -4 \\ \hline \end{array} \quad \begin{array}{r} -14 \\ +\ +4 \\ \hline -10 \end{array} \qquad \begin{array}{r} +20 \\ -\ -3 \\ \hline \end{array} \quad \begin{array}{r} +20 \\ +\ +3 \\ \hline +23 \end{array}$$

Multiplying and Dividing Signed Numbers

To multiply or divide signed numbers, treat them just like regular numbers but remember this rule: An odd number of negative signs will produce a negative answer. An even number of negative signs will produce a positive answer. *For example:*

$$(-3)(+8)(-5)(-1)(-2) = +240$$
$$(-3)(+8)(-1)(-2) = -48$$

$$\frac{-64}{-2} = +32$$

$$\frac{-64}{2} = -32$$

Parentheses

Parentheses are used to group numbers. Everything inside parentheses must be done before any other operations. *For example:*

$$50(2 + 6) = 50(8) = 400$$

When a parenthesis is preceded by a minus sign, change the minus to a plus by changing all the signs in front of each term inside the parentheses. Then remove the parentheses. *For example:*

$$6 - (-3 + a - 2b + c) =$$
$$6 + (+3 - a + 2b - c) =$$
$$6 + 3 - a + 2b - c = 9 - a + 2b - c$$

Order of Operations

If multiplication, division, powers, addition, parentheses, etc., are all contained in one problem, the order of operations is as follows:

1. parentheses
2. powers and square roots
3. multiplication⎫ whichever comes first, left to right
4. division ⎭
5. addition ⎫ whichever comes first, left to right
6. subtraction⎭

For example:

$10 - 3 \times 6 + 10^2 + (6 + 1) \times 4 =$
$10 - 3 \times 6 + 10^2 + (7) \times 4 =$ (parentheses first)
$10 - 3 \times 6 + 100 + (7) \times 4 =$ (powers next)
$10 - 18 + 100 + 28 =$ (multiplication)
$-8 + 100 + 28 =$ (addition/subtraction, left to right)
$92 + 28 = 120$

An easy way to remember the order of operations *after parentheses* is: *P*lease *M*y *D*ear *A*unt *S*arah (*P*owers, *M*ultiplication, *D*ivision, *A*ddition, *S*ubtraction).

ALGEBRA

ALGEBRA DIAGNOSTIC TEST

Questions

1. Solve for x: $x + 5 = 17$

2. Solve for x: $4x + 9 = 21$

3. Solve for x: $5x + 7 = 3x - 9$

4. Solve for x: $mx - n = y$

5. Solve for x: $\dfrac{r}{x} = \dfrac{s}{t}$

6. Solve for y: $\dfrac{3}{7} = \dfrac{y}{8}$

7. Evaluate: $3x^2 + 5y + 7$ if $x = -2$ and $y = 3$

8. Simplify: $8xy^2 + 3xy + 4xy^2 - 2xy =$

9. Simplify: $6x^2(4x^3y) =$

10. Simplify: $(5x + 2z) + (3x - 4z) =$

11. Simplify: $(4x - 7z) - (3x - 4z) =$

12. Factor: $ab + ac$

13. Solve for x: $2x + 3 \leq 11$

14. Solve for x: $3x + 4 \geq 5x - 8$

Answers

1. $x = 12$

2. $x = 3$

3. $x = -8$

4. $x = (y + n)/m$

5. $x = \dfrac{rt}{s}$

6. $y = {}^{24}\!/_{7}$ or $3\frac{3}{7}$

7. 34

8. $12xy^2 + xy$

9. $24x^5y$

10. $8x - 2z$

11. $x - 3z$

12. $a(b + c)$

13. $x \leq 4$

14. $x \leq 6$

104

ALGEBRA REVIEW

Equations

An *equation* is a relationship between numbers and/or symbols. It helps to remember that an equation is like a balance scale, with the equal sign ($=$) being the fulcrum, or center. Thus, if you do the *same thing to both sides* of the equal sign (say, add 5 to each side), the equation will still be balanced. To solve the equation $x - 5 = 23$, you must get x by itself on one side; therefore, add 5 to both sides:

$$\begin{array}{r} x - 5 = 23 \\ + 5 + 5 \\ \hline x \quad\ = 28 \end{array}$$

In the same manner, you may subtract, multiply, or divide *both* sides of an equation by the same (nonzero) number, and the equation will not change. Sometimes you may have to use more than one step to solve for an unknown. *For example:*

$$3x + 4 = 19$$

Subtract 4 from both sides to get the 3x by itself on one side:

$$\begin{array}{r} 3x + 4 = 19 \\ - 4 - 4 \\ \hline 3x \quad\ = 15 \end{array}$$

Then divide both sides by 3 to get x:

$$\frac{3x}{3} = \frac{15}{3}$$

$$x = 5$$

Remember: Solving an equation is using opposite operations, until the letter is on a side by itself (for addition, subtract; for multiplication, divide, etc.).

Understood Multiplying

When two or more letters, or a number and letters, are written next to each other, they are understood to be *multiplied*. Thus 8x means 8 times x. Or ab means a times b. Or 18ab means 18 times a times b.

Parentheses also represent multiplication. Thus (a)b means a times b. A raised dot also means multiplication. Thus $6 \cdot 5$ means 6 times 5.

Literal Equations

Literal equations have no numbers, only symbols (letters). *For example:*

$$\text{Solve for Q: } QP - X = Y$$

First add X to both sides:
$$\begin{array}{rl} QP - X &= Y \\ +X &\quad +X \\ \hline QP &= Y + X \end{array}$$

Then divide both sides by P:
$$\frac{QP}{P} = \frac{Y + X}{P}$$

$$Q = \frac{Y + X}{P}$$

Again opposite operations were used to isolate Q.

Cross Multiplying

$$\text{Solve for x: } \frac{b}{x} = \frac{p}{q}$$

To solve this equation quickly, you cross multiply. To cross multiply:

1. bring the denominators up next to the opposite side numerators and
2. multiply

$$\frac{b}{x} = \frac{p}{q}$$

$$bq = px$$

Then divide both sides by p to get x alone:

$$\frac{bq}{p} = \frac{px}{p}$$

$$\frac{bq}{p} = x \text{ or } x = \frac{bq}{p}$$

Cross multiplying can be used only when the format is: 2 fractions separated by an equal sign.

Proportions

Proportions are written as two fractions equal to each other.

$$\text{Solve this proportion for x: } \frac{p}{q} = \frac{x}{y}$$

This is read "p is to q as x is to y." Cross multiply and solve:

$$py = xq$$

$$\frac{py}{q} = \frac{xq}{q}$$

$$\frac{py}{q} = x \text{ or } x = \frac{py}{q}$$

Evaluating Expressions

To *evaluate* an expression, just insert the value for the unknowns and do the arithmetic. *For example:*

Evaluate: $2x^2 + 3y + 6$ if $x = 2$ and $y = 9$

$$2(2^2) + 3(9) + 6 =$$
$$2(4) + 27 + 6 =$$
$$8 + 27 + 6 = 41$$

Monomials and Polynomials

A *monomial* is an algebraic expression that consists of only one term. For instance, $9x$, $4a^2$, and $3mpxz^2$ are all monomials.

A *polynomial* consists of two or more terms; $x + y$, $y^2 - x^2$, and $x^2 + 3x + 5y^2$ are all polynomials.

Adding and Subtracting Monomials

To *add or subtract monomials,* follow the same rules as with regular signed numbers, provided that the *terms are alike:*

$$\begin{array}{r} 15x^2yz \\ -18x^2yz \\ \hline -3x^2yz \end{array} \qquad 3x + 2x = 5x$$

Multiplying and Dividing Monomials

To *multiply monomials,* add the exponents of the same terms:

$$(x^3)(x^4) = x^7$$

$$(x^2y)(x^3y^2) = x^5y^3$$

$$-4(m^2n)(-3m^4n^3) = 12m^6n^4 \text{ (multiply numbers)}$$

To *divide monomials*, subtract the exponents of the like terms:

$$\frac{y^{15}}{y^4} = y^{11} \qquad \frac{x^5y^2}{x^3y} = x^2y \qquad \frac{36a^4b^6}{-9ab} = -4a^3b^5$$

Remember: x is the same as x^1.

Adding and Subtracting Polynomials

To *add or subtract polynomials,* just arrange like terms in columns and then add or subtract:

$$\text{Add:} \qquad \begin{array}{r} a^2 + ab + b^2 \\ 3a^2 + 4ab - 2b^2 \\ \hline 4a^2 + 5ab - b^2 \end{array}$$

$$\text{Subtract:} \qquad \begin{array}{r} a^2 + b^2 \\ - 2a^2 - b^2 \\ \hline \end{array} \longrightarrow \begin{array}{r} a^2 + b^2 \\ + -2a^2 + b^2 \\ \hline -a^2 + 2b^2 \end{array}$$

Multiplying Polynomials

To *multiply polynomials,* multiply each term in one polynomial by each term in the other polynomial. Then simplify if necessary:

$(3x + a)(2x - 2a) =$

$$\begin{array}{r} 2x - 2a \\ \times 3x + a \\ \hline + 2ax - 2a^2 \\ 6x^2 - 6ax \\ \hline 6x^2 - 4ax - 2a^2 \end{array} \qquad \begin{array}{l} \text{similar to} \end{array} \qquad \begin{array}{r} 23 \\ \times 19 \\ \hline 207 \\ 23 \\ \hline 437 \end{array}$$

Factoring

To *factor* means to find two or more quantities whose product equals the original quantity. There are three kinds of factoring:

A. *Factoring out a common factor*

Factor: $2y^3 - 6y$

1. Find the largest common monomial factor of each term.
2. Divide the original polynomial by this factor to obtain the second factor. The second factor will be a polynomial. *For example:*

$$2y^3 - 6y = 2y(y^2 - 3)$$
$$x^5 - 4x^3 + x^2 = x^2(x^3 - 4x + 1)$$

B. *Factoring the difference between 2 squares*

Factor: $x^2 - 144$

1. Find the square root of the first term and the square root of the second term.
2. Express your answer as the product of: the sum of the quantities from step 1, times the difference of those quantities. *For example:*

$$x^2 - 144 = (x + 12)(x - 12)$$
$$a^2 - b^2 = (a + b)(a - b)$$

Inequalities

An *inequality* is a statement in which the relationships are not equal. Instead of using an equal sign $(=)$ as in an equation, we use $>$ (greater than) and $<$ (less than), or $\geq$ (greater than or equal to) and $\leq$ (less than or equal to).

When working with inequalities, treat them exactly like equations, EXCEPT: if you multiply or divide both sides by a negative number, you must *reverse* the direction of the sign. *For example:*

Solve for x: $2x + 4 > 6$

$$\begin{array}{r} 2x + 4 > 6 \\ -4 - 4 \\ \hline 2x \quad\; > 2 \end{array}$$

$$\frac{2x}{2} > \frac{2}{2}$$

$$x > 1$$

Solve for x: $-7x > 14$ (divide by -7 and reverse the sign)

$$\frac{-7x}{-7} < \frac{14}{-7}$$

$$x < -2$$

$3x + 2 \geq 5x - 10$ becomes $-2x \geq -12$ by opposite operations. Divide both sides by -2 and reverse the sign.

$$\frac{-2x}{-2} \leq \frac{-12}{-2}$$

$$x \leq 6$$

GEOMETRY

GEOMETRY DIAGNOSTIC TEST

Questions

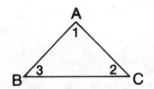

1. Name any angle of this triangle three different ways.

2. A(n)_____angle measures less than 90 degrees.

3. A(n)_____angle measures 90 degrees.

4. A(n)_____angle measures more than 90 degrees.

5. A(n) _____angle measures 180 degrees.

6. Two angles are complementary when their sum is _____.

7. Two angles are supplementary when their sum is _____.

8. In the diagram, find the measures of ∠a, ∠b, and ∠c.

9. Lines that stay the same distance apart and never meet are called _____lines.

10. Lines that meet to form 90 degree angles are called_____lines.

11. A(n)_____triangle has three equal sides. Therefore, each interior angle measures_____.

Questions 12 and 13

12. In the triangle, $\overline{AC}$ must be smaller than_____inches.

13. In the triangle, which angle is smaller, ∠A or ∠C?

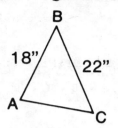

14. What is the measure of ∠ACD?

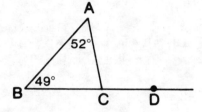

15. What is the length of $\overline{AC}$?

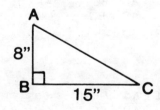

16. What is the length of $\overline{BC}$?

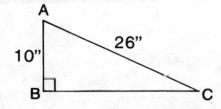

17. Name each of the following polygons:

(A) $\overline{AB} = \overline{BC} = \overline{AC}$
    $\angle A = \angle B = \angle C = 60°$

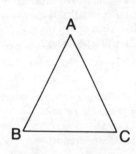

(B) $\overline{AB} = \overline{BC} = \overline{CD} = \overline{AD}$
    $\angle A = \angle B = \angle C = \angle D = 90°$

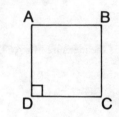

(C) $\overline{AB} \parallel \overline{DC}$
    $\overline{AB} = \overline{DC}$
    $\overline{AD} \parallel \overline{BC}$
    $\overline{AD} = \overline{BC}$
    $\angle A = \angle C$

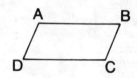

(D) $\overline{AB} = \overline{DC}$
    $\overline{AD} = \overline{BC}$
    $\angle A = \angle B = \angle C = \angle D = 90°$

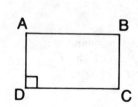

(E) $\overline{AB} \parallel \overline{DC}$

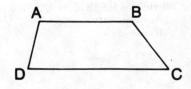

18. Fill in the blanks for circle R:
    (A) $\overline{RS}$ is called the _____.
    (B) $\overline{AB}$ is called the _____.
    (C) $\overline{CD}$ is called a _____.

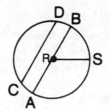

19. Find the area and circumference
    for the circle ($\pi \approx 22/7$):
    (A) area =
    (B) circumference =

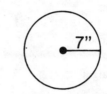

20. Find the area and perimeter
    of the figure:
    (A) area =
    (B) perimeter =

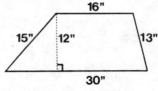

21. Find the area and perimeter of the
    figure (ABCD is a parallelogram):
    (A) area =
    (B) perimeter =

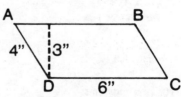

22. Find the volume of the figure
    if $V = (\pi r^2) h$
    (use 3.14 for π):

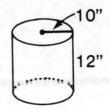

23. What is the surface area and
    volume of the cube?
    (A) surface area =
    (B) volume =

Answers

1. ∠3, ∠CBA, ∠ABC, ∠B
   ∠1, ∠BAC, ∠CAB, ∠A
   ∠2, ∠ACB, ∠BCA, ∠C

2. acute

3. right

4. obtuse

5. straight

6. 90°

7. 180°

8. a = 145°
   b = 35°
   c = 145°

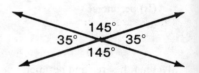

9. parallel

10. perpendicular

11. equilateral, 60°

12. 40 inches. Since $\overline{AB} + \overline{BC} = 40$ inches
    then $\overline{AC} < \overline{AB} + \overline{BC}$
    and $\overline{AC} < 40$ inches

13. ∠ C must be the smaller angle, since it is opposite the shorter side $\overline{AB}$.

14. ∠ ACD = 101°

15. $\overline{AC} = 17$ inches

16. Since $\triangle$ ABC is a right triangle, use the Pythagorean theorem:

$$a^2 + b^2 = c^2$$
$$10^2 + b^2 = 26^2$$
$$100 + b^2 = 676$$
$$b^2 = 576$$
$$b = 24''$$

17. (A) equilateral triangle   (D) rectangle
   (B) square   (E) trapezoid
   (C) parallelogram

18. (A) radius
   (B) diameter
   (C) chord

19. (A) area $= \pi r^2$
            $= \pi(7^2)$
            $= \frac{22}{7}(7)(7)$
            $= 154$ square inches

   (B) circumference $= \pi d$
                        $= \pi(14)$ $d = 14''$, since $r = 7''$
                        $= \frac{22}{7}(14)$
                        $= 22(2)$
                        $= 44$ inches

20. (A) area $= \frac{1}{2}(a + b)h$
             $= \frac{1}{2}(16 + 30)12$
             $= \frac{1}{2}(46)12$
             $= 23(12)$
             $= 276$ square inches
   (B) perimeter $= 16 + 13 + 30 + 15 = 74$ inches

21. (A) area $= bh$
             $= 6(3)$
             $= 18$ square inches
   (B) perimeter $= 6 + 4 + 6 + 4 = 20$ inches

22. Volume = $(\pi r^2)h$
    = $(\pi \cdot 10^2)(12)$
    = $3.14(100)(12)$
    = $314(12)$
    = 3,768 cubic inches

23. (A) All six surfaces have an area of 4×4, or 16 square inches, since each surface is a square. Therefore, $16(6) = 96$ square inches in the surface area.
    (B) Volume = side × side × side, or $4^3 = 64$ cubic inches.

GEOMETRY REVIEW

Plane geometry is the study of shapes and figures in two dimensions (the plane).

Solid geometry is the study of shapes and figures in three dimensions.

A point is the most fundamental idea in geometry. It is represented by a dot and named by a capital letter.

Lines

- A straight *line* is the shortest distance between two points. It continues forever in both directions. A line consists of an infinite number of points. It is named by any two points on the line. The symbol ↔ written on top of the two letters is used to denote that line.

This is line AB:

It is written: $\overleftrightarrow{AB}$

A line may also be named by one small letter. The symbol would not be used.

This is line *l*:

- A *line segment* is a piece of a line. A line segment has two endpoints. It is named by its two endpoints. The symbol — written on top of the two letters is used to denote that line segment.

This is line segment CD:

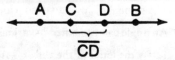

It is written: $\overline{CD}$
Note that it is a piece of $\overleftrightarrow{AB}$.

● A *ray* has only one endpoint and continues forever in one direction. A ray could be thought of as a half-line. It is named by the letter of its endpoint and any other point on the ray. The symbol → written on top of the two letters is used to denote that ray.

This is ray AB:

A   B

It is written: $\overrightarrow{AB}$

This is ray BC:

C   B

It is written: $\overrightarrow{BC}$ or $\overleftarrow{CB}$

Note that the direction of the symbol is the direction of the ray.

Angles

● An *angle* is formed by two rays that start from the same point. That point is called the *vertex;* the rays are called the *sides* of the angle. An angle is measured in degrees. The degrees indicate the size of the angle, from one side to the other.

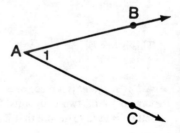

In the diagram, the angle is formed by rays $\overrightarrow{AB}$ and $\overrightarrow{AC}$. A is the vertex. $\overrightarrow{AB}$ and $\overrightarrow{AC}$ are the sides of the angle.

The symbol ∠ is used to denote an angle.

● An angle can be named in various ways:

1. By the letter of the vertex—therefore, the angle above could be named ∠A.
2. By the number (or small letter) in its interior—therefore, the angle above could be named ∠1.

3. By the letters of the three points that formed it—therefore, the angle above could be named ∠BAC, or ∠CAB. The center letter is always the letter of the vertex.

Types of Angles

- *Adjacent angles* are any angles that share a common side and a common vertex.

In the diagram, ∠1 and ∠2 are adjacent angles.

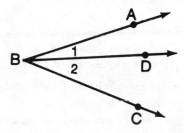

- A *right angle* has a measure of 90°. The symbol ⌐ in the interior of an angle designates the fact that a right angle is formed.

In the diagram, ∠ABC is a right angle.

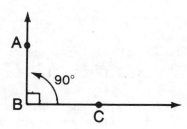

- Any angle whose measure is less than 90° is called an *acute angle*.

In the diagram, ∠b is acute.

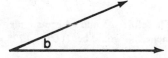

- Any angle whose measure is larger than 90°, but smaller than 180°, is called an *obtuse angle*.

In the diagram, ∠4 is an obtuse angle.

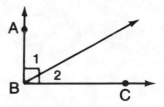

- A *straight angle* has a measure of 180°.

In the diagram, ∠BAC is a straight angle (also called a line).

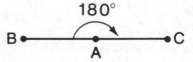

- Two angles whose sum is 90° are called *complementary angles*.

In the diagram, since ∠ABC is a right angle, ∠1 + ∠2 = 90°.

Therefore, ∠1 and ∠2 are complementary angles. If ∠1 = 55°, its complement, ∠2, would be: 90° − 55° = 35°.

- Two angles whose sum is 180° are called *supplementary angles*. Two adjacent angles that form a straight line are supplementary.

In the diagram, since ∠ABC is a straight angle, ∠3 + ∠4 = 180°.

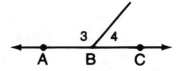

Therefore, ∠3 and ∠4 are supplementary angles. If ∠3 = 122°, its supplement, ∠4, would be: 180° − 122° = 58°.

- A ray from the vertex of an angle that divides the angle into two equal pieces is called an *angle bisector*.

In the diagram, $\overrightarrow{AB}$ is the angle bisector of ∠CAD.

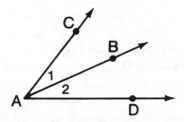

Therefore, ∠1 = ∠2.

- If two straight lines intersect, they do so at a point. Four angles are formed. Those angles opposite each other are called *vertical angles*. Those angles sharing a common side and a common vertex are, again, *adjacent angles*. Vertical angles are always equal.

In the diagram, line *l* and line *m* intersect at point Q. ∠1, ∠2, ∠3, and ∠4 are formed.

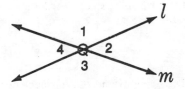

∠1 and ∠3 ⎱ are vertical
∠2 and ∠4 ⎰ angles

∠1 and ∠2 ⎫
∠2 and ∠3 ⎬ are adjacent
∠3 and ∠4 ⎪ angles
∠1 and ∠4 ⎭

Therefore, ∠1 = ∠3
∠2 = ∠4

Types of Lines

- Two or more lines that cross each other at a point are called *intersecting lines*. That point would be on each of those lines.

In the diagram, lines *l* and *m* intersect at Q.

- Two lines that meet to form right angles (90°) are called *perpendicular lines*. The symbol ⊥ is used to denote perpendicular lines.

In the diagram, line *l* ⊥ line *m*.

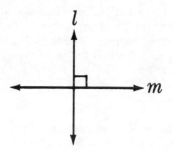

- Two or more lines that remain the same distance apart at all times are called *parallel lines*. Parallel lines never meet. The symbol ‖ is used to denote parallel lines.

In the diagram, *l* ‖ *m*.

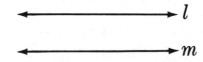

Polygons

- Closed shapes or figures with three or more sides are called *polygons*. (*Poly* means "many"; *gon* means "sides"; thus, *polygon* means "many sides.")

Triangles

- This section deals with those polygons having the fewest number of sides. A *triangle* is a three-sided polygon. It has three angles in its interior. The sum of these angles is *always* 180°. The symbol for triangle is △. A triangle is named by all three letters of its vertices.

This is △ ABC:

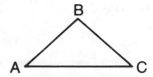

- Types of triangles:
  1. A triangle having all three sides equal (meaning all three sides have the same length) is called an *equilateral triangle*.
  2. A triangle having two sides equal is called an *isosceles triangle*.
  3. A triangle having none of its sides equal is called a *scalene triangle*.
  4. A triangle having a right (90°) angle in its interior is called a *right triangle*.

Facts about Triangles

- Every triangle has a base (bottom side) and a height (or altitude). Every height is the *perpendicular* (forms right angles) distance from a vertex to its opposite side (the base).

In this diagram of △ ABC, $\overline{BC}$ is the base, and $\overline{AE}$ is the height. $\overline{AE} \perp \overline{BC}$.

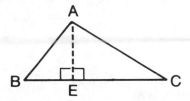

- Every triangle has a median. The median is the line segment drawn from a vertex to the midpoint of the opposite side.

In this diagram of △ ABC, E is
the midpoint of $\overline{BC}$.

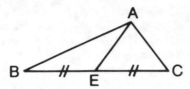

Therefore, $\overline{BE} = \overline{EC}$. $\overline{AE}$ is the median of ABC.

- In an equilateral triangle, all three sides are equal, and all three angles are
  equal. If all three angles are equal and their sum is 180°, the following
  must be true:

$$x + x + x = 180°$$
$$3x = 180°$$
$$x = 60°$$

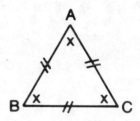

Every angle of an equilateral triangle always has a measure of 60°.

- In any triangle, the longest side is always opposite from the largest angle.
  Likewise, the shortest side is always opposite from the smallest angle. In a
  right triangle, the longest side will always be opposite from the right angle,
  as the right angle will be the largest angle in the triangle.

$\overline{AC}$ is the longest side of
right △ ABC.

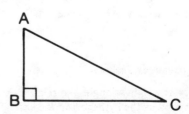

- The sum of the lengths of any two sides of a triangle must be larger than the length of the third side.

In the diagram of ABC:

$$\overline{AB} + \overline{BC} > \overline{AC}$$
$$\overline{AB} + \overline{AC} > \overline{BC}$$
$$\overline{AC} + \overline{BC} > \overline{AB}$$

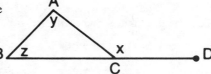

- If one side of a triangle is extended, the exterior angle formed by that extension is equal to the sum of the other two interior angles.

In the diagram of △ ABC, side BC is extended to D.

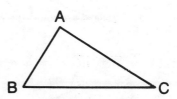

∠ACD is the exterior angle formed.
$\angle x = \angle y + \angle z$

$x = 82° + 41°$
$x = 123°$

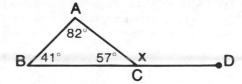

Pythagorean Theorem

- In any right triangle, the relationship between the lengths of the sides is stated by the Pythagorean theorem. The parts of a right triangle are:

∠C is the right angle.

The side opposite the right angle
is called the *hypotenuse* (side c).
(The hypotenuse will always be the
longest side.)

The other two sides are called the
legs (sides a and b).

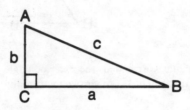

The three lengths a, b, and c will always be numbers such that:

$$a^2 + b^2 = c^2$$

For example:

If a = 3, b = 4, and c = 5,

$a^2 + b^2 = c^2$
$3^2 + 4^2 = 5^2$
$9 + 16 = 25$
$\quad\quad 25 = 25$

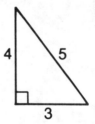

Therefore, 3-4-5 is called a Pythagorean triple. There are other values for
a, b, and c that will always work. Some are: 1-1-$\sqrt{2}$, 5-12-13, and 8-15-17.
Any multiple of one of these triples will also work. For example, using the
3-4-5: 6-8-10, 9-12-15, and 15-20-25 will also be Pythagorean triples.

- If perfect squares are known, the lengths of these sides can be determined easily. A knowledge of the use of algebraic equations can also be used to determine the lengths of the sides. *For example:*

$$a^2 + b^2 = c^2$$
$$x^2 + 10^2 = 15^2$$
$$x^2 + 100 = 225$$
$$x^2 = 125$$
$$x = \sqrt{125}$$
$$= \sqrt{25} \times \sqrt{5}$$
$$= 5\sqrt{5}$$

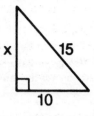

Quadrilaterals

- A polygon having four sides is called a *quadrilateral*. There are four angles in its interior. The sum of these interior angles will always be 360°. A quadrilateral is named by using the four letters of its vertices.

This is quadrilateral ABCD:

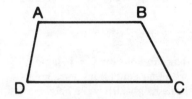

Types of Quadrilaterals

- The *square* has four equal sides and four right angles.

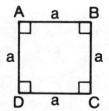

- The *rectangle* has opposite sides equal and four right angles.

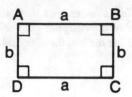

- The *parallelogram* has opposite sides equal and parallel, opposite angles equal, and consecutive angles supplementary. Every parallelogram has a height.

$\angle A = \angle C$
$\angle B = \angle D$
$\angle A + \angle B = 180°$
$\angle A + \angle D = 180°$
$\angle B + \angle C = 180°$
$\angle C + \angle D = 180°$

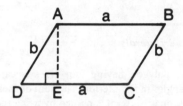

AE is the height of the parallelogram, $\overline{AB} \parallel \overline{CD}$, and $\overline{AD} \parallel \overline{BC}$.

- The *rhombus* is a parallelogram with four equal sides. A rhombus has a height. BE is the height.

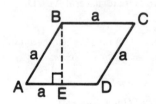

- The *trapezoid* has only one pair of parallel sides. A trapezoid has a height. AE is the height. $\overline{AB} \parallel \overline{DC}$.

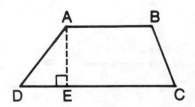

Other Polygons

- The *pentagon* is a five-sided polygon.
- The *hexagon* is a six-sided polygon.
- The *octagon* is an eight-sided polygon.
- The *nonagon* is a nine-sided polygon.
- The *decagon* is a ten-sided polygon.

Facts about Polygons

- *Regular* means all sides have the same length and all angles have the same measure. A regular three-sided polygon is the equilateral triangle. A regular four-sided polygon is the square. There are no other special names. Other polygons will just be described as regular, if they are. For example, a regular five-sided polygon is called a regular pentagon. A regular six-sided polygon is called a regular hexagon.

Perimeter

- *Perimeter* means the total distance all the way around the outside of any polygon. The perimeter of any polygon can be determined by adding up the lengths of all the sides. The total distance around will be the sum of all sides of the polygon. No special formulas are really necessary.

Area

Area (A) means the amount of space inside the polygon. The formulas for each area are as follows:

- Triangle: $A = \frac{1}{2}bh$

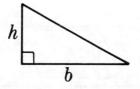   or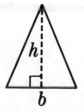

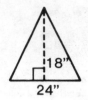

For example:
A = ½bh
A = ½(24)(18) = 216 sq in

- Square or rectangle: A = *lw*

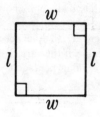   or

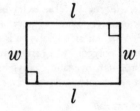

For example:

A = *l*(*w*) = 4(4) = 16 sq in

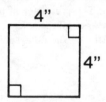

A = *l*(*w*) = 12(5) = 60 sq in

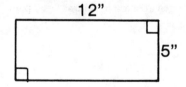

- Parallelogram: A = *bh*

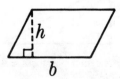

For example:
A = b(h)
A = 10(5) = 50 sq in

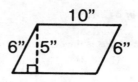

• Trapezoid: A = ½(a + b)h

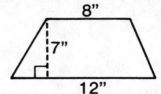

For example:
A = ½(a + b)h
A = ½(8 + 12)7
  = ½(20)7 = 70 sq in

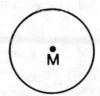

Circles

• A closed shape whose side is formed by one curved line all points of which are equidistant from the center point is called a *circle*. Circles are named by the letter of their center point.

This is circle M:

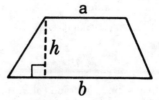

M is the center point, since it is the same distance away from any point on the circle.

Parts of a Circle

- The *radius* is the distance from the center to any point on the circle.

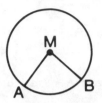

$\overline{MA}$ is a radius.
$\overline{MB}$ is a radius.

In any circle, all radii (plural) are the same length.

- The *diameter* of a circle is the distance across the circle, through the center.

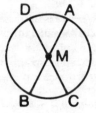

$\overline{AB}$ is a diameter.
$\overline{CD}$ is a diameter.

In any circle, all diameters are the same length. Each diameter is two radii.

- A *chord* of a circle is a line segment whose end points lie on the circle itself.

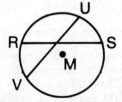

$\overline{RS}$ is a chord.
$\overline{UV}$ is a chord.

The diameter is the longest chord in any circle.

- An *arc* is the distance between any two points *on* the circle itself. An arc is a piece of the circle. The symbol ⌢ is used to denote an arc. It is written on top of the two endpoints that form the arc. Arcs are measured in degrees. There are 360° around the circle.

This is $\overset{\frown}{EF}$:

Minor $\overset{\frown}{EF}$ is the shorter distance between E and F.
Major $\overset{\frown}{EF}$ is the longer distance between E and F.
When $\overset{\frown}{EF}$ is written, the minor arc is assumed.

Area and Circumference

- *Circumference* is the distance around the circle. Since there are no sides to add up, a formula is needed. π (pi) is a Greek letter that represents a specific number. In fractional or decimal form, the commonly used approximations are: $\pi \simeq 3.14$ or $\pi \simeq {}^{22}/_7$. The formula for circumference is: $C = \pi d$ or $C = 2 \pi r$. *For example:*

In circle M, d = 8, since r = 4.

$C = \pi d$
$C = \pi (8)$
$C = 3.14(8)$
$C = 25.12$ inches

- The *area* of a circle can be determined by: $A = \pi r^2$. *For example:*

In circle M, r = 5, since d = 10.

$A = \pi(r^2)$
$A = \pi(5^2)$
$A = 3.14(25)$
$A = 78.5$ sq in

Volume

● In three dimensions there are different facts that can be determined about shapes. *Volume* is the capacity to hold. The formula for volume of each shape is different. The volume of any *prism* (a three-dimensional shape having many sides, but two bases) can be determined by: Volume (V) = (area of base) (height of prism).

Specifically for a rectangular solid:

$V = (lw)(h)$
$= lwh$

Specifically for a cylinder (circular bases):

$V = (\pi r^2)h$
$V = \pi r^2 h$

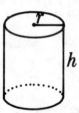

Volume is labeled "cubic" units.

Surface Area

● The *surface area* of a three-dimensional solid is the area of all of the surfaces that form the solid. Find the area of each surface, and then add up those areas. The surface area of a rectangular solid can be found by adding up the areas of all six surfaces. *For example:*

The surface area of this prism is:

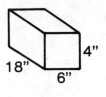

top	18 × 6 =	108
bottom	18 × 6 =	108
left side	6 × 4 =	24
right side	6 × 4 =	24
front	18 × 4 =	72
back	18 × 4 =	72
		408 sq in

PART IV: Practice-Review-Analyze-Practice

Three Full-Length Practice Tests

This section contains three full-length simulation CBESTs. The practice tests are followed by complete answers, explanations, and analysis techniques. The format, levels of difficulty, question structures, and number of questions are similar to those on the actual CBEST. The actual CBEST is copyrighted and may not be duplicated, and these questions are not taken directly from the actual tests.

When taking these exams, try to simulate the test conditions by following the time allotments carefully. Remember, the total testing time for each practice test is approximately 3 hours and 15 minutes. Be aware of the different time allotments for each section.

PRACTICE TEST 1

Section I: Reading Comprehension—65 Minutes, 50 Questions
Section II: Mathematics—70 Minutes; 50 Questions
Section III: Essay Writing—60 Minutes; 2 Essays

ANSWER SHEET FOR PRACTICE TEST 1
(Remove This Sheet and Use It to Mark Your Answers)

SECTION I: READING COMPREHENSION

1 Ⓐ Ⓑ Ⓒ Ⓓ Ⓔ	26 Ⓐ Ⓑ Ⓒ Ⓓ Ⓔ
2 Ⓐ Ⓑ Ⓒ Ⓓ Ⓔ	27 Ⓐ Ⓑ Ⓒ Ⓓ Ⓔ
3 Ⓐ Ⓑ Ⓒ Ⓓ Ⓔ	28 Ⓐ Ⓑ Ⓒ Ⓓ Ⓔ
4 Ⓐ Ⓑ Ⓒ Ⓓ Ⓔ	29 Ⓐ Ⓑ Ⓒ Ⓓ Ⓔ
5 Ⓐ Ⓑ Ⓒ Ⓓ Ⓔ	30 Ⓐ Ⓑ Ⓒ Ⓓ Ⓔ
6 Ⓐ Ⓑ Ⓒ Ⓓ Ⓔ	31 Ⓐ Ⓑ Ⓒ Ⓓ Ⓔ
7 Ⓐ Ⓑ Ⓒ Ⓓ Ⓔ	32 Ⓐ Ⓑ Ⓒ Ⓓ Ⓔ
8 Ⓐ Ⓑ Ⓒ Ⓓ Ⓔ	33 Ⓐ Ⓑ Ⓒ Ⓓ Ⓔ
9 Ⓐ Ⓑ Ⓒ Ⓓ Ⓔ	34 Ⓐ Ⓑ Ⓒ Ⓓ Ⓔ
10 Ⓐ Ⓑ Ⓒ Ⓓ Ⓔ	35 Ⓐ Ⓑ Ⓒ Ⓓ Ⓔ
11 Ⓐ Ⓑ Ⓒ Ⓓ Ⓔ	36 Ⓐ Ⓑ Ⓒ Ⓓ Ⓔ
12 Ⓐ Ⓑ Ⓒ Ⓓ Ⓔ	37 Ⓐ Ⓑ Ⓒ Ⓓ Ⓔ
13 Ⓐ Ⓑ Ⓒ Ⓓ Ⓔ	38 Ⓐ Ⓑ Ⓒ Ⓓ Ⓔ
14 Ⓐ Ⓑ Ⓒ Ⓓ Ⓔ	39 Ⓐ Ⓑ Ⓒ Ⓓ Ⓔ
15 Ⓐ Ⓑ Ⓒ Ⓓ Ⓔ	40 Ⓐ Ⓑ Ⓒ Ⓓ Ⓔ
16 Ⓐ Ⓑ Ⓒ Ⓓ Ⓔ	41 Ⓐ Ⓑ Ⓒ Ⓓ Ⓔ
17 Ⓐ Ⓑ Ⓒ Ⓓ Ⓔ	42 Ⓐ Ⓑ Ⓒ Ⓓ Ⓔ
18 Ⓐ Ⓑ Ⓒ Ⓓ Ⓔ	43 Ⓐ Ⓑ Ⓒ Ⓓ Ⓔ
19 Ⓐ Ⓑ Ⓒ Ⓓ Ⓔ	44 Ⓐ Ⓑ Ⓒ Ⓓ Ⓔ
20 Ⓐ Ⓑ Ⓒ Ⓓ Ⓔ	45 Ⓐ Ⓑ Ⓒ Ⓓ Ⓔ
21 Ⓐ Ⓓ Ⓒ Ⓓ Ⓒ	46 Ⓐ Ⓓ Ⓒ Ⓓ Ⓒ
22 Ⓐ Ⓑ Ⓒ Ⓓ Ⓔ	47 Ⓐ Ⓑ Ⓒ Ⓓ Ⓔ
23 Ⓐ Ⓑ Ⓒ Ⓓ Ⓔ	48 Ⓐ Ⓑ Ⓒ Ⓓ Ⓔ
24 Ⓐ Ⓑ Ⓒ Ⓓ Ⓔ	49 Ⓐ Ⓑ Ⓒ Ⓓ Ⓔ
25 Ⓐ Ⓑ Ⓒ Ⓓ Ⓔ	50 Ⓐ Ⓑ Ⓒ Ⓓ Ⓔ

SECTION II: MATHEMATICS

1 Ⓐ Ⓑ Ⓒ Ⓓ Ⓔ		26 Ⓐ Ⓑ Ⓒ Ⓓ Ⓔ
2 Ⓐ Ⓑ Ⓒ Ⓓ Ⓔ		27 Ⓐ Ⓑ Ⓒ Ⓓ Ⓔ
3 Ⓐ Ⓑ Ⓒ Ⓓ Ⓔ		28 Ⓐ Ⓑ Ⓒ Ⓓ Ⓔ
4 Ⓐ Ⓑ Ⓒ Ⓓ Ⓔ		29 Ⓐ Ⓑ Ⓒ Ⓓ Ⓔ
5 Ⓐ Ⓑ Ⓒ Ⓓ Ⓔ		30 Ⓐ Ⓑ Ⓒ Ⓓ Ⓔ
6 Ⓐ Ⓑ Ⓒ Ⓓ Ⓔ		31 Ⓐ Ⓑ Ⓒ Ⓓ Ⓔ
7 Ⓐ Ⓑ Ⓒ Ⓓ Ⓔ		32 Ⓐ Ⓑ Ⓒ Ⓓ Ⓔ
8 Ⓐ Ⓑ Ⓒ Ⓓ Ⓔ		33 Ⓐ Ⓑ Ⓒ Ⓓ Ⓔ
9 Ⓐ Ⓑ Ⓒ Ⓓ Ⓔ		34 Ⓐ Ⓑ Ⓒ Ⓓ Ⓔ
10 Ⓐ Ⓑ Ⓒ Ⓓ Ⓔ		35 Ⓐ Ⓑ Ⓒ Ⓓ Ⓔ
11 Ⓐ Ⓑ Ⓒ Ⓓ Ⓔ		36 Ⓐ Ⓑ Ⓒ Ⓓ Ⓔ
12 Ⓐ Ⓑ Ⓒ Ⓓ Ⓔ		37 Ⓐ Ⓑ Ⓒ Ⓓ Ⓔ
13 Ⓐ Ⓑ Ⓒ Ⓓ Ⓔ		38 Ⓐ Ⓑ Ⓒ Ⓓ Ⓔ
14 Ⓐ Ⓑ Ⓒ Ⓓ Ⓔ		39 Ⓐ Ⓑ Ⓒ Ⓓ Ⓔ
15 Ⓐ Ⓑ Ⓒ Ⓓ Ⓔ		40 Ⓐ Ⓑ Ⓒ Ⓓ Ⓔ
16 Ⓐ Ⓑ Ⓒ Ⓓ Ⓔ		41 Ⓐ Ⓑ Ⓒ Ⓓ Ⓔ
17 Ⓐ Ⓑ Ⓒ Ⓓ Ⓔ		42 Ⓐ Ⓑ Ⓒ Ⓓ Ⓔ
18 Ⓐ Ⓑ Ⓒ Ⓓ Ⓔ		43 Ⓐ Ⓑ Ⓒ Ⓓ Ⓔ
19 Ⓐ Ⓑ Ⓒ Ⓓ Ⓔ		44 Ⓐ Ⓑ Ⓒ Ⓓ Ⓔ
20 Ⓐ Ⓑ Ⓒ Ⓓ Ⓔ		45 Ⓐ Ⓑ Ⓒ Ⓓ Ⓔ
21 Ⓐ Ⓑ Ⓒ Ⓓ Ⓔ		46 Ⓐ Ⓑ Ⓒ Ⓓ Ⓔ
22 Ⓐ Ⓑ Ⓒ Ⓓ Ⓔ		47 Ⓐ Ⓑ Ⓒ Ⓓ Ⓔ
23 Ⓐ Ⓑ Ⓒ Ⓓ Ⓔ		48 Ⓐ Ⓑ Ⓒ Ⓓ Ⓔ
24 Ⓐ Ⓑ Ⓒ Ⓓ Ⓔ		49 Ⓐ Ⓑ Ⓒ Ⓓ Ⓔ
25 Ⓐ Ⓑ Ⓒ Ⓓ Ⓔ		50 Ⓐ Ⓑ Ⓒ Ⓓ Ⓔ

SECTION I: READING COMPREHENSION

Time: 65 Minutes
50 Questions

DIRECTIONS

A question or number of questions follow each of the statements or passages in this section. Using only the *stated* or *implied* information given in the statement or passage, answer the question or questions by choosing the *best* answer from among the five choices given.

The major function of social psychology as a behavioral science, and therefore as a discipline which can contribute to the solution of many social problems, is its investigation of the psychology of the individual in society. Thus, the scientist's main objective is to attempt to determine the influences of the social environment upon the personal behavior of individuals.

1. Which of the following best summarizes the passage?
    (A) Social psychology is a science in which the behavior of the scientist in the social environment is a major function.
    (B) The social environment influences the behavior of individuals.
    (C) Social psychology studies the ways in which people in society are affected by their surroundings.
    (D) Understanding human behavior, through the help of social psychology, leads to the eventual betterment of society.
    (E) A minor objective of social psychology is the solution of social problems.

The quiet child is one of our concerns today. Our philosophy about children and speaking in the classroom has flip-flopped. Today we are interested in what Ruth Strickland implies when she refers to the idea of "freeing the child to talk."

2. Which of the following is implied by this passage?
    (A) Teachers in the past have preferred quiet and reticent students.
    (B) The behavior of children in the classroom is a trivial concern that can change abruptly.
    (C) Whether or not a child is quiet determines the quality of his or her education.
    (D) Ruth Strickland never explicitly stated her opinions about children and speaking in the classroom.
    (E) There are fewer quiet children today than in the past.

143

For some, the term *creative writing* seems to imply precious writing, useless writing, flowery writing, writing that is a luxury rather than a necessity, something that is produced under the influence of drugs or leisure, a hobby.

3. By *precious* the author of this passage means
   (A) beloved   (D) valuable
   (B) costly   (E) affected
   (C) desirable

No matter how significant the speaker's message, and no matter how strongly he or she feels about it, it will be lost unless the listeners attend to it. Attention and perception are key concepts in communication.

4. The primary purpose of the statement is to
   (A) imply that some speakers without strong feelings find an attentive audience
   (B) note that some very important messages fall on deaf ears
   (C) stress the critical role of listening in oral communication
   (D) urge readers to listen more carefully to spoken language
   (E) argue that attention and perception are unimportant concepts in communication

Many of today's secondary school students will retire (either voluntarily or by coercion) from their careers or professions between the ages of forty and fifty. Indeed, by 1995 the problems of today's elderly are going to be the problems of the middle-aged.

5. If the above statement is true, then which of the following must also be true?
   (A) People are beginning to age more quickly.
   (B) There will be more leisure time available for more people in the future.
   (C) Today's secondary school students will be entering careers which require youthful stamina.
   (D) No one in the future will want to work during the second half of their lives.
   (E) Retirement will become a more attractive possibility in the future.

Questions 6 and 7 refer to the following passage.

In future decades, what is actually required is the development of a new type of citizen—an individual who possesses confidence in his or her own potential, a person who is not intimidated by the prospect of not actively pursuing a career after the age of forty-five, and an individual who comprehends that technology can produce an easier world but only mankind can produce a better one.

6. Which of the following is an unstated assumption made by the author of this passage?
    (A) Technology is the unrecognized key to a better future.
    (B) Present citizens are intimidated by the prospect of ending their careers in middle age.
    (C) Present citizens do not have limitless potentials.
    (D) Many people in the future will pursue at least two careers in the course of a lifetime.
    (E) An easier world is not necessarily a safer one.

7. The author of the passage would disagree with which of the following statements?
    (A) The new type of citizen described in the passage does not presently exist.
    (B) Future decades may bring about a change in the existing types of citizens.
    (C) A new type of citizen will become necessary in future decades.
    (D) Technology should be regarded as a source of a better life.
    (E) Human potential is not limited, and we should be especially careful not to think of our potential as limited.

Questions 8, 9, and 10 refer to the following passage.

The arts have been dismissed by some legislators as mere entertainment. As we strive not merely to amuse, but to reveal the great truths of human nature, we must remember that some regard our performances as "sound and fury, signifying nothing."

8. The author of this passage is probably
    (A) a citizen writing to a legislator
    (B) an actor writing to other actors
    (C) an actor playing a part
    (D) a painter writing to other painters
    (E) a philosopher writing to political scientists

9. The passage supports a concept of art as
    (A) a political activity
    (B) more than entertainment
    (C) empty of entertainment value
    (D) generously subsidized by the government
    (E) of no use to a serious audience

10. The author repeats *some* in order to indicate that
    (A) the problem described is a relatively small one
    (B) the legislators may be in the same group that regards performances as signifying nothing
    (C) the actor will never meet with a wholly sympathetic audience
    (D) the "sound and fury" on stage is paralleled in the legislature
    (E) most members of the audience are merely amused

Questions 11, 12, and 13 are based on the following passage.

If we must have evaluation, at least do it without grades. Grades are not good indicators of intellectual ability; we must abolish them. Then we will have students who are motivated by factors such as interest, factors more important than a letter on a transcript. And the abolition of grades will encourage us to concentrate less on evaluation and more on instruction.

11. In order to agree with this author's argument, we must presume that
    (A) wherever grades exist, instruction is poor
    (B) there are indicators of intellectual ability that are better than grades
    (C) graded students are not good students
    (D) intellectual ability can be measured only in a school situation
    (E) grades are the remaining hindrance to effective education

12. A reader of this passage might conclude that the author feels that graded students are not motivated by
    (A) the prospect of a high grade point average
    (B) interest in the subject matter of their course
    (C) the evaluation criteria established by their instructors
    (D) a thoroughly prepared instructor
    (E) the practicality of academic disciplines

13. This passage is most probably directed at which of the following audiences?
    (A) politicians   (D) teachers
    (B) parents   (E) civic leaders
    (C) students

Questions 14, 15, and 16 refer to the following passage.

We should spend more time enjoying life than preparing for its challenges, but sometimes we don't. For example, toward the end of every semester, all students at the university are tired and grumpy because they have spent long nights preparing for final exams. Consequently, they rarely look back on college as a time spent enjoying good fellowship and fine entertainment.

14. To agree with this author, we must accept which of the following implications of his or her argument?
    (A) It is only worthwhile to prepare for enjoyment.
    (B) School examinations do not require preparation.
    (C) Preparation is inappropriate only toward the end of the semester.
    (D) The result of preparation for exams is fatigue.
    (E) College students study too much.

15. According to this writer, the most memorable characteristic of college life should be
    (A) social interaction
    (B) academic fastidiousness
    (C) the value of sleep
    (D) more efficient exam preparation
    (E) a pleasant attitude

16. The author might have strengthened the argument without abandoning it by
    (A) changing *all* to *some*
    (B) advancing arguments in favor of studying all night
    (C) acknowledging that grumpiness is not necessarily related to fatigue
    (D) choosing a different example to illustrate the initial point
    (E) focusing the argument more explicitly on a particular audience

When asked by his students to comment on the value of steroids for increasing muscle size, the physical education teacher said, "Steroids can be very dangerous. Many bodybuilders use them for a short period before a contest. However, the long-term use of steroids might possibly cause severe damage to the reproductive system while it helps to build a beautiful body."

17. In this statement, the teacher is
    (A) categorically against the use of steroids
    (B) an advocate of steroids but not of reproduction
    (C) recommending the short-term use of steroids
    (D) trying not to condemn steroid users
    (E) preferring muscle definition to muscle size

Questions 18 and 19 refer to the following passage.

In modern society, those who are most adaptable to both an inflating economy and the decreasing value of the individual will survive in comfort. It is these survivors who will have the most value in the future.

18. The kind of value that the survivors possess is
    (A) inflating
    (B) decreasing
    (C) individual
    (D) comfortable
    (E) unstated

19. What conclusion about value must we accept if we accept the author's statement?
    (A) Value transcends the factors of time and place.
    (B) Survival is its own value.
    (C) Decreasing value must be tolerated.
    (D) Socioeconomic factors affect the definition of value.
    (E) Value is inversely proportional to the economy.

Questions 20 through 24 refer to the following passage.

Creative writing may serve many purposes for the writer. Above all, it is a means of self-expression. It is the individual's way of saying, "These are my thoughts and they are uniquely experienced by me." But creative writing can also serve as a safety valve for dormant tensions. This implies that a period of time has evolved in which the child gave an idea some deep thought and that the message on paper is revealing of this deep, inner thought. Finally, a worthwhile by-product of creative writing is the stimulus it gives students to do further reading and experimentation in their areas of interest. A child might become an ardent reader of good literature in order to satisfy an appetite whetted by a creative writing endeavor.

20. The primary purpose of the author of this passage is
    (A) to call attention to a widespread lack of self-expression
    (B) to address the increasing anxiety that plagues many individuals
    (C) to stress the value of good literature, both amateur and professional
    (D) to encourage the reader to try some creative writing
    — (E) to discuss some positive purposes and effects of creative writing

21. The content of the passage indicates that the passage would be least likely to appear in which of the following?
    (A) *Journal of English Teaching Techniques*
    (B) *Psychology Today*
    (C) *Journal of Technical Writing*
    (D) *Teaching English Today*
    (E) *The Creative Writer*

22. According to the passage, creative writing can help release dormant tensions because
    (A) the writer will usually write something autobiographical
    (B) understanding literature means understanding the tensions of the characters
    (C) creative writing can express what the writer has long held within
    (D) tensions are a by-product of writer's block
    (E) self-expression is never tense

23. All of the following are probably important to the ability to write creatively *except*
    (A) deep thought
    (B) time to think and ponder
    (C) spelling
    (D) reading
    (E) good literature

24. According to the passage, creative writing is most of all a
    (A) stimulus for further reading
    (B) release valve for dormant tensions
    (C) way of expressing one's feelings and thoughts
    (D) chance to let off steam
    (E) by-product of reading

Questions 25 through 30 are based on the following passage.

Throughout the history of mankind, predictions of future events have found receptive audiences: during the thirteenth century, the English scientist Roger Bacon discussed the development of such things as optical instruments and motor boats; in the fifteenth century, Leonardo da Vinci wrote about tanks and helicopters; in the nineteenth century, Jules Verne described trips to the moon. Man has always been interested in where he is going. Since humanity's continued existence is dependent upon its making intelligent decisions about the future, such fascination has taken on a very practical dimension. Along with the changes in social mores and attitudes, greater numbers of people are demanding a role in planning the future. The social studies curriculum must provide students with an understanding of how significant future challenges will be with regard to our national survival, social problems, religion, marriage and family life, and in our political processes.

It is vital that social studies teachers immerse themselves in the new field of futuristics—the study of future prospects and possibilities affecting the human condition. Futuristics, as an academic area, is already being taught at many major universities for the purpose of encouraging students to achieve an awareness that they can contribute to the development of a much better national and global society than they ever dreamed of. The perspective of futurism is very important for today's students, since they know they can do nothing about the past.

25. Which of the following is the intended audience for the passage?
   (A) students planning which courses to take in high school
   (B) teachers considering changing or enriching the curriculum
   (C) historians interested in the ways that the past reflects the future
   (D) politicians drafting future legislation that addresses present social problems
   (E) parents concerned about what their children should be learning

26. In order to show that "man has always been interested in where he is going," the author provides which of the following types of facts?
   (A) unfounded   (D) historical
   (B) extraterrestrial   (E) scientific
   (C) political

27. Which of the following is an assumption of the passage but is not explicitly stated?
   (A) Futuristic studies should take precedence over all other school studies.
   (B) Today's students know little about the past and less about the future.
   (C) Many social studies curriculums do not adequately acknowledge the importance of futurism.
   (D) Some figures in the past have been the equivalent of modern fortunetellers.
   (E) Social studies gives little thought to the future.

28. In the passage, the intended meaning of *global society* is which of the
   following?
   (A) a society well aware of the contributions of Bacon, da Vinci, and
   Verne
   (B) a society whose students have had courses in international rela-
   tions
   (C) a society able to communicate with other societies around the
   globe
   (D) a society including the globes of other solar systems
   (E) a society including all the nations of the earth

29. Which of the following statements, if true, would most weaken the
   author's argument?
   (A) Figures other than Bacon, da Vinci, and Verne might have been
   mentioned as well.
   (B) Apart from Bacon, da Vinci, and Verne, many others who have
   tried to "see into" the future have voiced prospects and possibilities
   that did not come true.
   (C) Those major universities not offering courses in futuristics are
   considering them.
   (D) Futuristics has been the nonacademic interest of great numbers of
   people for many centuries.
   (E) Futuristic predictions are the stock-in-trade of many sincere politicians trying to urge the passage of significant legislation.

30. The author of this passage would most likely be
   (A) a historian   (D) an educator
   (B) a traditionalist   (E) a pacifist
   (C) a high school teacher

Questions 31 through 35 refer to the following passage.

Possibly everyone at some point has been in a classroom where he or
she didn't dare express an idea for fear that it would be chopped off. And
if it was expressed, it was chopped off and no further ideas came forth.
Perhaps everyone at some time has been in a student group where a
participant started to express an insight but was nipped in the bud by a
teacher who corrected the student's usage. Perhaps some have been in a
classroom where a child was groping for just the right way to express a
thought only to have the teacher or another child supply the words. And
some have wondered why a certain child was so talkative at age five and
so reticent at sixteen.

31. The author implies which of the following in the passage?
    - (A) Wondering about human inhibitions will do little to solve the problem.
    - (B) Only certain children are either uninhibited at age five or inhibited at age sixteen.
    - (C) Sixteen-year-olds should spend more time in the classroom with five-year-olds.
    - (D) Attending school may cause children to become inhibited.
    - (E) Inhibitions go along with maturity.

32. Which of the following terms is an appropriate substitute for *chopped off*?
    - (A) put out
    - (B) removed
    - (C) severely criticized
    - (D) misunderstood
    - (E) cut back

33. Which of the following techniques is the author using to make the point that classroom situations can be very undesirable?
    - (A) an appeal to the personal experiences of the readers
    - (B) disguised references to recent educational theory
    - (C) unsubstantiated and illogical anecdotes
    - (D) a story
    - (E) references to his or her own experiences as a teacher

34. The author's attitude may be described as being
    - (A) supportive
    - (B) critical
    - (C) skeptical
    - (D) favorable
    - (E) affected

35. The author would probably most strongly agree with which of the following statements?
    - (A) Students should think carefully before expressing ideas in class.
    - (B) Teachers should be critical of students' expressions.
    - (C) Talkative students should be tactfully silenced.
    - (D) Teachers should be careful not to inhibit students' expressions.
    - (E) Teachers should assist students in completing their expressions.

Questions 36 through 42 refer to the following passage.

Learning disabilities are among the most frequently occurring of all childhood disorders. It is estimated that eight million children in the United States can be classified as learning disabled. And many more function ineffectually *throughout their entire lives* due to learning disabilities. The Department of Health, Education, and Welfare's National Advisory Committee on Dyslexia and Related Reading Disorders estimates that fifteen percent of children in public schools experience difficulty in learning to read. The majority of children identified as being learning disabled are so diagnosed because of difficulties in mastering the process of reading.

It is apparent that reading requires a number of intact auditory processing skills. All levels of auditory processing also require an intact sensorimotor system. In language acquisition, the child must be able to receive acoustical messages which make up the individual language system being acquired. In addition to requiring an adequate auditory mechanism, auditory processing involves a complex series of behaviors including but not limited to: the ability to focus attention on the content and the source of the message; the ability to detect and identify the selected message; the ability to transmit and conduct the message to the brain for analysis; the ability to store and retain the message by sorting out the appropriate perceptual or cognitive level; and the ability to retrieve and restore the message.

36. According to the passage above, the number of people who function ineffectually throughout their entire lives due to learning disabilities
    (A) can never be estimated
    (B) has never been estimated
    (C) has been estimated at less than eight million
    (D) has been estimated at just over eight million
    — (E) has been estimated at much greater than eight million

37. The content indicates that the passage would be most likely to appear in which of the following?
    (A) an article about successful classroom techniques for teaching reading
    (B) a book on the history of linguistic research in the United States
    (C) a budget report by the Department of Education
    (D) a book on auditory processing and learning disabilities
    (E) a technical manual for practicing audiologists

38. The author of the passage would agree with which of the following statements?
    (A) Auditory processing may be either simple or complex.
    (B) Those children who have difficulty reading probably have an adequately functioning sensorimotor system. ✓
    (C) For fewer than eight million individuals, learning disabilities are a lifelong impairment.
    (D) Poor reading may be a learning disability related to auditory processing skills.
    (E) Eight million individuals in the United States experience difficulty in learning to read.

39. The primary purpose of the passage is to
    (A) explain the process of language control
    (B) assure readers that a great number of individuals are not learning disabled
    (C) discuss relationships between learning disability, reading difficulty, and the sensorimotor system
    (D) relate the history of auditory processing
    (E) explain the criteria used to decide whether a child can spell or not

40. If the final statement of the passage is true, which of the following must also be true?
    (A) Reading difficulty may not have a simple cause.
    (B) Five and only five separate abilities comprise auditory processing. ✓
    (C) There are five components in an intact sensorimotor system.
    (D) Children may acquire different auditory processing skills at different ages.
    (E) More research into auditory processing remains to be done.

41. Which of the following conclusions is implied by the first sentence in the passage?
    (A) Childhood disorders are the most serious type of human psychological or physiological disorder.
    (B) Childhood disorders other than learning disabilities also exist.
    (C) Learning disabilities are the only childhood disorders that occur with any frequency.
    (D) The only handicapping childhood disorders are those which occur with some frequency.
    (E) Learning disabilities are almost always reading disabilities.

42. Which of the following best describes the author's attitude toward the subject discussed?
    (A) passive resignation   (D) moral outrage
    (B) hopeless frustration   (E) informed concern
    (C) whimsical skepticism

Over the last decade, teachers in elementary schools have received modest pay raises regularly, but considering inflation, their salaries have decreased twenty-three percent.

43. Which of the following best expresses the point of the statement above?
    (A) Being a teacher means living at or below the poverty line.
    (B) Many teachers must hold second jobs.
    (C) The effects of inflation can negate the benefits of a pay raise.
    (D) Teachers' salaries are not adequate.
    (E) Those who teach in elementary schools can live on less than those who teach in high schools.

For preschool children, television cartoons could serve to stimulate them to create their own drawings if their parents provided them with the graphic materials and the indispensable encouragement.

44. The author of the statement would probably agree with which of the following?
    (A) A decision to ban television cartoons as useless is not wise.
    (B) Television cartoons are the preschooler's primary source of creative inspiration.
    (C) For older children, cartoons have no educational value.
    (D) Cartoons are a viable substitute for parents when they are not available.
    (E) Cartoons accelerate a young child's learning of new words.

There are many people who, after experiencing severe disappointments, lose every vestige of self-esteem; they view themselves as failures in every respect; there is no more to do or to attempt.

45. The author stresses which of the following responses to disappointment?
    (A) rehabilitation   (D) happiness
    (B) hopelessness   (E) courage
    (C) optimism

It is clear that the first four or five years of a child's life are the period of most rapid change in physical and mental characteristics and greatest susceptibility to environmental influences. Attitudes are formed, values are learned, habits are developed, and innate abilities are fostered or retarded by conditions the child encounters during these early years.

46. Which of the following, if true, would most weaken the author's argument?
   (A) Many young children possess attitudes and habits similar to those of their peers.
   (B) There are significant, basic differences between a five-year-old from Samoa and one from New York.
   (C) "Midlife crisis" provokes many adults to change their entire personality structures within only a few months.
   (D) The environment continues to influence personal characteristics in adolescents.
   (E) Environmental influences can have either positive or negative effects on human development.

In order for an individual to judge whether two or more speech sounds are alike or different or to make more difficult judgments, the sounds must be kept in memory and retrieved for comparison.

47. The passage supports which of the following conclusions?
   (A) Most speech sounds are more different than they are alike.
   (B) Visual discrimination is easier than auditory discrimination.
   (C) A number of individuals cannot discriminate between different sounds.
   (D) People with good memories are also good listeners.
   (E) A person cannot compare two sounds at precisely the same time.

A two percent budget cut ordered by the governor will seriously hamper the operation of the state university system, but while education will be hurt, the state budget in general will remain relatively unaffected.

48. The author's attitude toward the governor's order is most likely
   (A) neutral   (D) supportive
   (B) antagonistic   (E) inconsistent
   (C) understanding

Questions 49 and 50 refer to the following passage.

Integrating sports into the elementary curriculum can have a far more beneficial effect than merely allowing students to "blow off steam" or providing an opportunity for physical exercise. The inclusion of a physical rather than a mental skill will allow those students less adept in the classroom to _____49_____ their physical proficiencies to their peers and to their teachers, thus allowing ego-enhancing experiences which they might not otherwise get sitting at their desks. The teachers' overall knowledge of their students will also be enhanced, and thus they will have more to draw upon when relating to their students and the students' _____50_____.

49. The word which best completes _____49_____ is
   (A) boast
   (B) display
   (C) give
   (D) relate
   (E) explain

50. The word which best completes _____50_____ is
   (A) grades
   (B) sports
   (C) work
   (D) exercise
   (E) games

STOP. IF YOU FINISH BEFORE TIME IS CALLED, CHECK YOUR WORK ON THIS SECTION ONLY. DO NOT WORK ON ANY OTHER SECTION IN THE TEST.

SECTION II: MATHEMATICS

Time: 70 Minutes
50 Questions

DIRECTIONS

In the questions or incomplete statements below, select the one *best* answer or completion of the five choices given.

1. What is the value of 342,499 rounded to the nearest <u>thousand?</u>
   (A) 342,000   (D) 343,000
   (B) 342,400   (E) 343,400
   (C) 342,500

2. Which of the following is the largest?
   (A) .09   (B) $\frac{1}{11}$ (C) 8½%   (D) .084   (E) $\frac{1}{13}$

$$9x^2 + 3y - 5$$

3. What would be the closest approximation to $\sqrt{83}$?
   (A) 8.3   (B) 8.9   (C) 9.1   (D) 9.7   (E) 41.5

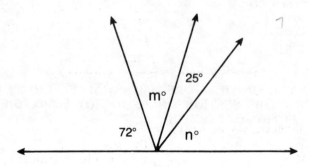

4. In the figure, what is the number of degrees in the sum of m + n?
   (A) 83   (D) 103
   (B) 93   (E) cannot be determined
   (C) 97

5. A square 4 inches on a side is cut up into smaller squares 1 inch on a side. What is the maximum number of such squares that can be formed?
   (A) 4   (B) 8   (C) 16   (D) 36   (E) 64

6. Given a number, x, add 4 to it, then multiply it by 4, then subtract 4 and divide this by 4. The result is
   (A) x + 3   (D) x − 2
   (B) x + 2   (E) x + 1
   (C) x

7. The length of a rectangle is 6*l* and the width is 4*w*. What is its perimeter?
   (A) 24*lw*   (D) 20*lw*
   (B) 10*lw*   (E) 12*l* + 8*w*
   (C) 6*l* + 4*w*

$$9x^2 + 3y - 5$$

8. If x = −3, and y = −2, then the value of the expression above is
   (A) −92   (D) 80
   (B) −65   (E) 82
   (C) 70

(*Note: figure not drawn to scale*)

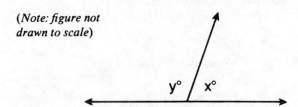

9. If, in the figure, y = 3x, then x =
   (A) 36   (D) 180
   (B) 45   (E) cannot be determined
   (C) 90

10. If x is between 0 and 1, which of the following statements is (are) true?

    I. $x^2 > 1$
    II. $x^2 > 0$
    III. $x^2 > x$

    (A) I only   (D) I and II
    (B) II only   (E) II and III
    (C) III only

11. Armand is making a salad from the following ingredients: three different kinds of lettuce, three different kinds of tomatoes, and four different kinds of beans. If he wishes to use only one kind of lettuce, one kind of tomato, and one kind of beans, how many different combinations of salads can he possibly make?
(A) 3   (B) 6   (C) 10   (D) 15   (E) 36

Sandra's weekly wage is $30 less than three times Harold's weekly wage. If Sandra's weekly wage is $90, what is Harold's weekly wage?

---

12. If t represents Harold's weekly wage, which of the following equations can be used to solve the problem above?
(A) $90 = 3t − $30
(B) $90 − $30 = 3t
(C) 3t − t − $30 = $90
(D) t − $30 = 3($90)
(E) 3t + t = $90

13. If 3/y = 18, then y + 2 =
(A) 2⅙   (B) 4⅙   (C) 6⅙   (D) 8⅙   (E) 12⅙

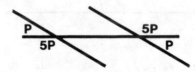

14. In the diagram above, what is the value of p?
(A) 30°   (B) 45°   (C) 60°   (D) 90°   (E) 120°

15. A color television set is marked down 20% to $320. Which of the following equations could be used to determine its original price, P?
(A) $320 − .20 = P
(B) .20P = $320
(C) P = $320 + .20
(D) .80P + .20P = $320
(E) .80P = $320

16. The areas of which of the following are equal?

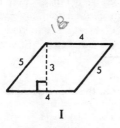
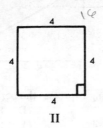
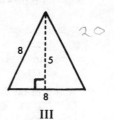

       I   II   III

(A) I and II
(B) I and III
(C) II and III
(D) I, II, and III
(E) none of them are equal

17. $\dfrac{x^2y}{wz} \div \dfrac{xy}{w^2z} =$

(A) $\dfrac{x^2y^2}{w^2z^2}$ (D) xw

(B) $\dfrac{x^3y^2}{w^3z^2}$ (E) $\dfrac{x}{w}$

(C) $\dfrac{wz}{x}$

18. Which of the following is the most appropriate unit for describing the weight of a bowling ball?
(A) milligrams   (D) decagrams
(B) centigrams   (E) kilograms
(C) grams

19. If a bus stops 4 times in every mile, how many stops does it make in 8 miles?
(A) 2   (D) 16
(B) 4   (E) 32
(C) 8

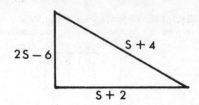

20. Which of the following expresses the perimeter of the above triangle?
    (A) $(2s - 6)(s + 4)$ (D) $4s + 12$
    (B) $\frac{1}{2}(2s - 6)(s + 4)$ (E) $4s - 12$
    (C) $4s$

21. Temperature increases 2 degrees for every 1,000 feet gained above sea level. How many degrees warmer is it at 6,000 feet above sea level than at 2,500 feet above sea level?
    (A) $3,500(2 - 1,000)$
    (B) $(6,000 - 2,500)2$
    (C) $\dfrac{3,500}{1,000 \times 2}$
    (D) $\dfrac{6,000 - 2,500}{1,000}(2)$
    (E) $(1,000 \times 6,000) - (2,500 \times 1,000) \div 2$

22. 90% of 80% of 70% is approximately equal to
    (A) 25%   (B) 40%   (C) 50%   (D) 65%   (E) 80%

23. How many buses are needed to carry 98 children to the park if each bus holds 42 children?
    (A) 2   (B) 2.14   (C) $2\frac{1}{3}$ (D) 3   (E) $3\frac{1}{2}$

24. If 5x is the average of two numbers, and one of the numbers is 3, what is the other number?
    (A) $5x$ (B) $10x$ (C) $10x - 7$ (D) $10x - 3$ (E) $10x + 7$

25. A school is going to build a new playground. State regulations require no more than 50% asphalt and no less than 20% grass for any school playground. If the school plans to build a playground of exactly 200 square feet, which of the following is acceptable?
    (A) 50 square feet grass, 110 square feet asphalt, and the rest sand
    (B) 30 square feet grass, 90 square feet asphalt, and the rest sand
    (C) 20 square feet grass, 95 square feet asphalt, and the rest sand
    (D) 50 square feet grass, 95 square feet asphalt, and the rest sand
    (E) 45 square feet grass, 115 square feet asphalt, and the rest sand

26. If a store purchases several items for $1.80 per dozen and sells them at 3 for $.85, what is the store's profit on 6 dozen of these items?
(A) $4.20   (D) $10.60
(B) $5.70   (E) $20.40
(C) $9.60

27. Arnold takes 8 weekly tests in his history class, and his scores range from a low of 72% to a high of 94%. Which of the following must be true regarding Arnold's average for all 8 tests?
(A) His average for all 8 tests is 83%.
(B) His average for all 8 tests is above 83%.
(C) His average for all 8 tests is lower than 83%.
(D) His average for all 8 tests is any score between 1% and 100%.
(E) His average for all 8 tests is between 72% and 94%.

28. What is the simple interest on a $40,000 savings account over 3 years if the interest rate is 2% quarterly?
(A) $800   (D) $9,600
(B) $2,400   (E) $32,000
(C) $3,200

29. Using the formula $F° = \frac{9}{5}C° + 32°$, where F = Fahrenheit temperature and C = centigrade temperature, what is the temperature in Fahrenheit degrees when the temperature is 25° centigrade?
(A) 77°   (B) 57°   (C) 45°   (D) 25°   (E) −7°

30. If 1 ml (milliliter) of water occupies 1 cc (cubic centimeter) of space, how many liters of water are needed to fill a tank with dimensions 25 cm × 10 cm × 8 cm? (1 liter = 1,000 milliliters; V = l × w × h)
(A) 2,000   (B) 200   (C) 20   (D) 2.0   (E) .020

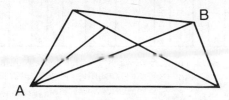

31. How many different ways are there to travel from A to B without going over a line more than once in any one attempt?
(A) less than 5   (D) 7
(B) 5   (E) more than 7
(C) 6

32. $2/3 + 1/5 + 1/6 = ?$ can be most efficiently answered by
    (A) using a common denominator of 90
    (B) using a common denominator of 15
    (C) using a common denominator of 30
    (D) using the "invert and multiply" technique
    (E) multiplying denominators

33. What is the probability of rolling two dice that total 7?
    (A) 1/6   (B) 1/4   (C) 11/36   (D) 1/3   (E) 1/2

Questions 34 and 35 refer to the following graph.

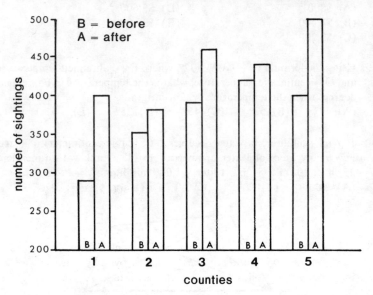

Number of Wild Bear Sightings Before and After Conservation Measures in Five Different Counties

34. According to the graph, which county had the most bear sightings before the conservation measures?
    (A) 1   (B) 2   (C) 3   (D) 4   (E) 5

35. To determine in which county the sightings increased by approximately 25%, one would
   (A) find the county which had 250 more sightings after the conservation measures
   (B) find the county which had 25 more sightings after the conservation measures
   (C) find the county in which the "B" bar is ¼ taller than the "A" bar
   (D) find the county in which the number of sightings indicated by the "A" bar is 250 more than those indicated by the "B" bar
   (E) find the county in which the number of sightings indicated by the "A" bar is ¼ more than those indicated by the "B" bar

36. How long will it take a school bus averaging 40 miles per hour to reach its destination 10 miles away?
   (A) 15 minutes
   (B) 20 minutes
   (C) 30 minutes
   (D) 1 hour
   (E) 4 hours

37. 68% is between
   (A) 3/8 and 2/5
   (B) 3/5 and 5/6
   (C) 1/2 and 2/3 ✓
   (D) 7/10 and 3/4 ✓
   (E) 4/5 and 9/10 ✓

38. A commission of $6.80 is paid for each $50 of sales. How much did sales total if the commissions equaled $156.40?
   (A) $1,100
   (B) $1,150
   (C) $1,200
   (D) $1,250
   (E) $1,300

39. There are 36 students in a certain geometry class. If two-thirds of the students are boys and three-fourths of the boys are under six feet tall, how many boys in the class are under six feet tall?
   (A) 6   (B) 12   (C) 18   (D) 24   (E) 27

40. An astronaut weighing 207 pounds on Earth would weigh 182 pounds on Venus. The weight of the astronaut on Venus would be approximately what percent of his weight on Earth?
   (A) 50%   (B) 60%   (C) 70%   (D) 80%   (E) 90%

41. Dividing by 2/4 is the same as
    (A) multiplying by 1/2
    (B) dividing by 2
    (C) multiplying by 2
    (D) multiplying by 2 and then dividing by 4
    (E) dividing by 50

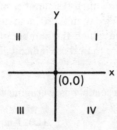

42. In the coordinate graph above, the point represented by $(-3,4)$ would be found in which quadrant?
    (A) I   (D) IV
    (B) II   (E) cannot be determined
    (C) III

43. In the flow chart, if $x = 3$, then what is the value of z?
    (A) -1
    (B) 0
    (C) 1
    (D) 3
    (E) 6

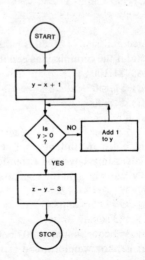

Robert's four paychecks total $840, and the largest paycheck is $100 more than the average for the four paychecks and $200 more than the smallest paycheck.

44. Which of the following *cannot* be determined from the information given above?
    (A) the average of the four paychecks
    (B) the largest paycheck
    (C) the smallest paycheck
    (D) the sum of the largest and the smallest paycheck
    (E) the sum of the two largest paychecks

45. To find the total surface area in square meters of a rectangular solid whose length is 7 meters, width is 6 meters, and depth is 3 meters, one would use the following calculation:
    (A) 7m × 6m × 3m
    (B) 2(7m × 6m) + 2(6m × 3m) + 2(7m × 3m)
    (C) 7m × 6m + 6m × 3m + 3m × 7m
    (D) 7m × 6m × 3m × 2
    (E) 7m × 3m × 2

46. Judith has a purse full of coins totaling $9.15. She has at least one of every U.S. coin (dollar, half-dollar, quarter, dime, nickel, and penny). What is the largest number of quarters she can have in her purse?
    (A) 25   (B) 27   (C) 28   (D) 29   (E) 30

47. Bob works twice as fast as Pete. When they work together they can complete a certain job in 8 hours. How fast could Pete have completed the same job if he were working alone?
    (A) 5⅓ hours   (D) 8 hours
    (B) 6 hours   (E) 24 hours
    (C) 7 hours

48. What is the volume of a right circular cylinder with a radius of 7? (V = $\pi r^2 h$)
    (A) 49π square units
    (B) 49π cubic units
    (C) 343 square units
    (D) 343 cubic units
    (E) cannot be determined

Questions 49 and 50 refer to the following graph.

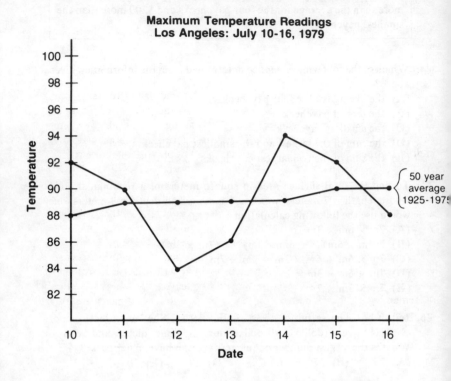

Maximum Temperature Readings
Los Angeles: July 10-16, 1979

49. Of the seven days shown, about what percent of the days did the maximum temperature exceed the average temperature?
    (A) 3%   (B) 4%   (C) 43%   (D) 57%   (E) 93%

50. Between which two dates shown was the greatest increase in maximum temperature?
    (A) July 11–12   (D) July 14–15
    (B) July 12–13   (E) July 15–16
    (C) July 13–14

STOP. IF YOU FINISH BEFORE TIME IS CALLED, CHECK YOUR WORK ON THIS SECTION ONLY. DO NOT WORK ON ANY OTHER SECTION IN THE TEST.

SECTION III: ESSAY WRITING

Time: 60 Minutes
2 Essays

DIRECTIONS

In this section, you will have 60 minutes to plan and write two essays, one for each topic given. You may use the bottom of this and the following page to organize and plan your essay before you begin writing. You should plan your time wisely. Read each topic carefully to make sure that you are properly addressing the issue or situation. YOU MUST WRITE ON THE SPECIFIED TOPIC. AN ESSAY ON ANOTHER TOPIC WILL NOT BE ACCEPTABLE.

The two essay questions included in this section are designed to give you an opportunity to write clearly and effectively. Use specific examples whenever appropriate to aid in supporting your ideas. Keep in mind that the quality of your writing is much more important than the quantity.

Your essays are to be written on the special answer sheets provided. No other paper may be used. Your writing should be neat and legible. Because you have only a limited amount of space in which to write, please do NOT skip lines, do NOT write excessively large, and do NOT leave wide margins.

Remember, use the bottom of this and the following page for any organizational notes you may wish to make.

Topic 1

What particular experience had the greatest impact on your decision to enter education? Explain why that particular experience was so important.

FOR EACH ESSAY, USE TWO SIDES OF AN 8½″ BY 11″ LINED SHEET OF PAPER.

Topic 2

Some educators believe that the most important trait a teacher can have is self-acceptance. It allows the teacher to better relate to his or her students, to better deal with student problems, and to better provide a positive and constructive role model.

Present your arguments in agreement with this statement, or, if you disagree, present your viewpoints as to what you believe *is* the most important quality for a teacher to have.

FOR EACH ESSAY, USE TWO SIDES OF AN 8½″ BY 11″ LINED SHEET OF PAPER.

ANSWER KEY FOR PRACTICE TEST 1

	SECTION I			SECTION II	
	READING COMPREHENSION			MATHEMATICS	
1. C	18. E	35. D	1. A	18. E	35. E
2. A	19. D	36. E	2. B	19. E	36. A
3. E	20. E	37. D	3. C	20. C	37. B
4. C	21. C	38. D	4. A	21. D	38. B
5. B	22. C	39. C	5. C	22. C	39. C
6. B	23. C	40. A	6. A	23. D	40. E
7. D	24. C	41. B	7. E	24. D	41. C
8. B	25. B	42. E	8. C	25. D	42. B
9. B	26. D	43. C	9. B	26. C	43. C
10. B	27. C	44. A	10. B	27. E	44. E
11. B	28. E	45. B	11. E	28. D	45. B
12. B	29. B	46. C	12. A	29. A	46. D
13. D	30. D	47. E	13. A	30. D	47. E
14. E	31. D	48. B	14. A	31. E	48. E
15. A	32. C	49. B	15. E	32. C	49. D
16. D	33. A	50. C	16. E	33. A	50. C
17. D	34. B		17. D	34. D	

SCORING YOUR CBEST PRACTICE TEST 1

To score your CBEST Practice Test 1, total the number of correct responses for each section of the test separately. Do not subtract any points for questions attempted but missed, as there is no penalty for guessing. The score for each section is then scaled from 20 to 80. (About 70% right is a passing score.)

ANALYZING YOUR TEST RESULTS

The charts on the following page should be used to carefully analyze your results and spot your strengths and weaknesses. The complete process of analyzing each subject area and each individual question should be completed for this Practice Test. These results should be reexamined for trends in types of error (repeated errors) or poor results in specific subject areas. THIS REEXAMINATION AND ANALYSIS IS OF TREMENDOUS IMPORTANCE FOR EFFECTIVE TEST PREPARATION.

PRACTICE TEST 1: SUBJECT AREA ANALYSIS SHEET

	Possible	Completed	Right	Wrong
Reading Comprehension	50	50	39	11
Mathematics	50	50	39	11
TOTAL	100	100	78	22

ANALYSIS—TALLY SHEET FOR QUESTIONS MISSED

One of the most important parts of test preparation is analyzing WHY you missed a question so that you can reduce the number of mistakes. Now that you have taken Practice Test 1 and corrected your answers, carefully tally your mistakes by marking them in the proper column.

		REASON FOR MISTAKE		
	Total Missed	Simple Mistake	Misread Problem	Lack of Knowledge
Reading Comprehension	11	5	4	2
Mathematics	11	5	0	6
TOTAL	22	10	4	8

Reviewing the above data should help you determine WHY you are missing certain questions. Now that you have pinpointed the type of error, when you take Practice Test 2, focus on avoiding your most common type.

ESSAY TOPIC 1 CHECKLIST

Use this checklist to evaluate your Topic 1 essay.

Diagnosis/Prescription for Timed Writing Exercise

A good essay will:

_____	address the assignment
	be well focused
_____	be well organized
	smooth transitions between paragraphs
	coherent, unified
_____	be well developed
	contain specific examples to support points
_____	be grammatically sound (only minor flaws)
	correct sentence structure
	correct punctuation
	use of standard written English
_____	use language skillfully
	variety of sentence types
	variety of words
_____	be legible
	clear handwriting
	neat

ESSAY TOPIC 2 CHECKLIST

Use this checklist to evaluate your Topic 2 essay.

Diagnosis/Prescription for Timed Writing Exercise

A good essay will:

_____	address the assignment
	be well focused
_____	be well organized
	smooth transitions between paragraphs
	coherent, unified
_____	be well developed
	contain specific examples to support points
_____	be grammatically sound (only minor flaws)
	correct sentence structure
	correct punctuation
	use of standard written English
_____	use language skillfully
	variety of sentence types
	variety of words
_____	be legible
	clear handwriting
	neat

ANSWERS AND COMPLETE EXPLANATIONS
FOR PRACTICE TEST 1

SECTION I: READING COMPREHENSION

1. (C) Choices (D) and (E) address subsidiary points only. Choice (A) mentions the behavior of the scientist, rather than the behavior of individuals, and (B) does not even mention social psychology. Only (C) is both comprehensive and accurate.

2. (A) The final sentence expresses an interest in and appreciation for *talking* children, thus implying that the "flip-flop" is a change from the past preference for quiet children.

3. (E) All of the other terms stress negative attitudes toward creative writing, and choice (E) maintains this emphasis on the negative at the same time as it expresses one meaning of *precious*.

4. (C) Each of the other choices either describes a secondary rather than primary point or assigns a purpose (to urge) that is beyond the scope of the passage. And choice (E) is obviously incorrect.

5. (B) The passage portrays early retirement as an unattractive, problematic occurrence that will affect many but not all; (D) and (E) contradict the unattractive connotations of early retirement; and (A) and (C) state conclusions which are neither expressed nor implied in the passage.

6. (B) By saying that the *new* type of citizen will not be intimidated by ending careers, the author assumes that *present* citizens *are* intimidated. Incorrect choices either state an implication rather than an assumption— (D)—or draw conclusions beyond the scope of the passage—(A), (C), and (E).

7. (D) Toward the end of the passage, the author expresses a skeptical, qualified view of the value of technology; each of the other choices is consistent with the author's views.

8. (B) The *we* in the passage tells us that the author counts himself or herself among those who give performances.

9. (B) As the author says, art is *not merely to amuse.*

10. (B) The repeat of *some* recalls the earlier mention of *some legislators* and indicates that the legislators may be part of those who do not appreciate the full value of art.

11. (B) In order to accept an argument abolishing grades, we must presume that there are viable alternatives; none of the other choices is a necessary condition for agreement with the argument.

12. (B) By saying that the abolition of grades will increase student interest in subject matter, the author implies that graded students are less interested in and motivated by subject matter.

13. (D) The words *we will have students* indicate that the author is a teacher talking to teachers; so does *us* in the third sentence.

14. (E) Although choice (D) is part of the author's argument, acknowledging that exams cause fatigue will not make us accept the overall argument stressing fun over study. To accept that argument, we must accept the fact that students study too much—(E).

15. (A) The author stresses the value of *good fellowship and fine entertainment,* both social characteristics.

16. (D) Taking a negative view of studying, the author does not pick as strong and generally acceptable an example of enjoying life as might have been presented. Choices (A) and (C) would weaken rather than strengthen the argument, and (B) contradicts the argument. Choice (E) is too vague, not specifying *which* audience, so we cannot tell what effect such a change would have.

17. (D) The teacher does not advocate, recommend, or prefer anything in particular; nor is he categorically for or against steroids. Therefore (A), (B), (C), and (E) should be eliminated because they assign an *absolute* point of view that is not expressed.

18. (E) The author says that survivors will be adaptable but does not specify the way in which adaptability will be a value.

19. (D) Each of the other choices goes beyond the scope of the passage. Choice (D) is directly relevant to the author's assertion that the economy is a significant factor.

20. (E) This is the most comprehensive choice, describing the overall purpose of the passage rather than secondary purposes and implications.

21. (C) A discussion of creative writing is relevant to English and psychology but not to technical writing.

22. (C) The passage states that dormant tensions may be released through the revealing of a *deep, inner thought.* Choice (C) refers to this idea.

23. (C) Spelling is the one characteristic that the author neither expresses nor implies as relevant to creative writing.

24. (C) The passage explicitly states that creative writing is, *above all, . . . a means of self-expression.*

25. **(B)** The passage stresses ways of changing the social studies curriculum, thus designating its audience as those who can effect such changes— teachers.

26. **(D)** *Man has always been interested in where he is going* is preceded by a series of historical facts—that is, facts about occurrences of the past.

27. **(C)** By advocating the addition of futurism to the social studies curriculum, the author assumes that futurism is not adequately acknowledged. Without that assumption, the author would have no reason to make the argument.

28. **(E)** By distinguishing *global* from *national* in the passage, the author suggests that a global society is larger and more inclusive than a national one but does not go so far as to suggest that such a society necessarily includes outer space.

29. **(B)** Choices (C) and (D) would strengthen the argument for the value of futurism. Choices (A) and (E) are irrelevant to the strength or weakness of the argument. Choice (C) weakens the passage by calling into question those futurists of the past.

30. **(D)** The overall stress on changes in education indicates that the author is an educator.

31. **(D)** Through presenting a series of school situations in which students are discouraged from expressing themselves, the author implies that attending school may cause children to become inhibited.

32. **(C)** The passage overall suggests that students are inhibited by being severely criticized or corrected; the meaning of *chopped off* given by (C) is consistent with this overall view.

33. **(A)** The author repeatedly addresses the common experiences of *everyone*.

34. **(B)** By citing a number of negative situations, the author leaves no question that he or she is critical of the practices described.

35. **(D)** Choices (A), (B), and (C) contradict the implied argument of the passage, and (E) *may* contradict the implied argument because the meaning of *assist* is not made clear and possibly suggests that the teacher should supply words for the student. Choice (D) repeats the author's overall point.

36. **(E)** In the second sentence, the author states that *approximately eight million children in the U.S. can be classified as learning disabled.* The third sentence states that *many more function ineffectually throughout their entire lives.*

37. (D) The passage explicitly addresses auditory processing and learning disabilities and is not so technical that it would be intended for practicing audiologists—(E).

38. (D) The second paragraph generally supports this point. Choices (A) and (B) contradict the passage, and (C) and (E) go beyond the scope of the passage.

39. (C) Choice (C) is the most comprehensive statement; other choices express secondary rather than primary purposes—(B)—or are simply incorrect.

40. (A) The final statement of the passage explicitly stresses the complexity of auditory processing related to reading but it does not restrict this complexity to only five causes. Therefore, (B) and (C) are incorrect. Choices (D) and (E) are irrelevant to the final statement.

41. (B) The first sentence states that learning disabilities are *among* childhood disorders, thus implying that other disorders exist as well.

42. (E) Choices (A), (B), and (C) all connote an uninvolved, unconcerned attitude not at all expressed in the passage. Choice (D) suggests that the author is angry, which is not supported by the tone of the passage.

43. (C) Each of the other choices is beyond the scope of the passage.

44. (A) Choices (C) and (E) make statements beyond the scope of the passage; (D) contradicts the passage (the parents' contribution is said to be *indispensable*); and (B) makes cartoons a *primary* source of inspiration. The author would agree that cartoons have some value and should not be banned.

45. (B) The author stresses a severely negative response to disappointment, and only (B) supplies a negative term.

46. (C) Choice (C) weakens the stress on early childhood as a time of rapid change by saying that midlife may be a time of rapid change as well.

47. (E) By stressing the separateness of speech sounds in memory, the author supports the conclusion of (E). Each of the other conclusions is beyond the scope of the passage.

48. (B) The author's negative assessment suggests a negative attitude, and (B) offers the only negative choice.

49. (B) *Display* best fits the meaning of the sentence.

50. (C) *Work* best fits the meaning of the sentence.

SECTION II: MATHEMATICS

1. **(A)** 500 or above rounds *up* to the next highest thousand. 499 or below rounds *down* to the previous thousand. Thus, 342,499 rounds down to 342,000. Note that choices (B), (C), and (E) could have been quickly eliminated, as they were rounded to nearest hundreds not thousands.

2. **(B)** Converting all the terms to decimals gives

   (A) .09   (B) .0909   (C) .085   (D) .084   (E) .077

   Note that (E) could have been eliminated quickly, as it is smaller than (B). Choice (D) is smaller than (A) and also could have been eliminated quickly.

3. **(C)** Note that $\sqrt{83}$ is just slightly more than $\sqrt{81}$. Since $\sqrt{81}$ equals exactly 9, the best answer is (C) 9.1.

4. **(A)** Since the sum of the angles is 180°, we have

$$
\begin{aligned}
m + n + 72 + 25 &= 180 \\
m + n + 97 &= 180 \\
m + n &= 180 - 97 \\
m + n &= 83
\end{aligned}
$$

   Hence the sum of m + n is 83°

5. **(C)** The maximum number of squares 1 inch by 1 inch will be 16.

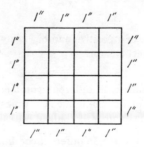

6. **(A)** Let x = the number;

   adding 4 gives x + 4;

   multiplying by 4 gives 4(x + 4) or 4x + 16;

   subtracting 4 gives 4x + 16 − 4 or 4x + 12;

181

and finally, dividing by 4 gives $\dfrac{4x + 12}{4}$ or $x + 3$

You could also plug in any number for x, and the end result would be $x + 3$ or the number plus 3.

7. **(E)** The perimeter of a rectangle is equal to the sum of its sides. For this rectangle we have

$$\text{perimeter} = 6l + 4w + 6l + 4w$$
$$= 6l + 6l + 4w + 4w$$
$$= 12l + 8w$$

8. **(C)** Plugging in the values for x and y into the expression

$9x^2 + 3y - 5 =$
$9(-3)^2 + 3(-2) - 5 =$
$9(9) + (-6) - 5 =$
$81 + (-6) - 5 = 70$

9. **(B)** $x + y = 180°$ (x plus y form a straight line, or straight angle); since $y = 3x$, substituting gives

$$3x + x = 180°$$
$$4x = 180°$$
$$x = 45°$$

10. **(B)** Since the square of a positive number is always a positive number, choice (B) is the correct answer.

11. **(E)** To find the number of different combinations possible, simply multiply the number of kinds of lettuce (3) times the number of kinds of tomatoes (3) times the number of kinds of beans (4).

$$3 \times 3 \times 4 = 36 \text{ different combinations}$$

12. **(A)** Change the sentence word for word into an equation.

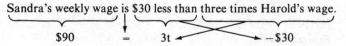

Sandra's weekly wage is $30 less than three times Harold's wage.

$90   =   3t   -$30

13. **(A)** Solving the equation

$$\frac{3}{y} = 18$$

$$\frac{3}{y} = \frac{18}{1}$$

Cross multiply $18y = 3$

$$y = \frac{3}{18}$$

$$y = \frac{1}{6}$$

Therefore $y + 2 = \frac{1}{6} + 2 = 2\frac{1}{6}$

14. **(A)** Since the number of degrees in a straight angle (straight line) equals 180,

$$p + 5p = 180°$$
$$6p = 180°$$
$$p = 30°$$

15. **(E)** If the color television is marked down 20%, then its current price is 80% of its original price. Thus, $.80P = \$320$.

16. **(E)** The area of I, the parallelogram, equals bh or $4 \times 3 = 12$. The area of II, the square, equals s^2, or $4^2 = 16$. The area of III, the triangle, equals $\frac{1}{2}bh$, or $\frac{1}{2}(8)(5) = 20$. Thus, none of their areas are equal.

17. **(D)** When dividing fractions, invert the divisor and then multiply.

$$\frac{x^2y}{wz} \div \frac{xy}{w^2z} = \frac{x^2y}{wz} \times \frac{w^2z}{xy} = \frac{x^2yw^2z}{xywz} = xw$$

18. **(E)** Kilograms could be used to approximate the weight of a bowling ball. The other units all weigh far less than a pound.

19. **(E)** Since the bus stops 4 times each mile, the total number of stops will equal the number of miles times 4. Thus, 8 miles $\times$ 4 stops each mile = 32 total stops.

20. **(C)** Perimeter is the sum of all sides. Thus, $(2s - 6) + (s + 4) + (s + 2)$ = perimeter.

$$2s - 6$$
$$s + 4$$
$$\underline{s + 2}$$
$$4s + 0 = 4s$$

21. **(D)** To determine the difference in temperature you first must know the difference in altitude. Thus $6,000 - 2,500$. Now that you know the difference in altitude, you multiply by 2 degrees for each thousand feet. Thus,

$$\frac{6,000 - 2,500}{1,000} \text{ times } 2$$

Answer (D) is correct.

22. **(C)** The word *of* means *multiply*. Thus, 90% of 80% of 70% is $(.90)(.80)(.70) = .504$, or approximately 50%.

23. **(D)** Since each bus carries a maximum of 42 children, 3 buses will be able to carry all 98 children. Remember, a fractional bus (for instance, $1/3$ bus) is not a logical answer.

24. **(D)** If two numbers average to 5x, the sum of the two numbers must be 10x, since 10x divided by the two numbers gives 5x for an average. Therefore

$$\text{one number} + \text{other number} = 10x$$
$$3 \quad + \quad ? \quad = 10x$$

Subtract 3 from both sides.

$$? \quad = 10x - 3$$

Therefore, the other number is $10x - 3$.

25. **(D)** The state requires no more than 50% asphalt. So 50% of 200 square feet is 100 square feet of asphalt *maximum*. Notice that this maximum limit eliminates choices (A) and (E). The other requirement is no less than 20% grass. So 20% of 200 is 40 square feet of grass as a *minimum*. This eliminates choices (B) and (C). Only choice (D) provides no more than 50% asphalt and no less than 20% grass.

26. **(C)** The selling price for 1 dozen at 3 for $.85 is $3 \times 4 = 12 = 1$ dozen $= \$.85 \times 4 = \$3.40$. Hence, 6 dozen will yield $\$3.40 \times 6 = \$20.40$. The cost for 6 dozen at $1.80 per dozen is $\$1.80 \times 6 = \$10.80$. Hence, the profit on 6 dozen of these items will be $\$20.40 - \$10.80$, or $9.60.

27. **(E)** Since his scores were all between 72% and 94%, Arnold's average for the 8 tests must fall between the highest and lowest scores. The average for all 8 tests, however, does not necessarily have to be 83%, the average of only the highest and lowest scores.

28. **(D)** Simple interest is calculated with this formula:

$$I = \text{principal} \times \text{annual rate} \times \text{time in years}$$

But notice that a 2% quarterly rate is actually an 8% annual rate. Plugging into the formula we get

$$I = \$40,000 \times .08 \times 3 = \$9,600$$

29. **(A)** To change centigrade degrees to Fahrenheit degrees, simply plug into the formula and solve:

$$F° = \tfrac{9}{5}C + 32°$$
$$F° = \tfrac{9}{5}(25°) + 32°$$
$$F° = 45° + 32°$$
$$F° = 77°$$

30. **(D)** Volume equals length × width × height, or 25 cm × 10 cm × 8 cm = 2,000 cc. Since 2,000 milliliters of water equals 2,000 cc of space, exactly 2 liters are needed (since 1 liter = 1,000 milliliters).

31. **(E)** The following diagrams show eight ways of going from A to B along the lines, and there are many more.

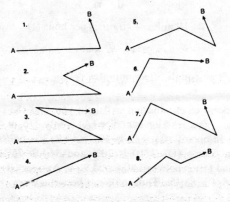

32. (C) To solve an addition problem containing fractions with different denominators, a common denominator must be found. Both 90 (choice A) and 30 (choice C) are common denominators, but only 30 is the *lowest* common denominator. Using 30 for the denominator eliminates the necessity of reducing your final answer and also minimizes the size of the numbers in your computations.

33. (A) There are 36 possible combinations of two dice (see page 30). Of these 36 combinations, only six combinations equal 7 (1,6; 2,5; 3,4; 4,3; 5,2; 6,1). Thus, 6 out of 36 equals 6/36, or 1/6.

34. (D) According to the graph, the tallest "B" (before) bar is county 4.

35. (E) To determine a 25% increase, find the county in which the increase in number of sightings equals ¼ of the original number of sightings.

$$\text{percent change} = \frac{\text{increase or change}}{\text{original number}}$$

$$25\% \text{ (or } \tfrac{1}{4}) = \frac{A - B}{B}$$

Note that merely approximating the size of the bars will not work, as the bars do not begin at 0 (they begin at 200).

36. (A) Problems of distance, speed, and time can be solved using d = rt, where d is distance; r is rate, or speed; and t is time. So

$$d = rt$$

$$10 \text{ miles} = 40 \text{ miles per hour (t)}$$

$$t = \tfrac{1}{4} \text{ hour}$$

Note that ¼ hour equals fifteen minutes.

37. (B) The process of elimination will help you find the correct answer. Note that the bigger fraction in choice (A) is only 2/5, or 40%. Thus, (A) is incorrect. In choice (C), 1/2 is 50% and 2/3 is 66⅔%. Thus (C) is incorrect. In choice (D) 7/10 is 70% and 3/4 is 75%. Thus, (D) is incorrect. And (E) is between 80% and 90%. Answer (B) is correct: 3/5 is 60%, and 5/6 is 83⅓%. Thus, 68% lies between them.

38. (B) Dividing the amount of commissions by $6.80 will give the number of $50 sales:

$$\frac{\$156.40}{\$6.80} = 23$$

Thus, 23 × $50 = $1,150.

39. (C) Since two-thirds of the students are boys, we have $\frac{2}{3}(36) = 24$ boys in the class. Out of the 24 boys in the class, three-fourths are under six feet tall, or $\frac{3}{4}(24) = 18$ boys under six feet tall.

40. (E)

$$\frac{\text{weight on Venus}}{\text{weight on Earth}} = \frac{182}{207} \approx 88\%, \text{ or approximately } 90\%$$

41. (C) Dividing by a fraction is the same as multiplying by the reciprocal of the fraction (the fraction inverted, or turned upside down). This procedure is used in division of fraction problems; the second fraction is inverted and then multiplied. For instance,

$$\frac{3}{4} \div \frac{1}{2} =$$

$$\frac{3}{4} \times \frac{2}{1} = \frac{6}{4} = \frac{3}{2}$$

Therefore, dividing by 2/4 is the same as multiplying by 4/2, or multiplying by 2.

42. (B) Points plotted on a coordinate graph are expressed (x,y) where x indicates the distance forward or backward and y indicates the distance up or down. Thus, $(-3,4)$ means 3 "steps" back and then 4 "steps" up. This will place the point within quadrant II.

43. (C) Plug in 3 for x:

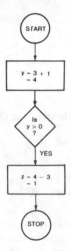

44. (E) Since Robert's four paychecks total $840, the average of the four paychecks is $210. If the largest is $100 more than the average, the largest paycheck is $310, and if the largest is $200 more than the smallest, the smallest paycheck must be $110. We cannot determine, however, the second or third largest paycheck.

45. (B) To calculate total surface area of a rectangular solid, one must find the area of each of six faces. One face is 7m × 6m. Note that the face directly opposite that face also equals 7m × 6m. The same is true with the other two different faces. Therefore, each of the areas of the three different faces must be doubled and added together.

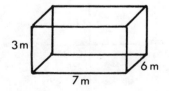

46. (D) First add the value of one of each coin:

$$1.00 + .50 + .25 + .10 + .05 + .01 = \$1.91$$

That leaves $9.15 − $1.91, or $7.24, for the rest of the quarters.

$$\frac{\$7.24}{.25} = 28^{24}\!/_{25}, \text{ or 28 additional quarters}$$

Add the 28 additional quarters to the 1 original quarter. Thus, 29 is the largest number of quarters she can have.

47. (E) If Pete and Jim work together, they will complete the job in 8 hours. Therefore, if Pete works alone, it should take longer without help to complete the job. Thus, the only reasonable answer choice is (E)—24 hours. Scanning your answer choices and eliminating the unreasonable choices is the best way to answer this problem.

48. (E) The formula for the volume of a right circular cylinder is V = area of circle times height of cylinder. Since the height of the cylinder is not given, the volume cannot be determined.

49. (D) There were 4 days (July 10, 11, 14, and 15) on which the maximum temperature exceeded the average; thus, 4/7 is approximately 57%.

50. (C) The maximum temperature rose from 86° to 94° from July 13 to July 14. This was the greatest increase.

PRACTICE TEST 2

Section I: Reading Comprehension—65 Minutes; 50 Questions
Section II: Mathematics—70 Minutes; 50 Questions
Section III: Essay Writing—60 Minutes; 2 Essays

SECTION I: READING COMPREHENSION

1 Ⓐ Ⓑ Ⓒ Ⓓ Ⓔ	26 Ⓐ Ⓑ Ⓒ Ⓓ Ⓔ
2 Ⓐ Ⓑ Ⓒ Ⓓ Ⓔ	27 Ⓐ Ⓑ Ⓒ Ⓓ Ⓔ
3 Ⓐ Ⓑ Ⓒ Ⓓ Ⓔ	28 Ⓐ Ⓑ Ⓒ Ⓓ Ⓔ
4 Ⓐ Ⓑ Ⓒ Ⓓ Ⓔ	29 Ⓐ Ⓑ Ⓒ Ⓓ Ⓔ
5 Ⓐ Ⓑ Ⓒ Ⓓ Ⓔ	30 Ⓐ Ⓑ Ⓒ Ⓓ Ⓔ
6 Ⓐ Ⓑ Ⓒ Ⓓ Ⓔ	31 Ⓐ Ⓑ Ⓒ Ⓓ Ⓔ
7 Ⓐ Ⓑ Ⓒ Ⓓ Ⓔ	32 Ⓐ Ⓑ Ⓒ Ⓓ Ⓔ
8 Ⓐ Ⓑ Ⓒ Ⓓ Ⓔ	33 Ⓐ Ⓑ Ⓒ Ⓓ Ⓔ
9 Ⓐ Ⓑ Ⓒ Ⓓ Ⓔ	34 Ⓐ Ⓑ Ⓒ Ⓓ Ⓔ
10 Ⓐ Ⓑ Ⓒ Ⓓ Ⓔ	35 Ⓐ Ⓑ Ⓒ Ⓓ Ⓔ
11 Ⓐ Ⓑ Ⓒ Ⓓ Ⓔ	36 Ⓐ Ⓑ Ⓒ Ⓓ Ⓔ
12 Ⓐ Ⓑ Ⓒ Ⓓ Ⓔ	37 Ⓐ Ⓑ Ⓒ Ⓓ Ⓔ
13 Ⓐ Ⓑ Ⓒ Ⓓ Ⓔ	38 Ⓐ Ⓑ Ⓒ Ⓓ Ⓔ
14 Ⓐ Ⓑ Ⓒ Ⓓ Ⓔ	39 Ⓐ Ⓑ Ⓒ Ⓓ Ⓔ
15 Ⓐ Ⓑ Ⓒ Ⓓ Ⓔ	40 Ⓐ Ⓑ Ⓒ Ⓓ Ⓔ
16 Ⓐ Ⓑ Ⓒ Ⓓ Ⓔ	41 Ⓐ Ⓑ Ⓒ Ⓓ Ⓔ
17 Ⓐ Ⓑ Ⓒ Ⓓ Ⓔ	42 Ⓐ Ⓑ Ⓒ Ⓓ Ⓔ
18 Ⓐ Ⓑ Ⓒ Ⓓ Ⓔ	43 Ⓐ Ⓑ Ⓒ Ⓓ Ⓔ
19 Ⓐ Ⓑ Ⓒ Ⓓ Ⓔ	44 Ⓐ Ⓑ Ⓒ Ⓓ Ⓔ
20 Ⓐ Ⓑ Ⓒ Ⓓ Ⓔ	45 Ⓐ Ⓑ Ⓒ Ⓓ Ⓔ
21 Ⓐ Ⓑ Ⓒ Ⓓ Ⓔ	46 Ⓐ Ⓑ Ⓒ Ⓓ Ⓔ
22 Ⓐ Ⓑ Ⓒ Ⓓ Ⓔ	47 Ⓐ Ⓑ Ⓒ Ⓓ Ⓔ
23 Ⓐ Ⓑ Ⓒ Ⓓ Ⓔ	48 Ⓐ Ⓑ Ⓒ Ⓓ Ⓔ
24 Ⓐ Ⓑ Ⓒ Ⓓ Ⓔ	49 Ⓐ Ⓑ Ⓒ Ⓓ Ⓔ
25 Ⓐ Ⓑ Ⓒ Ⓓ Ⓔ	50 Ⓐ Ⓑ Ⓒ Ⓓ Ⓔ

SECTION II: MATHEMATICS

1 Ⓐ Ⓑ Ⓒ Ⓓ Ⓔ		26 Ⓐ Ⓑ Ⓒ Ⓓ Ⓔ
2 Ⓐ Ⓑ Ⓒ Ⓓ Ⓔ		27 Ⓐ Ⓑ Ⓒ Ⓓ Ⓔ
3 Ⓐ Ⓑ Ⓒ Ⓓ Ⓔ		28 Ⓐ Ⓑ Ⓒ Ⓓ Ⓔ
4 Ⓐ Ⓑ Ⓒ Ⓓ Ⓔ		29 Ⓐ Ⓑ Ⓒ Ⓓ Ⓔ
5 Ⓐ Ⓑ Ⓒ Ⓓ Ⓔ		30 Ⓐ Ⓑ Ⓒ Ⓓ Ⓔ
6 Ⓐ Ⓑ Ⓒ Ⓓ Ⓔ		31 Ⓐ Ⓑ Ⓒ Ⓓ Ⓔ
7 Ⓐ Ⓑ Ⓒ Ⓓ Ⓔ		32 Ⓐ Ⓑ Ⓒ Ⓓ Ⓔ
8 Ⓐ Ⓑ Ⓒ Ⓓ Ⓔ		33 Ⓐ Ⓑ Ⓒ Ⓓ Ⓔ
9 Ⓐ Ⓑ Ⓒ Ⓓ Ⓔ		34 Ⓐ Ⓑ Ⓒ Ⓓ Ⓔ
10 Ⓐ Ⓑ Ⓒ Ⓓ Ⓔ		35 Ⓐ Ⓑ Ⓒ Ⓓ Ⓔ
11 Ⓐ Ⓑ Ⓒ Ⓓ Ⓔ		36 Ⓐ Ⓑ Ⓒ Ⓓ Ⓔ
12 Ⓐ Ⓑ Ⓒ Ⓓ Ⓔ		37 Ⓐ Ⓑ Ⓒ Ⓓ Ⓔ
13 Ⓐ Ⓑ Ⓒ Ⓓ Ⓔ		38 Ⓐ Ⓑ Ⓒ Ⓓ Ⓔ
14 Ⓐ Ⓑ Ⓒ Ⓓ Ⓔ		39 Ⓐ Ⓑ Ⓒ Ⓓ Ⓔ
15 Ⓐ Ⓑ Ⓒ Ⓓ Ⓔ		40 Ⓐ Ⓑ Ⓒ Ⓓ Ⓔ
16 Ⓐ Ⓑ Ⓒ Ⓓ Ⓔ		41 Ⓐ Ⓑ Ⓒ Ⓓ Ⓔ
17 Ⓐ Ⓑ Ⓒ Ⓓ Ⓔ		42 Ⓐ Ⓑ Ⓒ Ⓓ Ⓔ
18 Ⓐ Ⓑ Ⓒ Ⓓ Ⓔ		43 Ⓐ Ⓑ Ⓒ Ⓓ Ⓔ
19 Ⓐ Ⓑ Ⓒ Ⓓ Ⓔ		44 Ⓐ Ⓑ Ⓒ Ⓓ Ⓔ
20 Ⓐ Ⓑ Ⓒ Ⓓ Ⓔ		45 Ⓐ Ⓑ Ⓒ Ⓓ Ⓔ
21 Ⓐ Ⓑ Ⓒ Ⓓ Ⓔ		46 Ⓐ Ⓑ Ⓒ Ⓓ Ⓔ
22 Ⓐ Ⓑ Ⓒ Ⓓ Ⓔ		47 Ⓐ Ⓑ Ⓒ Ⓓ Ⓔ
23 Ⓐ Ⓑ Ⓒ Ⓓ Ⓔ		48 Ⓐ Ⓑ Ⓒ Ⓓ Ⓔ
24 Ⓐ Ⓑ Ⓒ Ⓓ Ⓔ		49 Ⓐ Ⓑ Ⓒ Ⓓ Ⓔ
25 Ⓐ Ⓑ Ⓒ Ⓓ Ⓔ		50 Ⓐ Ⓑ Ⓒ Ⓓ Ⓔ

SECTION I: READING COMPREHENSION

Time: 65 Minutes
50 Questions

DIRECTIONS

A question or number of questions follow each of the statements or passages in this section. Using only the *stated* or *implied* information given in the statement or passage, answer the question or questions by choosing the *best* answer from among the five choices given.

Questions 1 and 2 refer to the following passage.

Parallax is a range-finding technique used to measure the distance to some nearby stars from the annual angular displacement of a nearby star against the background of more distant, relatively fixed stars. Behold parallax by noting the apparent position of a vertical pencil in front of your face with only your right eye, then your left eye; the pencil shifts across the background.

1. In order to make this passage clear to a general audience, the author can do which of the following?
   (A) concede that parallax is not the only range-finding technique used by astronomers
   (B) define *angular displacement* in nontechnical terms
   (C) cite references in *Scientific American*
   (D) explain that stars are never even "relatively" fixed
   (E) eliminate the demonstration using a pencil

2. In the second sentence, the author suggests which of the following?
   (A) Most people have never really considered the position of a pencil.
   (B) The perceived position of any object varies according to the point from which it is observed.
   (C) Parallax is also a technique used by nonscientists.
   (D) The right eye is a more reliable observer than the left eye.
   (E) A pencil is very similar to a star.

Questions 3 and 4 refer to the following passage.

At the outset of the Civil War, the North possessed a large population, a superior rail system, a greater industrial capacity, greater capital assets, and a larger food-production capability than did the South. Despite the North's apparent economic superiority, the South did possess a few military advantages. Among them were fighting a defensive war on their home ground and an established military tradition. Most of the leaders of the pre-War army were from the South, while the North had to train a new military leadership.

3. The final sentence of this passage functions in which of the following ways?

   (A) to support the general contention that most of the talent in the United States is concentrated in the South

   (B) to hint that the North found many of its military leaders in the South

   (C) to argue that the North entered the war without leaders

   (D) to further explain the South's "established military tradition"

   (E) to show that the South probably should have won the war

4. The author implies which of the following points in the passage?

   (A) The North did not have an economic advantage at the end of the war.

   (B) Previous to the beginning of the war, the South was already fighting another war and seasoning its leaders.

   (C) Almost all the banks in the United States were located in the North.

   (D) Military advantages are much more important than economic advantages.

   (E) The North had a greater capacity for enduring a prolonged conflict.

Few opticians have recognized the value of target practice for stimulating the eyes and improving vision. The value of a day on the rifle range surpasses that of a whole crop of fresh carrots.

5. The writer assumes that his or her readers are already convinced that

   (A) poor eyesight is a widespread problem

   (B) target practice is enjoyable and useful

   (C) carrots are good for the eyes

   (D) most people should own guns

   (E) the *day* mentioned is an eight-hour day

Questions 6, 7, and 8 refer to the following passage.

The doctrine of association had been the basis for explaining memories and how one idea leads to another. Aristotle provided the basic law, association by contiguity. We remember something because in the past we had experienced that something together with something else. Seeing a shotgun may remind you of a murder, or it may remind you of a hunting experience in Wyoming, depending on your history. When you hear the word *table* you are likely to think of *chair. Carrots* makes you think of *peas; bread* makes you think *butter;* and so on. In each case the two items had for you been *experienced* contiguously—in the same place or at the same time or both. Today the terms stimulus and response are used to describe the two units which have been associated by contiguity.

6. The author of the passage would agree with which of the following statements?
   (A) Many of the associations which Aristotle posited have become part of modern experience.
   (B) There are a number of adults who have had no experiences and who therefore have no memories.
   (C) When one smells coffee, one is not likely to think of eating a donut.
   (D) No one thing is necessarily associated with any other thing in particular.
   (E) Guns always remind people of an experience in which someone or something was killed.

7. Which of the following statements, if true, would most weaken the argument of the passage?
   (A) Many people tend to become depressed when the weather is rainy.
   (B) Only a very few researchers question the doctrine of association.
   (C) More recent studies show that word-association responses are random and not determined by experience.
   (D) Of 100 people tested, 96 of those given the word *bread* responded with the word *butter.*
   (E) Psychologists have found that we have many common associations.

8. The argument of the passage is best strengthened by which of the following statements?
   (A) It is certainly possible to experience more than two items contiguously.
   (B) The terms stimulus and response were never used by Aristotle.
   (C) Those Londoners who endured the German "bombings" of World War II still become fearful when they hear a loud noise.
   (D) Some people think of *butter* when they hear *carrots.*
   (E) Aristotle's own writing is full of very uncommon and unexplained associations.

All experts on testing and learning admit that multiple choice tests measure knowledge only within limits. And yet the fact remains that multiple choice tests are used, both in school and out of school, as significant indicators of intellectual ability and the capacity for learning.

9. The passage implies which of the following statements?
   (A) The administration of tests is a more cost-effective measure than the exploration of other modes of measurement.
   (B) Tests are appropriate only when the students tested have limited knowledge.
   (C) One's capacity for learning cannot be measured by any sort of test.
   (D) Those who work first-hand with tests must know something that the experts do not.
   (E) Those who administer tests may not be experts on testing.

Questions 10 through 13 refer to the following passage.

Ostensibly punishment is used to reduce tendencies to behave in certain ways. We spank and scold children for misbehavior; we fine, lock up, or assign to hard labor adults who break laws; we threaten, censure, disapprove, ostracize, and coerce in our efforts to control social behaviors. Does punishment, in fact, do what it is supposed to do?

The effects of punishment, it has been found, are not the opposite of reward. It does not subtract reponses where reinforcement adds them. Rather it appears to temporarily suppress a behavior, and when punishment is discontinued, eventually responses will reappear. But this is only one aspect of the topic. Let us look at it in further detail.

Skinner defines punishment in two ways, first as the withdrawal of a positive reinforcer and, second, as the presentation of a negative reinforcer or aversive stimulus. We take candy away from a child or we spank him. Note that the arrangement in punishment is the opposite of that in reinforcement, where a positive reinforcer is presented and a negative reinforcer is removed.

Since we remove positive reinforcers to extinguish a response and also to punish it, a distinction must be made. When a response is made and no reinforcement follows, i.e., *nothing* happens, the response gradually extinguishes. However, if we *withdraw* a reinforcer and the withdrawal of a reinforcer is contingent on a response, responding is suppressed more rapidly. The latter is punishment. Sometimes we withdraw a privilege from a child to control his behavior. A teacher might keep a child in the classroom during recess or cancel a field trip as a result of misbehavior. Turning off television when a child puts his thumb in his mouth may effectively suppress thumbsucking. Most punishments of this sort utilize conditioned or generalized reinforcers. Quite frequently one sees adults withdraw attention or affection as punishment for misbehavior, sometimes in subtle ways.

10. The passage equates taking candy away from a child with
    (A) only one of many categories of punishment
    (B) the presentation of a negative reinforcer
    (C) the presentation of an aversion stimulus
    (D) withdrawal of negative reinforcement
    (E) withdrawal of positive reinforcement

11. Which of the following may be concluded from the last paragraph of the passage?
    (A) Most children regard the classroom as a prison.
    (B) It is usually best to ignore whatever bothers us.
    (C) The author considers recess and field trips to be privileges.
    (D) The withdrawal of affection is an unconscious form of punishment.
    (E) Children who do not like television are harder to punish.

12. The passage does not do which of the following?
    (A) give a definite answer to the question posed in the first paragraph
    (B) discuss generally some of the effects of punishment
    (C) provide examples of some common forms of punishment
    (D) distinguish punishment from reinforcement
    (E) mention the temporary suppression of behavior

13. Which of the following facts, if true, supports one of the author's contentions about punishment?
    (A) Those who were spanked as children may not praise the benefits of such discipline.
    (B) Imposing longer jail terms on criminals does not necessarily permanently reduce their tendency to return to crime.
    (C) Any species or race which is consistently punished will eventually become extinct.
    (D) The temporary suppression of a negative behavior is a fine accomplishment.
    (E) People who are consistently rewarded are incapable of punishing others.

Questions 14 through 18 refer to the following passage.

The question might be asked: how can we know what is "really" real? Defined phenomenologically, "reality" becomes purely a hypothetical concept which accounts for the totality of all conditions imposed by the external world upon an individual. But since other individuals are included in each of our fields of experience, it does become possible as we make identification of similarly perceived phenomena to form consensus groups. In fact, we often tend to ignore and even push out of awareness those persons and their assumptions regarding what is real which do not correspond to our own. However, such a lack of consensus also affords us the opportunity of checking our hypothesis about reality. We may change our concepts about reality and thus in doing so facilitate changes in our phenomenal world of experience. Scientists, for instance, deliberately set out to get a consensus of both their procedures and their conclusions. If they are successful in this quest, their conclusions are considered by the consensus group as constituting an addition to a factual body of sharable knowledge. This process is somewhat in contrast, for example, to those religious experiences considered to be mystical. By their nature they are not always available for communication to others. However, even the scientific reasearcher must finally evaluate the consequences of his research in his own, personal phenomenological field. To use a cliché: truth as beauty exists in the eyes of the beholder.

14. Which of the following is a specific example supporting the point of the passage?
    (A) Certain established scientific facts have not changed for hundreds of years.
    (B) Part of the phrase in the last sentence is from a poem by Keats.
    (C) Reality is a given, unique experience in an individual's phenomenal world.
    (D) We think of our enemies in war as cruel and regard our own soldiers as virtuous.
    (E) The fans at baseball games often see things exactly as the umpire sees them.

15. Applying the argument of the passage, we might define a political party as
    (A) a political group to which few scientists belong
    (B) a consensus group whose individuals share a similar view of political reality
    (C) a consensus group whose members are deluded about what is really "real" politically
    (D) in touch with reality if it is a majority party and out of touch with reality if it is a minority party
    (E) a collection of individuals who are each fundamentally unsure about what political reality is

16. When the author says that "reality" is a "hypothetical concept," he or she means that
    (A) as for reality, there is none
    (B) we can think about reality but never really experience it
    (C) "reality" is not objective
    (D) "reality" is a figment of your imagination
    (E) "reality" is only known by scientists

17. According to the passage, one difference between a scientist and a mystic is that
    (A) the scientist sees truth as facts, the mystic sees truth as beauty
    (B) scientists are unwilling and unable to lend importance to religious experiences
    (C) the work of the mystic does not have consequences that affect individuals
    (D) the scientist is concerned with sharable knowledge and the mystic may not be
    (E) the scientists cannot believe in anything mystical

18. To the question "How can we know what is 'really' real?" this author would probably answer in which of the following ways?
    (A) If no one sees things our way, we are detached from reality.
    (B) Whatever we are aware of can legitimately be called real.
    (C) What is really real is whatever a group of individuals believe.
    (D) We can, if we use the scientific method.
    (E) We cannot know what is "really" real because reality varies with individual perspective.

Questions 19 through 23 refer to the following passage.

He who lets the world, or his own portion of it, choose his plan of life for him has no need of any other faculty than the ape-like one of imitation. He who chooses his plan for himself employs all his faculties. He must use observation to see, reasoning and judgment to foresee, activity to gather materials for decision, discrimination to decide, and when he has decided, firmness and self-control to hold to his decision. And these qualities he requires and exercises exactly in proportion as the part of his conduct which he determines according to his own judgment and feelings is a large one. It is possible that he might be guided in some good path, and kept out of harm's way, without any of these things. But what will be his comparative worth as a human being? It really is of importance, not only what men do, but also what manner of men they are that do it. Among the works of man, which human life is rightly employed in perfecting and beautifying, the first in importance surely is man himself. Supposing it were possible to get houses built, corn grown, battles fought, causes tried, and even churches erected and prayers said, by machinery—by automatons in human form—it would be a considerable loss to exchange for these automatons even the men and women who at present inhabit the more civilized parts of the world, and who assuredly are but starved specimens of what nature can and will produce. Human nature is not a machine to be built after a model, and set to do exactly the work prescribed for it, but a tree, which requires to grow and develop itself on all sides, according to the tendency of the inward forces which make it a living thing.

19. One major distinction in this passage is between
   (A) automatons and machines
   (B) people and machines
   (C) beauty and perfection
   (D) apes and machines
   (E) growing food and fighting battles

20. Which of the following groups represents the type of person that the author calls an *automaton?*
   (A) comedians
   (B) botanists
   (C) workers on an assembly line
   (D) a team of physicians in surgery
   (E) students who consistently ask challenging questions

21. Which of the following is an unstated assumption of the passage?
   (A) Mankind will probably never improve.
   (B) The essence of people themselves is more important than what people do.
   (C) It is desirable to let modern technology do some of our more unpleasant tasks.
   (D) Some people in the world do not select their own life plans.
   (E) What man produces is really no different than man himself.

22. The author would agree that a major benefit of letting the world choose for you your plan of life is
    (A) simplicity
    (B) profit
    (C) friendship
    (D) progress
    (E) happiness

23. The author would probably agree with each of the following statements *except*
    (A) To conform to custom, merely *as* custom, does not educate or develop one.
    (B) Human beings should use and interpret experience in their own way.
    (C) More good may always be made of an energetic nature than of an indolent and impassive one.
    (D) Persons whose desires and impulses are their own are said to have character.
    (E) It makes good sense to choose the easy life of conformity.

Questions 24 and 25 refer to the following passage.

   Charles Darwin was both a naturalist and a scientist. Darwin's *Origin of Species* (1859) was based on twenty-five years of research in testing and checking his theory of evolution. "Darwinism" had a profound effect on the natural sciences, the social sciences, and the humanities. Churchmen who feared for the survival of religious institutions rushed to attack him. However Darwin never attempted to apply his laws of evolution to human society. It was the social Darwinists who expanded the theory of evolution to include society as a whole. The social Darwinists viewed society as a "struggle for existence" with only the "fittest" members of society able to survive. They espoused basically a racist and elitist doctrine. Some people were naturally superior to others; it was in the "nature of things" for big business to take over "less fit," smaller concerns.

24. The final sentence of the passage beginning "Some people. . ." is the author's attempt to
    (A) discredit Charles Darwin's theory
    (B) voice his or her own point of view
    (C) summarize one point of view
    (D) give social Darwinism a fair shake
    (E) explain the modern prominence of big business

25. The author's primary purpose in this passage is to
    (A) warn of the dangers of having one's ideas abused
    (B) show that Darwin was unconcerned with human society
    (C) defend Darwin against modern charges of racism and elitism
    (D) explain how Darwin's theory was applied to society
    (E) give an example of Darwinian evolution

Current evidence suggests that there is a marked tendency for children with superior IQs to be more mature both socially and physically than children of average ability. Also, educational research shows that gifted children also appear superior in moral or trait tests to children of average IQ.

26. In the above passage, the author is using *gifted children* to mean children
    (A) from a traditional moral background
    (B) who are in no way average
    (C) with superior IQs
    (D) who have submitted to educational research
    (E) who build social relationships earlier

Prior to the 1960s, educational psychologists were primarily concerned with specific social, motivational, and aptitudinal aspects of learning. The intellectual structure of class activities, in addition to curriculum problems, has been comprehensively studied only in the last two decades.

27. One of the author's points in this passage is that
    (A) prior to the 1960s, no one noticed that the concerns of educational psychologists were limited
    (B) educational psychologists tend to shift their interests as a group
    (C) after 1960, psychologists lost interest in the social, motivational, and aptitudinal aspects of learning
    (D) the academic significance of classroom activities themselves has not been the concern of educational psychologists until fairly recently
    (E) the decades preceding the 1960s were marked by poorly thought out, poorly implemented classroom activities

Pestalozzi (1746–1827) was influenced by Rousseau in adopting an educational philosophy based on the needs of the child. Pestalozzi recognized the dependence of the child on society for the development of effective personal growth. His most famous work was *Leonard and Gertrude* (1781).

28. The passage is *least* likely to appear in which of the following?
    (A) an introduction to Pestalozzi's *Leonard and Gertrude*
    (B) an article surveying the influence of society on the personal growth of children
    (C) an essay describing the influence of Rousseau's educational philosophy
    (D) a journal of the history of education
    (E) the history of seventeenth-century Italy

Questions 29 and 30 refer to the following passage.

A lesson plan is basically a tool for effective teaching. Its primary importance is to present objectives and content in a logical and systematic manner; as such, it is an integral part of the instructional process.

29. Which of the following is an unstated assumption made by the author of this passage?
    (A) All features of the instructional process should have the same logical, systematic qualities as the lesson plan.
    (B) Students learn best when material is not presented in a disorganized or unplanned manner.
    (C) A teacher who is not a logical, systematic thinker has no place in the instructional process.
    (D) The lesson plan is by far the most important tool for effective teaching.
    (E) Teachers should not deviate from the lesson plan in any case.

30. The author uses *integral* to mean
    (A) original
    (B) whole
    (C) essential
    (D) not segregated
    (E) modern

Questions 31, 32, and 33 refer to the following statements.

Five children in a family of six children have freckles.
Three children in the family are girls.
Four children in the family have blue eyes.

31. Which of the following *must* be true?

    I. All of the girls have freckles.
    II. At least one of the girls has blue eyes.

  (A) I only   (D) both I and II
  (B) II only   (E) neither I nor II
  (C) either I or II but not both

32. Which of the following *must* be false?

    I. All of the blue-eyed girls have freckles.
    II. No children with freckles have blue eyes.

  (A) I only   (D) both I and II
  (B) II only   (E) neither I nor II
  (C) either I or II but not both

33. Which of the following can be deduced from the statements?
  (A) None of the girls have freckles.
  (B) Three of the blue-eyed children have freckles.
  (C) One girl has no freckles.
  (D) All of the girls have blue eyes.
  (E) none of the above

Rewards tend to be more effective than punishment in controlling student behavior. Negative reinforcement often is accompanied by emotional side effects that may cause continued learning disabilities.

34. The author implies which of the following?
  (A) The same student who is punished frequently may have difficulty learning.
  (B) In society at large, rewards are not given nearly as often as they should be.
  (C) Negative reinforcement is much more useful out of school than it is in school.
  (D) The most effective punishment is that which is followed by a reward.
  (E) Learning disabilities often lead to emotional problems.

It is an important guideline to avoid discussing other students during a parent-teacher conference. Such comments often result in an emotional reaction by the parent and can interfere with the purpose of the conference.

35. Which of the following facts, if true, would most strengthen the argument of the passage?
    (A) The discussion of other students gives many parents a comfortable sense that the teacher understands the whole classroom "scene."
    (B) Most parents avoid taking the trouble to attend a conference.
    (C) The child's relationship with other students is most often the cause of problems that necessitate a conference.
    (D) Researchers witnessing parent-teacher conferences have verified that parents become angry in 90% of the conferences in which other students are discussed.
    (E) Emotional reactions by parents must be understood as the parents' legitimate expression of deeply felt concerns.

A test is valid if it measures what it is intended to measure. A test is reliable if it is consistent. Therefore, a test may be consistent even though it does not measure what it is intended to measure.

36. The author's primary purpose in this passage is to
    (A) contribute to recent research in testing validity and reliability
    (B) question whether we should use the terms *valid* and *reliable* to describe tests
    (C) insist that all tests must be both valid and reliable
    (D) call for the abolition of invalid tests
    (E) explain the difference between validity and reliability

Teacher salaries account for approximately seventy percent of a school budget. Any major proposal designed to reduce educational expenditures will ultimately necessitate a cut in teaching staff.

37. Neighborhood High School is staffed by fifty teachers, and its administration has just ordered a reduction in educational expenditures. According to the above passage, which of the following will be one result of the reduction?
    (A) a reduction in both administrative and teaching salaries
    (B) a teaching staff dependent on fewer educational materials
    (C) a teaching staff of fewer than fifty teachers
    (D) a teaching staff of only fifteen teachers
    (E) a substantial change in the quality of education

"Open houses" should be offered, as they enable a school district to present the school programs to the community. Effective open-house activities can further community participation in the educational process.

38. Which of the following is an unstated assumption of the author of this passage?
    (A) Most participants in open-house activities do not take a whole-hearted interest in the enterprise.
    (B) Without an open house, no members of the community would be aware of the available school programs.
    (C) Open-house activities are very rarely effective.
    (D) Community participation has a positive effect on the educational process.
    (E) Many school districts never hold an open house.

The failure of the progressive movement to adjust to the transformation of American society spelled its ultimate collapse. The progressive educational theories of the early 1900s did not take into consideration the technological expertise of the nuclear age.

39. Which of the following best expresses the point of this passage?
    (A) At one time, the progressive movement served well the needs of American education.
    (B) The progressive theories were not adaptable to late-twentieth-century progress.
    (C) The progressive movement collapsed soon after its heyday in the early 1900s.
    (D) The progressive movement was motivated by theories too conservative to be useful.
    (E) No American student these days could possibly benefit from progressive educational theory.

Graduate students who expect to specialize in The Teaching of Writing must take English 600, either English 500 (Advanced Composition) or 504 (Writing of Criticism), at least three literature courses concentrating on the same single century only, English 740 (Teaching of Writing), English 741 (Classical Rhetoric), and English 742 (Modern Rhetorical Theory).

40. According to the statement above, which of the following schedules does *not* belong to a specialist in The Teaching of Writing?
    (A) English 740–42, Advanced Composition, twentieth-century drama, twentieth-century poetry, twentieth-century novels, English 600
    (B) English 740–42, eighteenth-century poetry, eighteenth-century prose fiction, eighteenth-century drama, English 504, English 600
    (C) English 600, Victorian poetry, Victorian prose fiction, Victorian novels, English 500, English 740, 741, and 742
    (D) English 500, seventeenth-century poetry, seventeenth-century drama, Victorian novels, English 740, 741, and 742
    (E) English 740, Classical Rhetoric, Modern Rhetorical Theory, English 500, English 600, Victorian poetry, Victorian prose fiction, Victorian novels

Questions 41 through 46 refer to the following passage.

[1]The Morrill Act (1862) extended the principle of federal support for public education, the earliest attempt being the Northwest Ordinance of 1787. [2]The Morrill Act established land-grant colleges in each state and specified a curriculum based on agriculture and mechanical arts. [3]Land-grant colleges often were a state's first institution of public higher education. [4]Public support and public control strengthened the concept of the state-university system. [5]The Civil Rights Act of 1875 was the first federal attempt to provide equal educational opportunity. [6]The progressive theories of John Dewey also had a profound effect on public education. [7]Dewey believed that education included the home, shop, neighborhood, church, and school. [8]However, industrialization was destroying the educational functions of these institutions. [9]Dewey believed that the public schools must be society's instrument for "shaping its own destiny." [10]To do this the schools had to be transformed in order to serve the interests of democracy.

41. If this passage were divided into two paragraphs, the second paragraph would begin with sentence number
    (A) 3   (B) 5   (C) 6   (D) 7   (E) 8

42. The passage implies that one significant contrast between the Morrill Act and Dewey's theories was
    (A) Dewey's lack of faith in land-grant colleges
    (B) the fact that the Morrill Act was not a democratic law
    (C) the neglect in the Morrill Act of education's relationship to society
    (D) Dewey's lack of knowledge about the Morrill Act
    (E) the Morrill Act's stress on a heavily agricultural and mechanical curriculum

43. The word *also* in sentence 6 does which of the following?
   (A) opens the question concerning whether Dewey himself would have supported certain government acts concerning education
   (B) makes clear that Dewey's theories were innovative and inconsistent with government policy
   (C) makes the point that Dewey's theories were somewhat identical to material in the Morrill Act
   (D) suggests that the Morrill Act, Northwest Ordinance, and Civil Rights Act had a profound effect on public education.
   (E) suggests that Dewey's theories did more than affect public education

44. Which of the following statements, if true, would best support sentences 7 and 8?
   (A) Home, shop, neighborhood, church, and school each played an ever-increasing role in the world of learning.
   (B) Learning was equated exclusively with industrial progress, while moral, social, and artistic growth were undervalued.
   (C) Industry was shaping the destiny of the citizens, and Dewey was a strong industrial supporter.
   (D) Industry was transforming the schools so that they could serve the interests of democracy.
   (E) sentence 3

45. This passage would be *least* likely to appear in which of the following?
   (A) an encyclopedia article summarizing the major legislation of the nineteenth century
   (B) a brief survey of legislation and theories that significantly affected education
   (C) an introduction to the theories of John Dewey
   (D) an argument about the benefits of both progressive legislation and progressive educational theory
   (E) a discussion of the relationship between social needs and school curriculum

46. The passage allows us to conclude which of the following?
   (A) Beyond the legislation discussed in the passage, no other government acts addressed the issue of public education.
   (B) Theorists always have a more significant effect on education than legislators.
   (C) The framers of the Morrill Act did not appreciate the value of moral education.
   (D) Dewey succeeded to some extent in transforming public education.
   (E) The state-university system was a concept long before it became a reality.

**Students Involved in Extracurricular
Activities at Mercy High School**

	Sports	Music/ Drama	Newspaper/ Yearbook	Miscellaneous
Sophomore Girls	53%	22%	13%	12%
Sophomore Boys	62%	23%	10%	5%
Junior Girls	42%	25%	13%	20%
Junior Boys	58%	20%	10%	12%
Senior Girls	51%	26%	14%	9%
Senior Boys	63%	20%	10%	7%

47. Which of the following can be derived from the information in the chart above?
    (A) There is a greater percentage of senior girls involved in sports than sophomore girls involved in sports.
    (B) There is a greater percentage of junior girls involved in newspaper/yearbook than senior girls involved in newspaper/yearbook.
    (C) There is a greater percentage of sophomore boys involved in music/drama than senior girls involved in music/drama.
    (D) There is a greater percentage of junior girls involved in newspaper/yearbook than sophomore girls involved in newspaper/yearbook.
    (E) There is a greater percentage of senior boys involved in sports than sophomore boys involved in sports.

Psychology is often considered a science of the mind. As a science, it aims to generate comprehensive theories to explain behavior. Despite its status as a science, the "methods" of psychology sometimes seem more mystical than rational and analytical.

48. Which of the following functions does the second sentence perform?
    (A) provides an example
    (B) provides more information
    (C) denies the truth of the first sentence
    (D) uses a metaphor
    (E) adds an inconsistency

Twenty years ago, most television programs were shown in black and white. These days, the brightly colored clothes most of us wear signal that the medium has changed.

49. The author implies which of the following in the above passage?
    (A) Twenty years ago, people wore only black and white clothes.
    (B) Most people no longer will tolerate black and white television.
    (C) There is only a slight relationship between our self-image and the images we see on television.
    (D) Color television is significantly responsible for our preference for brightly colored clothes.
    (E) Clothing technology, like television, was relatively primitive twenty years ago.

The political party is a voluntary association of voters whose purpose in a democracy is to control the policies of government by electing to public office persons of its membership.

50. The above passage would be most likely to appear in which of the following?
    (A) an introductory text on political science
    (B) a general interest magazine
    (C) a manual of rules for legislators
    (D) a piece of campaign literature
    (E) a brief essay discussing the president's most recent news conference

STOP: IF YOU FINISH BEFORE TIME IS CALLED, CHECK YOUR WORK ON THIS SECTION ONLY. DO NOT WORK ON ANY OTHER SECTION IN THE TEST.

SECTION II: MATHEMATICS

Time: 70 Minutes
50 Questions

DIRECTIONS

In the questions or incomplete statements below, select the one *best* answer or completion of the five choices given.

1. What number is 15% of 80?
   (A) 11½   (B) 12   (C) 15   (D) 16½   (E) 18

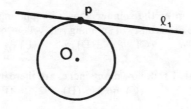

2. If line ℓ_1 is tangent to circle O at point p, above, which of the following must be true about a line drawn perpendicular to ℓ_1 at point p?
   (A) It bisects line ℓ_1.
   (B) It is parallel to line ℓ_1.
   (C) It passes through the center of circle O.
   (D) It is half the diameter.
   (E) none of the above

3. Solve: $(7 + 8) \div 2/3 =$
   (A) 22½   (B) 15⅔   (C) 10   (D) 6²⁄₁₀   (E) 6¹⁄₁₆

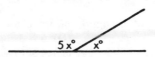

4. What is the degree measure of angle x?
   (A) 20°   (B) 30°   (C) 40°   (D) 60°   (E) 90°

5 Which of the following fractions is the largest?
   (A) 25/52   (D) 51/103
   (B) 31/60   (E) 43/90
   (C) 19/40

6. If 7 pounds of bananas cost $1.68, at the same rate how much do 9 pounds of bananas cost?

(A) $1.76

(B) $1.92

(C) $1.98

(D) $2.16

(E) $2.35

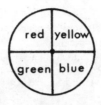

7. From the diagram of the spinner above, in spinning the spinner only once, what is the probability of spinning red, yellow, or blue?

(A) ¼   (B) ⅓   (C) ½   (D) ¾   (E) 3/2

8. If 16½ feet equals 1 rod, how many inches are there in 4 rods?

(A) 5½   (B) 22   (C) 66   (D) 792   (E) 2,376

9. Approximate √94.

(A) 9   (B) 10   (C) 11   (D) 30   (E) √9.4

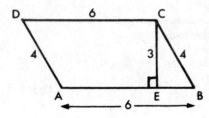

10. To compute the area of this figure, one would use

(A) 6 × 4

(B) 12 × 3

(C) 6 × 3

(D) 6 + 3

(E) 4 × (6 + 3)

11. All of the following ratios are equal *except*

(A) 1 to 4

(B) 3 to 8

(C) 2 to 8

(D) 3 to 12

(E) 4 to 16

12. Which of the following could be expressed by the following number sentence? 825.50 + 435.00 = 1,260.50
    (A) the difference in the cost of housing in two cities, Chicago and Indianapolis
    (B) the total amount of money earned in each of two months during the summer vacation
    (C) the average of two months' earnings
    (D) 435.00 is the result of subtracting the weight of 824.50 pounds minus some unknown
    (E) the total of funding received by a school district of 435 students at $825.50 per student

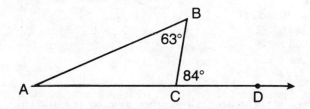

13. Given △ABC with ∠BCD = 84° and ∠B = 63°, find the measure of ∠A in degrees.
    (A) 21   (B) 27   (C) 84   (D) 96   (E) 116

14. If Juan works 8 hours and receives $3.75 per hour and Mary works 24 hours and receives a total of $110, which of the following *cannot* be derived from the above statement?
    (A) Juan's total
    (B) Mary's wage per hour
    (C) the difference received between Juan and Mary
    (D) the average total received by Juan and Mary
    (E) the hours Mary worked each day

15. If $3c = d$, then $c =$
    (A) $3 + d$ (D) $1/3d$
    (B) $3d$ (E) $(1 + d)/3$
    (C) $d/3$

16. On a map, 1 centimeter represents 35 kilometers. Two cities 245 kilometers apart would be separated on the map by how many centimeters?
    (A) 5   (B) 7   (C) 9   (D) 210   (E) 280

17. Round off to the nearest tenth: 4,316.136
    (A) 4,320
    (B) 4,316.14
    (C) 4,316.13
    (D) 4,316.106
    (E) 4,316.1

18. Which of the following is a prime number?
    (A) 15   (B) 17   (C) 39   (D) 93   (E) 129

19. The fraction 1/8 is between the numbers listed in which of the following pairs?
    (A) 1/10 and 2/17
    (B) .1 and .12
    (C) .08 and .1
    (D) 1 and 2
    (E) 1/9 and 2/15

20. A class of 30 students all together have 60 pencils. Which of the following *must* be true?
    (A) Each student has 2 pencils.
    (B) Every student has a pencil.
    (C) Some students have only 1 pencil.
    (D) Some students have more pencils than other students.
    (E) The class averages 2 pencils per student.

21. A pint of salad dressing has 3 parts oil for every 1 part vinegar. How could you calculate the number of ounces of vinegar in 3 pints of salad dressing? (16 ounces = 1 pint)
    (A) ($3/4 \times 32$) 3
    (B) $16 \times 1/3$
    (C) ($1/4 \times 16$) 3
    (D) ($32 - 16$)($4 - 1/4$)
    (E) $32 \times 3/4$

22. A man purchased 4 pounds of steak priced at $3.89 per pound. How much change did he receive from a twenty-dollar bill?
    (A) $4.34   (D) $15.56
    (B) $4.44   (E) $44.66
    (C) $4.46

23. In the series 8, 9, 12, 17, 24, . . . , the next number would be
    (A) 29   (B) 30   (C) 33   (D) 35   (E) 41

24. Assume that inflation will increase the prices of everything at a rate of
    10% a year over the next ten years. What will be the price of a now-$100
    stereo in three years?
    (A) $121.00
    (B) $126.00
    (C) $130.00
    (D) $133.10
    (E) $146.41

25. If the edges of a 2″ by 3″ photograph are each enlarged by 20%, what is
    the area of the new photograph?
    (A) 6.82 square inches
    (B) 7.2 square inches
    (C) 8.64 square inches
    (D) 9.2 square inches
    (E) 12 square inches

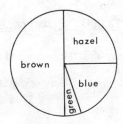

26. Sam tries to construct a pie graph representing eye color of his
    classmates. In his class of 24 students, 6 students have blue eyes, 12
    students have brown eyes, 5 students have hazel eyes, and 1 student has
    green eyes. His teacher tells him that his graph (shown above) is not
    correct. In order to fix the graph, Sam should
    (A) increase the amount of green and decrease the amount of blue
    (B) increase the amount of blue and decrease the amount of hazel
    (C) decrease the amount of blue and increase the amount of brown
    (D) decrease the amount of hazel and increase the amount of brown
    (E) increase the amount of hazel and increase the amount of blue

27. If D is between A and B on $\overleftrightarrow{AB}$, which of the following must be true?

(A) AD = DB

(B) DB = AB − AD

(C) AD = AB + DB

(D) DB = AD + AB

(E) AB = AD = BD

Questions 28 and 29 are based on the following graph.

AVERAGE FAMILY'S EXPENSES

1970	1975
Average Income $12,000	**Average Income $16,000**

28. How much more money did the average family spend on medical expenses in 1975 than in 1970?

(A) $500–$600

(B) $600–$700

(C) $700–$800

(D) $800–$900

(E) $900–$1,000

29. What was the approximate increase from 1970 to 1975 in the percentage spent on food and drink?

(A) 4%   (B) 18%   (C) 22%   (D) 40%   (E) 50%

30. The length of rectangle ABCD is twice as long as the side of square WXYZ. The width of rectangle ABCD is two-thirds as long as the side of square WXYZ. If the area of the square is 36 square inches, what is the perimeter of the rectangle?

(A) 50 inches

(B) 48 inches

(C) 32 inches

(D) 24 inches

(E) 12 inches

31. How many inches are there in m yards and n feet?
    - (A) m + n
    - (B) 36m + 12n
    - (C) 36(m + n)
    - (D) 3m + n
    - (E) 12(m + n)

32. In a senior class of 800, only 240 decide to attend the senior prom. What percentage of the senior class attended the senior prom?
    - (A) 8%
    - (B) 24%
    - (C) 30%
    - (D) 33%
    - (E) 80%

33. What is the probability of tossing a penny twice so that both times it lands heads up?
    - (A) 1/8   (B) 1/4   (C) 1/3   (D) 1/2   (E) 2/3

34. .0074 is how many times smaller than 740,000?
    - (A) 1,000,000
    - (B) 10,000,000
    - (C) 100,000,000
    - (D) 1,000,000,000
    - (E) 10,000,000,000

35. A suit that originally sold for $120 is on sale for $90. What is the rate of discount?
    - (A) 20%
    - (B) 25%
    - (C) 30%
    - (D) 33⅓%
    - (E) 75%

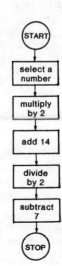

36. In this flow chart, regardless of the number you select, the number at the end is always
    - (A) 5
    - (B) less than 14
    - (C) the same as the original number
    - (D) twice the original number
    - (E) an odd number

37. To change 3 miles to inches, you should
    (A) multiply 3 times 5,280
    (B) multiply 3 times 5,280 and then divide by 12
    (C) multiply 3 times 5,280 and then multiply by 12
    (D) divide 3 into 5,280 and then multiply by 12
    (E) divide 3 into 12 and then multiply by 5,280

38. What is the largest integer if the sum of three consecutive even integers is 318?
    (A) 100   (B) 104   (C) 106   (D) 108   (E) 111

39. In a certain classroom, girls account for 40% of the students. Also in that classroom, 1 out of every 3 boys has red hair. If there are Q students in that classroom, the best expression for boys without red hair would be
    (A) $(.6Q)\frac{2}{3}$
    (B) $\frac{1}{3}Q - 40$
    (C) $(\frac{1}{3}Q)(.6)$
    (D) $(.4Q)\frac{2}{3}$
    (E) $(Q/.6)2$

40. A basketball is fully inflated to 24 pounds per square inch. A football is fully inflated to 16 pounds per square inch. The air pressure in the basketball is what percentage of the air pressure in the football?
    (A) 50%   (B) 66%   (C) 100%   (D) 125%   (E) 150%

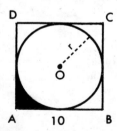

41. Circle O is inscribed in square ABCD as shown above. The area of the shaded region is approximately
    (A) 10   (B) 25   (C) 30   (D) 50   (E) 75

42. Today is Lucy's fourteenth birthday. Last year she was three years older than twice Charlie's age at that time. Using C for Charlie's age now, which of the following can be used to determine Charlie's age now?

(A) $13 - 3 = 2(C - 1)$

(B) $14 - 3 = 2C$

(C) $13 - 3 = 2C$

(D) $13 + 3 = 2C$

(E) $13 + 3 = 2(C - 1)$

43. If 15 students in a class average 80% on an English exam and 10 students average 90% on the same exam, what is the average in percent for all 25 students?

(A) 83%   (B) $83\frac{1}{2}$%   (C) 84%   (D) 85%   (E) $86\frac{2}{3}$%

44. Lucre Savings and Loan pays 8% annual interest. InterGuild Federal Credit Union pays 12% annual interest. What would be the difference in the amount of simple interest earned over three years on $1200 if it were invested in the Credit Union instead of in the Savings and Loan? $(I = Prt)$

(A) $48   (B) $144   (C) $432   (D) $480   (E) $960

45. Angela has nickels and dimes in her pocket. She has twice as many dimes as nickels. What is the best expression of the amount of money she has in cents if x equals the number of nickels she has?

(A) $25x$

(B) $10x + 5(2x)$

(C) $x + 2x$

(D) $5(3x)$

(E) $20(x + 5)$

46. In the Junior Olympics, first place is worth 5 points, second place is worth 3 points, and third place is worth 1 point. No points are awarded for any other place, and there are no ties. Tim always finished just behind Tom in each of the five events. If Tom finished first, second, and third each at least once, then how many points did Tim have if Tom finished with 19?

(A) 7   (B) 10   (C) 11   (D) 14   (E) 15

47. Four construction workers build a house containing 16 rooms. If the house has 4 floors and they take exactly 4 months (without stopping) to build it, then which of the following *must* be true?

  I. They build 4 rooms each month.
 II. Each floor has 4 rooms.
III. They build an average of 1 floor per month.
IV. The house averages 4 rooms per floor.

(A) I and II

(B) I, II, and III

(C) II and III

(D) III and IV

(E) I, II, III, and IV

Questions 48 and 49 refer to the following information.

In the number represented by xy, x is the digit in the tens place and y is the digit in the ones place.

48. If the digits were reversed, which of the following *must* be true?

    I.   x > y
    II. y > x
    III. xy > yx

    (A) I only   (D) II and III
    (C) II only   (E) none of these
    (C) I and II

49. What is the largest difference possible between xy and yx?
    (A) 46   (D) 99
    (B) 72   (E) cannot be determined
    (C) 81

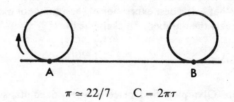

$\pi \simeq 22/7$ $C = 2\pi r$

50. The tire above rolls one complete revolution from point A to point B without slipping. If the radius of the tire is 5 inches, then the distance in inches from A to B is
    (A) 10 × 22/7   (D) 5 × (22/7)²
    (B) 25 × 22/7   (E) cannot be determined
    (C) 20 × 22/7

STOP. IF YOU FINISH BEFORE TIME IS CALLED, CHECK YOUR WORK ON THIS SECTION ONLY. DO NOT WORK ON ANY OTHER SECTION IN THE TEST.

SECTION III: ESSAY WRITING

Time: 60 Minutes
2 Essays

DIRECTIONS

In this section, you will have 60 minutes to plan and write two essays, one for each topic given. You may use the bottom of this and the following page to organize and plan your essay before you begin writing. You should plan your time wisely. Read each topic carefully to make sure that you are properly addressing the issue or situation. YOU MUST WRITE ON THE SPECIFIED TOPIC. AN ESSAY ON ANOTHER TOPIC WILL NOT BE ACCEPTABLE.

The two essay questions included in this section are designed to give you an opportunity to write clearly and effectively. Use specific examples whenever appropriate to aid in supporting your ideas. Keep in mind that the quality of your writing is much more important than the quantity.

Your essays are to be written on the special answer sheets provided. No other paper may be used. Your writing should be neat and legible. Because you have only a limited amount of space in which to write, please do NOT skip lines, do NOT write excessively large, and do NOT leave wide margins.

Remember, use the bottom of this and the following page for any organizational notes you may wish to make.

Topic 1

Reflect upon a good friend and select the one character trait that you feel to be the most important. Describe and explain why that particular trait is more important than any other.

FOR EACH ESSAY, USE TWO SIDES OF AN $8\frac{1}{2}''$ BY $11''$ LINED SHEET OF PAPER.

Topic 2

Some American public schools have removed the "A" to "F" grading system and substituted "Pass-Fail" grading with the instructor adding a written statement about the student's progress. Comment on the pros or cons of such a system.

ANSWER KEY FOR PRACTICE TEST 2

	SECTION I READING COMPREHENSION			SECTION II MATHEMATICS	
1. B	18. E	35. D	1. B	18. B	35. B
2. B	19. B	36. E	2. C	19. E	36. C
3. D	20. C	37. C	3. A	20. E	37. C
4. E	21. D	38. D	4. B	21. C	38. D
5. C	22. A	39. B	5. B	22. B	39. A
6. D	23. E	40. D	6. D	23. C	40. E
7. C	24. C	41. C	7. D	24. D	41. A
8. C	25. D	42. E	8. D	25. C	42. A
9. E	26. C	43. D	9. B	26. B	43. C
10. E	27. D	44. B	10. C	27. B	44. B
11. C	28. E	45. A	11. B	28. C	45. A
12. A	29. B	46. D	12. B	29. A	46. B
13. B	30. C	47. E	13. A	30. C	47. D
14. D	31. B	48. B	14. E	31. B	48. E
15. B	32. B	49. D	15. C	32. C	49. C
16. C	33. E	50. A	16. B	33. B	50. A
17. D	34. A		17. E	34. C	

SCORING YOUR CBEST PRACTICE TEST 2

To score your CBEST Practice Test 2, total the number of correct responses for each section of the test separately. Do not subtract any points for questions attempted but missed, as there is no penalty for guessing. The score for each section is then scaled from 20 to 80. (About 70% right is a passing score.)

ANALYZING YOUR TEST RESULTS

The charts on the following page should be used to carefully analyze your results and spot your strengths and weaknesses. The complete process of analyzing each subject area and each individual question should be completed for this Practice Test. These results should be reexamined for trends in types of error (repeated errors) or poor results in specific subject areas. THIS REEXAMINATION AND ANALYSIS IS OF TREMENDOUS IMPORTANCE FOR EFFECTIVE TEST PREPARATION.

PRACTICE TEST 2: SUBJECT AREA ANALYSIS SHEET

	Possible	Completed	Right	Wrong
Reading Comprehension	50			
Mathematics	50			
TOTAL	100			

ANALYSIS—TALLY SHEET FOR QUESTIONS MISSED

One of the most important parts of test preparation is analyzing WHY you missed a question so that you can reduce the number of mistakes. Now that you have taken Practice Test 2 and corrected your answers, carefully tally your mistakes by marking them in the proper column.

	REASON FOR MISTAKE			
	Total Missed	Simple Mistake	Misread Problem	Lack of Knowledge
Reading Comprehension				
Mathematics				
TOTAL				

Reviewing the above data should help you determine WHY you are missing certain questions. Now that you have pinpointed the type of error, when you take Practice Test 3, focus on avoiding your most common type.

ESSAY TOPIC 1 CHECKLIST

Use this checklist to evaluate your Topic 1 essay.

Diagnosis/Prescription for Timed Writing Exercise

A good essay will:

_____ address the assignment
           be well focused
_____ be well organized
           smooth transitions between paragraphs
           coherent, unified
_____ be well developed
           contain specific examples to support points
_____ be grammatically sound (only minor flaws)
           correct sentence structure
           correct punctuation
           use of standard written English
_____ use language skillfully
           variety of sentence types
           variety of words
_____ be legible
           clear handwriting
           neat

ESSAY TOPIC 2 CHECKLIST

Use this checklist to evaluate your Topic 2 essay.

Diagnosis/Prescription for Timed Writing Exercise

A good essay will:
_____ address the assignment
              be well focused
_____ be well organized
              smooth transitions between paragraphs
              coherent, unified
_____ be well developed
               contain specific examples to support points
_____ be grammatically sound (only minor flaws)
              correct sentence structure
              correct punctuation
              use of standard written English
_____ use language skillfully
              variety of sentence types
              variety of words
_____ be legible
              clear handwriting
              neat

ANSWERS AND COMPLETE EXPLANATIONS
FOR PRACTICE TEST 2

SECTION I: READING COMPREHENSION

1. (B) Clarifying the confusing term *angular displacement* would help make the passage clearer.

2. (B) The position of the pencil seemingly shifts according to which eye is seeing it—that is, according to the point from which it is observed.

3. (D) The sentence explains that the established military tradition supplied the South with military leaders.

4. (E) The Northern advantages are all long-term, especially food production. Each of the other choices draws a conclusion beyond any implications in the passage.

5. (C) By mentioning carrots in connection with improved eyesight and not explaining that implied connection, the author is assuming that readers readily see the connection.

6. (D) Choice (C) flatly contradicts the argument of the passage, and (A) and (B) present information not touched on in the passage. Choice (E) is weak because associations are not universal; they depend on each individual's personal experience. This point—that associations are personal rather than universal—is expressed by (D).

7. (C) Choice (C) directly contradicts the point of the passage, which is that associations are determined by experience.

8. (C) Choices (D) and (E) neither weaken nor strengthen the passage, simply suggesting other examples of associations without explaining the stimulus which produced them; (A) and (B) are irrelevant issues. Choice (C) strengthens the argument of the passage by citing an example of experience reinforcing an association—or in other words, stimulating a response.

9. (E) The passage implies that those who administer the tests are different from experts on testing because the administrators do not see that the tests are limited measurements.

10. (E) According to paragraph 3, taking candy away is the withdrawal of a positive reinforcer, and spanking is the presentation of a negative reinforcer.

11. (C) The mention of recess and field trips follows this sentence: "Sometimes we withdraw a privilege from a child to control his behavior." Therefore, we can conclude that the author is using recess and field trips as *examples* of such privileges.

12. (A) The question posed in the first paragraph—*Does punishment, in fact, do what it is supposed to do?*—is not answered in a definite way. The first sentence of the passage says that *punishment is used to reduce tendencies to behave in certain ways.* The second paragraph goes on to state that punishment *seems to temporarily suppress a behavior.* This is a less than definite answer to the question.

13. (B) Each of the other choices draws conclusions beyond the scope of the passage. The author suggests in paragraph 3 that imposing punishment does not seem to have any *permanent* effect.

14. (D) The point of the passage is that "reality" varies according to who experiences it and what "consensus group" he or she is a member of. Along this line, a war is a conflict between two different consensus groups, and so the example given by (D) is appropriate.

15. (B) Both choices (B) and (C) mention consensus group, but (C) says that the members of the group are deluded about reality, which contradicts the author's argument that no view of reality is, strictly speaking, a delusion.

16. (C) Once again, the point of the passage is that different people or groups acquire different versions of reality based on their differing experiences. Reality is, therefore, subjective, but not a mere figment of imagination.

17. (D) This choice is validated by sentences 8 and 9 of the passage.

18. (E) This choice has been explained above in the discussions of questions 14 and 16.

19. (B) The author says that *human nature is not a machine* and stresses this point throughout the passage.

20. (C) One way in which the author describes an automaton is a human machine *set to do exactly the work prescribed for it.* This description corresponds most closely to workers on an assembly line.

21. (D) The author develops arguments in favor of *he who chooses his plan for himself;* therefore, the author must assume that there are those who need to hear this argument—namely, those who do not select their own life plans.

22. (A) Early in the passage, the author shows that those who choose their own life plans must have complex skills, whereas those whose plan of life is chosen may live simply, with *no need of any other faculty than the ape-like one of imitation.*

23. (E) The passage is an extended argument *against* the easy life of conformity.

24. (C) The final sentence summarizes the *racist and elitist doctrine* mentioned in the sentence which precedes it.

25. (D) The fourth sentence of the passage focuses on the relevance of Darwin's theory to human society, and the bulk of the passage develops this connection.

26. (C) The second sentence distinguishes gifted children from children of average IQ and thereby equates gifted children with the *children with superior IQs* mentioned in the first sentence.

27. (D) The author contrasts an early concern with social, motivational, and aptitudinal aspects of learning with the more recent interest in class activities. None of the other choices is an explicit point of the passage.

28. (E) Since the passage describes the life and work of a man living in the eighteenth and nineteenth centuries, it would not be likely to appear in a seventeenth-century history.

29. (B) By citing the value of planning the presentation of material in an orderly way, the author must assume that such organized instruction is beneficial. Each of the other choices draws conclusions beyond the scope of the passage.

30. (C) None of the other choices makes good sense when substituted for *integral,* and *essential* is one of the meanings of *integral.*

31. (B) Since four out of six children have blue eyes, two children do not have blue eyes. Those two children could be two of the three girls, leaving one girl who *must* have blue eyes (statement II). Note that statement I may be false because one of the girls could be freckleless.

32. (B) Since five of the six children have freckles and four of the six have blue eyes, statement II must be false, as some of the children will be both blue eyed and freckled. Note, however, that statement I could possibly be true—the three girls could be both blue eyed and freckled.

33. (E) None of the choices—(A), (B), (C), or (D)—could be deduced from the statements. (B), (C), and (D) could possibly be true but aren't necessarily true. Choice (A) is false.

34. (A) Understanding punishment to be a type of negative reinforcement, we may infer that punishment may cause *continued learning disabilities.*

35. (D) The passage states that discussion of other students has a negative effect on parents and on the conference; the fact expressed in choice (D) directly validates this assertion.

36. (E) Each of the other choices introduces information well beyond the scope of the passage.

37. (C) The passage says that budget cuts result in teaching staff cuts; choices (C) and (D) mention a staff cut, but (D) is a weak answer because it is overly specific and not necessarily true.

38. (D) The author favors community participation in education; therefore, he or she must assume that such participation has a positive effect.

39. (B) If we replace *late-twentieth-century progress* in choice (B) with the synonymous term used in the passage, *technological expertise of the nuclear age,* we see that (B) clearly reiterates the point of the passage.

40. (D) This choice can be eliminated because it includes three literature courses *not* within the same century.

41. (C) Sentence 6 introduces a new topic; it shifts from a discussion of education legislation in general to a discussion of John Dewey in particular.

42. (E) Sentence 7 stresses Dewey's belief that education is concerned with many areas and experiences; this belief contrasts with the Morrill Act's stress on agricultural and mechanical arts as primary educational areas.

43. (D) *Also* indicates that Dewey's theories are being discussed in addition to previous information and that reference to the previous information is included in the statement about Dewey.

44. (B) Dewey's belief in a comprehensive education is inconsistent with a focus on industrialization, and choice (B) explains that inconsistency, thus supporting the statement that industrialization is destructive.

45. (A) The passage is about education and some related legislation but not about legislation in general.

46. (D) We are told that Dewey's theories *had a profound effect on public education.* Each of the other choices draws a conclusion beyond the scope of the passage.

47. (E) 63% of senior boys are involved in sports. Only 62% of sophomore boys are involved in sports.

48. (B) The second sentence adds more information about the "methods" of psychology.

49. (D) The author sketches parallel changes in television and clothes, implying that the medium (TV) is responsible for changing taste in clothes.

50. (A) The definition of a political party belongs in a text which explains such organizations and systems—namely, an introductory text on political science.

SECTION II: MATHEMATICS

1. **(B)** "What number is 15% of 80" can be changed into an equation:

$$N = .15 \times 80$$
$$N = 12$$

2. Since a tangent to a circle is always perpendicular with the radius that meets at the tangent, the perpendicular drawn to line ℓ_1 at point p will pass through the center of circle O.

3. **(A)**
$$(7 + 8) \div 2/3 =$$
$$15 \div 2/3 =$$
$$15 \times 3/2 = 45/2 = 22\frac{1}{2}$$

4. **(B)** Since a straight line equals 180°, $5x + x = 180°$, $6x = 180°$. Thus, angle $x = 30°$.

5. **(B)** Only choice **(B)**, 31/60, is greater than ½. All the other choices are less than ½.

6. **(D)** Set up the ratio:

$$\frac{7}{\$1.68} = \frac{9}{x}$$
$$7x = \$15.12$$
$$x = \$2.16$$

Or simply divide 7 into $1.68 and multiply the result by 9.

7. **(D)** There are 3 chances out of 4 of spinning either red, yellow, or blue. Thus, the correct answer is ¾.

8. **(D)** 4 rods = $(4)(16\frac{1}{2}$ feet$)$ = 66 feet
66 feet $\times$ 12 = 792 inches

9. **(B)** $\sqrt{94}$ is closer to $\sqrt{100}$ than $\sqrt{81}$. Therefore, it most nearly approximates 10.

10. **(C)** Figure ABCD is a parallelogram. The formula for the area of a parallelogram is area = base times height. Since the base is 6 and the

height (a perpendicular drawn to the base) is 3, the area would be computed by 6 × 3, or answer (C).

11. **(B)** Ratios may be expressed as fractions. Thus (A) 1 to 4 may be expressed as 1/4. Notice that (C), (D), and (E) are all fractions that reduce to 1/4.

$$2/8 = 1/4$$
$$3/12 = 1/4$$
$$4/16 = 1/4$$

Only **(B)** 3/8 does not equal 1/4.

12. **(B)** The number sentence is an addition problem (825.50 + 435.00). The only choice which expresses a problem in addition is **(B)**.

13. **(A)** ∠BCD = ∠A + ∠B (exterior angle of a triangle equals the sum of the opposite two angles). Then 84° = ∠A + 63°, and ∠A = 21°.

14. **(E)** Mary worked a total of 24 hours, but we do not know in how many days. Therefore we cannot derive the number of hours she worked each day. Each of the other choices can be derived from the statement.

15. **(C)**

$$3c = d$$

$$\frac{3c}{3} = \frac{d}{3}$$

$$c = \frac{d}{3}$$

16. **(B)**

$$\frac{245}{35} = 7 \text{ cm}$$

17. **(E)** The tenth place is the number immediately to the right of the decimal point. To round off to the nearest tenth, check the hundredth place (two places to the right of the decimal point). If the hundredth number is a 5 or higher, round the tenth up to the next number. For instance, .36 would round to .4. If the hundredth is a 4 or lower, simply drop any places after the tenth place. For instance, .74356 would round to .7. Thus, 4,316.136 rounded to the nearest tenth is 4,316.1—which is answer choice (E).

18. **(B)** A prime number is a number which can be divided evenly only by itself and the number 1. Choices (A), (C), (D), and (E) can all be divided evenly by 3. Answer choice (B)—17—can be divided only by itself and 1.

19. **(E)** The fraction ⅛ equals .125.

$$8\overline{)1.000}^{\,.125}$$

Thus, it would lie between ⅑ (.111) and ²⁄₁₅ (.133).

20. **(E)** The only statement which *must* be true is (E). The class averages 2 pencils per student. Notice that 30 students could each have 2 pencils; so (C) and (D) may be false. Likewise, just one of the students could have all 60 pencils; therefore (A) and (B) may be false. Only (E) *must* be true.

21. **(C)** In each pint, if 1 part out of the 4 parts are vinegar, then ¼ of the pint is vinegar. Thus, ¼ × 16 tells the number of ounces of vinegar in each pint. Then multiply that by the number of pints (3). Thus, the correct answer is (¼ × 16)3.

22. **(B)** Four pounds of steak at $3.89 per pound cost $15.56. Change from a twenty-dollar bill would therefore be $20.00 − $15.56, or $4.44.

23. **(C)** In the series 8, 9, 12, 17, 24, . . . , note the changes, or differences, between numbers:

$$9 - 8 = 1$$
$$12 - 9 = 3$$
$$17 - 12 = 5$$
$$24 - 17 = 7$$

Hence, the difference between the next term and 24 must be 9, or x − 24 = 9, and x = 33. Therefore, the next term in the series must be 33.

24. **(D)** Price today = $100

In 1 year = $100 + 10% of $100 = $110

In 2 years = $110 + 10% of $110 = $121

In 3 years = $121 + 10% of $121 = $133.10

25. **(C)** Enlarging each dimension by 20%, or $\frac{1}{5}$, the new dimensions would be 2.4″ and 3.6″. Therefore, the new area would be 2.4×3.6, or 8.64 square inches.

26. **(B)** In order to have the pie graph represent blue-eyed students as 6 out of 24, the piece of the "pie" representing blue-eyed students should be 6/24 or 1/4. So the blue piece needs to be increased. Likewise, for hazel to represent 5/24, its piece of the pie should be slightly less than 6/24, so its size should be decreased.

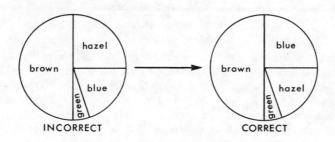

27. **(B)** Since D is between A and B on $\overleftrightarrow{AB}$, we know that the sum of the lengths of the smaller segments $\overline{AD}$ and $\overline{DB}$ is equal to the length of the larger segment $\overline{AB}$.

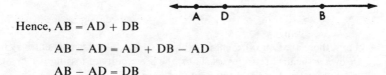

   Hence, $AB = AD + DB$

   $$AB - AD = AD + DB - AD$$

   $$AB - AD = DB$$

28. **(C)** In 1970, 10% of $12,000, or $1,200, was spent on medical. In 1975, 12% of $16,000, or $1,920, was spent on medical. Thus, there was an increase of $720.

29. **(A)** There was an increase from 18% to 22%, or 4%.

30. **(C)** If the area of the square is 36 square inches, then the side of the square must be 6 inches. Thus, the length of the rectangle must be 12 inches (since it is twice as long as the side of the square). The width of the rectangle is 4 inches (since it is two-thirds the side of the square). So the perimeter of the rectangle equals $12 + 12 + 4 + 4$, or 32 inches.

31. **(B)** Since m yards = 36m inches, and n feet = 12n inches, m yards and n feet = (36m + 12n) inches.

32. **(C)** 240 out of 800 can be expressed 240/80, which reduces to 3/10 or 30%.

33. **(B)** The probability of throwing a head in one throw is

$$\frac{\text{chance of a head}}{\text{total chances (1 head + 1 tail)}} = \frac{1}{2}$$

Since you are trying to throw a head *twice,* multiply the probability for the first toss ($\frac{1}{2}$) times the probability for the second toss (again $\frac{1}{2}$). Thus, $\frac{1}{2} \times \frac{1}{2} = \frac{1}{4}$, and $\frac{1}{4}$ is the probability of throwing heads twice in two tosses. Another way of approaching this problem is to look at the total number of possible outcomes:

	First Toss	*Second Toss*
1.	H	H
2.	H	T
3.	T	H
4.	T	T

Thus, there are four different possible outcomes. There is only one way to throw two heads in two tosses. Thus, the probability of tossing two heads in two tosses is 1 out of 4 total outcomes, or $\frac{1}{4}$.

34. **(C)** Changing 740,000 to .0074 requires moving the decimal 8 places to the left. This is the same as multiplying by 1/100,000,000.

35. **(B)** The amount of discount was $120 − $90 = $30. The rate of discount equals

$$\frac{\text{change}}{\text{starting point}} = \frac{30}{120} = \frac{1}{4} = 25\%$$

36. (C) The final number is always the same as the number selected. For instance, try 10:

$$10 \times 2 = 20$$
$$20 + 14 = 34$$
$$34 \div 2 = 17$$
$$17 - 7 = 10$$

37. (C) To change 3 miles to feet, simply multiply 3 times 5,280 (since 5,280 is the number of feet in a mile). This will give the number of feet in 3 miles. Then multiply this product by 12, since there are 12 inches in each foot. The resulting product will be the number of inches in 3 miles.

38. (D) If the first integer is x, then the next consecutive even integer must be x + 2. The third consecutive even integer must then be x + 4. Since their sum is 318,

$$(x) + (x + 2) + (x + 4) = 318$$
$$3x + 6 = 318$$
$$3x = 312$$
$$x = 104$$

The largest integer of the three is thus x + 4, or 108.

39. (A) First calculate the number of boys in the classroom. Since 40% are girls, then 60% must be boys, or .6Q (60% of the total number of students). Now, of those boys, two-thirds do not have red hair; therefore, the best expression of boys without red hair would be (.6Q)⅔, or answer (A).

40. (E) To compute percentage simply plug into the formula:

$$\frac{\text{is}}{\text{of}} = \text{percentage}$$

Note that the question reads: The *air pressure in the basketball IS* what percentage *OF the air pressure in the football?* Thus,

$$\frac{\text{air pressure in basketball}}{\text{air pressure in football}} = \frac{24}{16} = 1.50 = 150\%$$

41. **(A)** There are several approaches to this problem. One solution is to first find the area of the square: $10 \times 10 = 100$. Then subtract the approximate area of the circle: $A = \pi(r^2) \approx 3(5^2) = 3(25) = 75$. Therefore, the total area inside the square but outside the circle is approximately 25. One quarter of that area is shaded. Therefore, 25/4 is approximately the shaded area. The closest answer is (A)—10.

A more efficient method is to first find the area of the square: $10 \times 10 = 100$. The divide the square into 4 equal sections as follows:

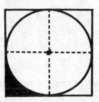

Since a quarter of the square is 25, the only possible answer choice for the shaded area is (A)—10.

42. **(A)** If today Lucy is 14, then last year she was 13. Likewise, if Charlie's age now is C, then last year he was $C - 1$. Now put these into an equation

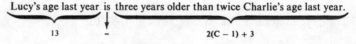

Lucy's age last year is three years older than twice Charlie's age last year.

$$13 \qquad = \qquad 2(C - 1) + 3$$

Transposing, $13 - 3 = 2(C - 1)$.

43. **(C)** In this type of problem (weighted average), you must multiply the number of students times their respective scores and divide this total by the number of students as follows:

$$
\begin{array}{r}
15 \times 80 = 1,200 \\
10 \times 90 = 900 \\
\hline
\text{total } 25 \qquad 2,100
\end{array}
$$

Now divide 25 into 2,100. This gives an average of 84%; therefore, the correct answer is (C).

44. **(B)** The difference in the amounts invested would be $12\% - 8\%$ or 4% of the principal ($1200) over three years.

$$
\begin{aligned}
I &= Prt \\
I &= (\$1200)(.04)(3) \\
I &= \$144
\end{aligned}
$$

45. (A) The number of nickels that Angela has is x. Thus, the total value of those nickels (in cents) is 5x. Angela also has twice as many dimes as nickels, or 2x. The total value in cents of those dimes is 2x(10), or 20x. Adding together the value of the nickels and dimes gives 5x + 20x, or 25x.

46. (B) For Tom to finish with 19 points in the five events, he must have finished with 3 first places, 1 second place, and 1 third place. Thus, Tim would have finished with 3 second places (worth 9 points), 1 third place (worth 1 point), and 1 fourth place (worth no points). Tim would then finish with 10 points.

47. (D) Only statements III and IV *must* be true. If the house has 4 floors and it takes exactly 4 months to build the house, the workers average 1 floor per month. And since the house has 16 rooms on 4 floors, the house averages 4 rooms per floor (16/4 = 4). However, I and II may not necessarily be true. To build 16 rooms in 4 months' time, the workers may not necessarily work at a steady pace, building 4 each month. They may, for example, build 5 rooms one month and 3 the next. Although they *average* 4 rooms per month, they don't have to build exactly 4 rooms each month. Likewise in II—just because a house *averages* 4 rooms on each floor does not mean the house necessarily has exactly 4 rooms on each floor. For example, the house could be built to have 6 rooms on the first floor, 3 rooms on the second and third floors, and 4 rooms on the top floor, which gives a total of 16 rooms.

48. (E) There is no way of knowing what numbers the digits x and y represent. Thus, none of the statements must be true.

49. (C) The number xy could represent 90. In that case, yx would represent 09. Thus, their difference would be 81. This is the largest difference possible between xy and yx.

50. (A) The distance traveled from A to B is actually the circumference of the circle. The formula for the circumference of a circle is circumference = 2 (π)radius. Thus, $2 \times 22/7 \times 5$, which is the same as $2 \times 5 \times 22/7$, or $10 \times 22/7$.

PRACTICE TEST 3

Section I: Reading Comprehension—65 Minutes; 50 Questions
Section II: Mathematics—70 Minutes; 50 Questions
Section III: Essay Writing—60 Minutes; 2 Essays

ANSWER SHEET FOR PRACTICE TEST 3
(Remove This Sheet and Use It to Mark Your Answers)

SECTION I: READING COMPREHENSION

1 Ⓐ Ⓑ Ⓒ Ⓓ Ⓔ		26 Ⓐ Ⓑ Ⓒ Ⓓ Ⓔ
2 Ⓐ Ⓑ Ⓒ Ⓓ Ⓔ		27 Ⓐ Ⓑ Ⓒ Ⓓ Ⓔ
3 Ⓐ Ⓑ Ⓒ Ⓓ Ⓔ		28 Ⓐ Ⓑ Ⓒ Ⓓ Ⓔ
4 Ⓐ Ⓑ Ⓒ Ⓓ Ⓔ		29 Ⓐ Ⓑ Ⓒ Ⓓ Ⓔ
5 Ⓐ Ⓑ Ⓒ Ⓓ Ⓔ		30 Ⓐ Ⓑ Ⓒ Ⓓ Ⓔ
6 Ⓐ Ⓑ Ⓒ Ⓓ Ⓔ		31 Ⓐ Ⓑ Ⓒ Ⓓ Ⓔ
7 Ⓐ Ⓑ Ⓒ Ⓓ Ⓔ		32 Ⓐ Ⓑ Ⓒ Ⓓ Ⓔ
8 Ⓐ Ⓑ Ⓒ Ⓓ Ⓔ		33 Ⓐ Ⓑ Ⓒ Ⓓ Ⓔ
9 Ⓐ Ⓑ Ⓒ Ⓓ Ⓔ		34 Ⓐ Ⓑ Ⓒ Ⓓ Ⓔ
10 Ⓐ Ⓑ Ⓒ Ⓓ Ⓔ		35 Ⓐ Ⓑ Ⓒ Ⓓ Ⓔ
11 Ⓐ Ⓑ Ⓒ Ⓓ Ⓔ		36 Ⓐ Ⓑ Ⓒ Ⓓ Ⓔ
12 Ⓐ Ⓑ Ⓒ Ⓓ Ⓔ		37 Ⓐ Ⓑ Ⓒ Ⓓ Ⓔ
13 Ⓐ Ⓑ Ⓒ Ⓓ Ⓔ		38 Ⓐ Ⓑ Ⓒ Ⓓ Ⓔ
14 Ⓐ Ⓑ Ⓒ Ⓓ Ⓔ		39 Ⓐ Ⓑ Ⓒ Ⓓ Ⓔ
15 Ⓐ Ⓑ Ⓒ Ⓓ Ⓔ		40 Ⓐ Ⓑ Ⓒ Ⓓ Ⓔ
16 Ⓐ Ⓑ Ⓒ Ⓓ Ⓔ		41 Ⓐ Ⓑ Ⓒ Ⓓ Ⓔ
17 Ⓐ Ⓑ Ⓒ Ⓓ Ⓔ		42 Ⓐ Ⓑ Ⓒ Ⓓ Ⓔ
18 Ⓐ Ⓑ Ⓒ Ⓓ Ⓔ		43 Ⓐ Ⓑ Ⓒ Ⓓ Ⓔ
19 Ⓐ Ⓑ Ⓒ Ⓓ Ⓔ		44 Ⓐ Ⓑ Ⓒ Ⓓ Ⓔ
20 Ⓐ Ⓑ Ⓒ Ⓓ Ⓔ		45 Ⓐ Ⓑ Ⓒ Ⓓ Ⓔ
21 Ⓐ Ⓑ Ⓒ Ⓓ Ⓔ		46 Ⓐ Ⓑ Ⓒ Ⓓ Ⓔ
22 Ⓐ Ⓑ Ⓒ Ⓓ Ⓔ		47 Ⓐ Ⓑ Ⓒ Ⓓ Ⓔ
23 Ⓐ Ⓑ Ⓒ Ⓓ Ⓔ		48 Ⓐ Ⓑ Ⓒ Ⓓ Ⓔ
24 Ⓐ Ⓑ Ⓒ Ⓓ Ⓔ		49 Ⓐ Ⓑ Ⓒ Ⓓ Ⓔ
25 Ⓐ Ⓑ Ⓒ Ⓓ Ⓔ		50 Ⓐ Ⓑ Ⓒ Ⓓ Ⓔ

SECTION II: MATHEMATICS

1 Ⓐ Ⓑ Ⓒ Ⓓ Ⓔ	26 Ⓐ Ⓑ Ⓒ Ⓓ Ⓔ
2 Ⓐ Ⓑ Ⓒ Ⓓ Ⓔ	27 Ⓐ Ⓑ Ⓒ Ⓓ Ⓔ
3 Ⓐ Ⓑ Ⓒ Ⓓ Ⓔ	28 Ⓐ Ⓑ Ⓒ Ⓓ Ⓔ
4 Ⓐ Ⓑ Ⓒ Ⓓ Ⓔ	29 Ⓐ Ⓑ Ⓒ Ⓓ Ⓔ
5 Ⓐ Ⓑ Ⓒ Ⓓ Ⓔ	30 Ⓐ Ⓑ Ⓒ Ⓓ Ⓔ
6 Ⓐ Ⓑ Ⓒ Ⓓ Ⓔ	31 Ⓐ Ⓑ Ⓒ Ⓓ Ⓔ
7 Ⓐ Ⓑ Ⓒ Ⓓ Ⓔ	32 Ⓐ Ⓑ Ⓒ Ⓓ Ⓔ
8 Ⓐ Ⓑ Ⓒ Ⓓ Ⓔ	33 Ⓐ Ⓑ Ⓒ Ⓓ Ⓔ
9 Ⓐ Ⓑ Ⓒ Ⓓ Ⓔ	34 Ⓐ Ⓑ Ⓒ Ⓓ Ⓔ
10 Ⓐ Ⓑ Ⓒ Ⓓ Ⓔ	35 Ⓐ Ⓑ Ⓒ Ⓓ Ⓔ
11 Ⓐ Ⓑ Ⓒ Ⓓ Ⓔ	36 Ⓐ Ⓑ Ⓒ Ⓓ Ⓔ
12 Ⓐ Ⓑ Ⓒ Ⓓ Ⓔ	37 Ⓐ Ⓑ Ⓒ Ⓓ Ⓔ
13 Ⓐ Ⓑ Ⓒ Ⓓ Ⓔ	38 Ⓐ Ⓑ Ⓒ Ⓓ Ⓔ
14 Ⓐ Ⓑ Ⓒ Ⓓ Ⓔ	39 Ⓐ Ⓑ Ⓒ Ⓓ Ⓔ
15 Ⓐ Ⓑ Ⓒ Ⓓ Ⓔ	40 Ⓐ Ⓑ Ⓒ Ⓓ Ⓔ
16 Ⓐ Ⓑ Ⓒ Ⓓ Ⓔ	41 Ⓐ Ⓑ Ⓒ Ⓓ Ⓔ
17 Ⓐ Ⓑ Ⓒ Ⓓ Ⓔ	42 Ⓐ Ⓑ Ⓒ Ⓓ Ⓔ
18 Ⓐ Ⓑ Ⓒ Ⓓ Ⓔ	43 Ⓐ Ⓑ Ⓒ Ⓓ Ⓔ
19 Ⓐ Ⓑ Ⓒ Ⓓ Ⓔ	44 Ⓐ Ⓑ Ⓒ Ⓓ Ⓔ
20 Ⓐ Ⓑ Ⓒ Ⓓ Ⓔ	45 Ⓐ Ⓑ Ⓒ Ⓓ Ⓔ
21 Ⓐ Ⓑ Ⓒ Ⓓ Ⓔ	46 Ⓐ Ⓑ Ⓒ Ⓓ Ⓔ
22 Ⓐ Ⓑ Ⓒ Ⓓ Ⓔ	47 Ⓐ Ⓑ Ⓒ Ⓓ Ⓔ
23 Ⓐ Ⓑ Ⓒ Ⓓ Ⓔ	48 Ⓐ Ⓑ Ⓒ Ⓓ Ⓔ
24 Ⓐ Ⓑ Ⓒ Ⓓ Ⓔ	49 Ⓐ Ⓑ Ⓒ Ⓓ Ⓔ
25 Ⓐ Ⓑ Ⓒ Ⓓ Ⓔ	50 Ⓐ Ⓑ Ⓒ Ⓓ Ⓔ

SECTION I: READING COMPREHENSION

Time: 65 Minutes
50 Questions

DIRECTIONS

A question or number of questions follow each of the statements or passages in this section. Using only the *stated* or *implied* information given in the statement or passage, answer the question or questions by choosing the *best* answer from among the five choices given.

Recent studies show that aptitude test scores are declining because of lack of family stability and students' preoccupation with out-of-school activities. Therefore, not only the student's attitude but also his or her home environment must be changed to stop this downward trend.

1. Which of the following is one assumption of the above argument?
   (A) Recent studies have refuted previous studies.
   (B) Heredity is more important than environment.
   (C) Aptitude test scores should stop declining soon.
   (D) The accuracy of the recent studies cited is not an issue.
   (E) More out-of-school activities are available than ever before.

Once again, our City Council has shown all the firmness of a bowl of oatmeal in deciding to seek a "compromise" on sheep grazing in the city. As it is wont to do more often than not, the council overturned a Planning Commission recommendation, this time to ban sheep grazing in the city.

2. The passage above uses the term *bowl of oatmeal* in order to
   (A) condemn the actions taken by the City Council
   (B) add levity to the otherwise tragic situation
   (C) imply that grazing sheep would prefer oats
   (D) praise the City Council for its recent vote
   (E) urge the City Council to overturn the Planning Commission

Question 3, 4, and 5 refer to the following passage.

Recent studies indicate that at the present rate of increase, within two years a single-family dwelling will be unaffordable by the average family. Therefore, apartment living will increase noticeably in the near future.

249

3. Which of the following statements is deducible from the argument?
   (A) The recent studies were for a five-year period.
   (B) Condominiums are expensive but plentiful.
   (C) The average family income will decrease in the next two years.
   (D) Home costs are increasing more rapidly than average family incomes.
   (E) The average family will increase within the next two years.

4. The argument would be weakened by the fact(s) that

   I. many inexpensive single-family dwellings are presently being built
   II. bank loan interest rates have increased
   III. apartment living is also becoming very expensive

   (A) I   (D) I and III
   (B) II   (E) II and III
   (C) III

5. The argument presented assumes that

   I. the present rate of price increase will continue
   II. families will turn to renting apartments instead of buying homes
   III. construction of apartments will double within the next two years

   (A) I   (D) I and II
   (B) II   (E) II and III
   (C) III

Questions 6 through 9 refer to the following passage.

From the U.S. Supreme Court now comes an extraordinary decision permitting inquiries into the "state of mind" of journalists and the editorial process of news organizations. This is perhaps the most alarming evidence so far of a determination by the nation's highest court to weaken the protection of the First Amendment for those who gather and report the news.

The court last year upheld the right of police to invade newspaper offices in search of evidence, and reporters in other cases have gone to jail to protect the confidentiality of their notebooks. Under the recent 6–3 ruling in a libel case, they now face a challenge to the privacy of their minds.

Few would argue that the First Amendment guarantees absolute freedom of speech or freedom of the press. Slander and libel laws stand to the contrary as a protection of an individual's reputation against the irresponsible dissemination of falsehoods. The effect of this latest decision, however, is to make the libel suit, or the threat of one, a clear invasion by the courts into the private decision-making that constitutes news and editorial judgement.

In landmark decisions of 1964 and 1967, the Supreme Court established that public officials or public figures bringing libel actions must prove that a damaging falsehood was published with "actual malice"— that is, with knowledge that the statements were false, or with reckless disregard of whether they were true or not.

Justice Byron R. White, writing for the new majority in the new ruling, says it is not enough to examine all the circumstances of publication that would indicate whether there was malicious intent or not. It is proper and constitutional, he says, for "state-of-mind evidence" to be introduced. The court is thus ordering a CBS television producer to answer questions about the thought processes that went into the preparation and airing of a segment of "60 Minutes."

That six justices of the Supreme Court fail to see this as a breach of the First Amendment is frightening. The novelist George Orwell may have been mistaken only in the timing of his vision of a Big Brother government practicing mind-control.

6. This article deals principally with
   (A) the U.S. Supreme Court's decisions
   (B) explaining the First Amendment to the Constitution
   (C) an attack on the freedom of the press
   (D) slander and libel laws
   (E) Big Brother in government

7. How many justices would have to change their minds to reverse this decision?
   (A) one   (D) four
   (B) two   (E) five
   (C) three

8. This writer feels the Supreme Court is wrong in this case because
   (A) newspapers were unsophisticated when the First Amendment was written
   (B) reporters are entitled to special rights
   (C) it challenges the privacy of a journalist's mind
   (D) Judge White has himself been accused of slander and libel
   (E) the Supreme Court is capable of malicious intent

9. What does *actual malice* (fourth paragraph) mean?
   (A) knowledge that the statements were false
   (B) reckless disregard of whether the statements were true or not
   (C) either (A) or (B)
   (D) libel
   (E) none of these

Questions 10 and 11 refer to the following passage.

Sometimes the U.S. government goes out of its way to prove it can be an absolute nuisance. Take the case of Southern Clay, Inc., which has a factory at Paris, Tennessee, putting out a clay product for cat-boxes best known as "Kitty Litter."

It's a simple enough process, but the federal Mine Safety and Health Administration insists that since clay comes from the ground—an excavation half a mile from the Kitty Litter plant—the company actually is engaged in mining and milling. Therefore, says MSHA, Southern Clay is subject to all the rules that govern, say, coal mines working in shafts several hundred feet down.

The company has been told to devise an escape system and fire-fighting procedure in case there is a fire in its "mine." Southern Clay estimates it will lose 6,000 man-hours in production time giving its 250 factory workers special training in how to escape from a mine disaster.

One thing that has always impressed us about cats, in addition to their tidiness, is that they seem to watch the human world with a sense of wise and detached superiority, as though they wondered what the hustle and bustle is all about. If they grin from time to time, as some people insist, it's no wonder.

10. The author's purpose in writing this article is to
    (A) explain how Kitty Litter is produced
    (B) describe the Mine Safety and Health Administration
    (C) show how tidy cats are
    (D) show that the government can sometimes be a nuisance
    (E) describe how to prevent fires in mines

11. What does the author mean by the article's last sentence?
    (A) Cats sometimes laugh at their own tidiness.
    (B) Cats sometimes seem to be amused by human antics.
    (C) People sometimes appear to be laughing at the antics of cats.
    (D) Some people think cats are laughing at the Kitty Litter plant.
    (E) Some people think cats are laughing at the futility of fire-fighting procedures.

The Jesuit Antonio Vieira, missionary, diplomat, voluminous writer, repeated the triumphs he had gained in Bahia and Lisbon in Rome, which proclaimed him the prince of Catholic orators. His two hundred sermons are a mine of learning and experience, and they stand out from all others by their imaginative power, originality of view, variety of treatment, and audacity of expression.

12. The author's attitude toward Vieira may be described as
   (A) spiritual   (D) admiring
   (B) idolatrous   (E) critical
   (C) indifferent

The 55-mile-per-hour speed limit has not only lowered the number of accidents, it has also saved many lives. Yet, auto insurance rates have not reflected this decrease. Therefore, insurance companies are making profits rather than lowering premiums.

13. This argument implies that
   (A) the 55-mile-per-hour limit is unfair
   (B) auto manufacturers agree with insurance companies' policies
   (C) insurance companies are taking advantage of drivers
   (D) saving lives is of more importance than lowering premiums
   (E) driving skills have improved greatly since the 55-mile-per-hour limit has been in effect

Questions 14 and 15 refer to the following passage.

It may be true that there are two sides to every question, but it is also true that there are two sides to a sheet of flypaper and it makes a big difference to the fly which side he chooses.

14. This statement suggests that
   (A) every question has only one answer
   (B) the choice of questions is very important
   (C) flypaper is not useful
   (D) every question may be interpreted in more than one way
   (E) every question is answered

15. Which of the following is true?
   I. The statement uses an analogy to make a point.
   II. The statement emphasizes the importance of choice.
   III. The statement points out the ways of getting stuck on a question.

   (A) I   (B) II   (C) III   (D) I and III   (E) I and II

Questions 16 and 17 refer to the following chart.

SUPER SALE ON MATTRESSES

	Original Price	Sale Price	Bonus Discount	Your Final Cost With Bonus
Regal:				
Twin, each piece	299.95	149.00	15.00	134.00
Full, each piece	399.95	199.00	20.00	179.00
Queen, 2-piece set	949.95	499.00	50.00	449.00
King, 3-piece set	1199.95	699.00	70.00	629.00
Extra Firm:				
Twin, each piece	329.95	179.95	18.00	161.95
Full, each piece	429.95	249.95	25.00	224.95
Queen, 2-piece set	999.95	549.95	55.00	494.95
King, 3-piece set	1249.95	749.95	75.00	674.95
Royal Satin:				
Twin, each piece	329.95	219.95	22.00	197.95
Full, each piece	399.95	279.95	28.00	251.95
Queen, 2-piece set	1019.95	699.00	70.00	629.00
King, 3-piece set	1339.95	899.95	90.00	809.95

16. As shown on the chart, the largest bonus discount for Extra Firm mattresses is
   (A) 55.00
   (B) 75.00
   (C) 90.00
   (D) 674.95
   (E) 809.95

17. According to the chart, for which two items was the sale price the same?
   (A) Regal, Full, and Royal Satin, Full
   (B) Extra Firm, Twin, and Royal Satin, Twin
   (C) Regal, King, and Royal Satin, Queen
   (D) Extra Firm, King, and Regal, King
   (E) Extra Firm, Queen, and Regal, Queen

Questions 18 through 22 refer to the following passage.

Some parents, teachers, and educators have tried to spoil the centennial celebration of one of America's greatest novels, *The Adventures of Huckleberry Finn,* by claiming that it and author Mark Twain were racist.

Most readers over the years have viewed this masterpiece as anything but offensive to blacks. Beneath the surface of a darn good yarn, it is one of several major writings by Twain that condemn the brutality of slavery. For some who suddenly find the novel offensive, the misunderstanding may lie in Twain's unmatched use of irony and the crude vernacular of river folk to tell the story of the friendship between a runaway Negro slave and young Huck—through the eyes of the uneducated boy.

Any doubts about Mr. Twain's views on slavery should have been dispelled by an even later work published in 1894, *Pudd'nhead Wilson.* The famous murder trial story also shows how slavery damages the human personality. But silly detractors apparently need more than the unspoiled and color-blind innocence of Huck or the eccentric but clever lawyer Wilson. For them, we have a letter from Mr. Twain himself, or rather Samuel L. Clemens, the writer's real name.

Written the same year as *The Adventures of Huckleberry Finn,* the letter details Twain's offer to pay the expenses of one of the first black students at Yale Law School. The student Twain befriended and financially assisted, Warner T. McGuinn, was the commencement orator at his graduation and went on to a distinguished legal and political career in Baltimore.

"I do not believe I would very cheerfully help a white student who would ask a benevolence of a stranger, but I do not feel so about the other color. We have ground the manhood out of them and the shame is ours, not theirs; and we should pay for it," Mr. Clemens wrote Francis Wayland, the law school dean.

In addition to being a critic of slavery, Mark Twain was fascinated with the subject of transmogrification. On this 150th anniversary of his birth, Twain might find ironic delight in the timing of the publication of a letter vindicating his commitment to racial progress.

18. The passage above was written
   (A) to promote the sale of *The Adventures of Huckleberry Finn*
   (B) one hundred and fifty years after Mark Twain's birth
   (C) to exonerate those who claim Twain's writing was racist
   (D) to explain the misunderstandings in Twain's philosophy
   (E) as a condemnation of the principle of transmogrification

19. Mark Twain offered to pay the expenses of a Yale Law School student because the student
   (A) was commencement orator at his graduation
   (B) would go on to a distinguished law career
   (C) was rightfully owed the assistance of whites
   (D) was very needy and couldn't afford the tuition
   (E) was also a severe critic of slavery

20. The *irony* referred to in the second paragraph appears to have
    (A) confused some readers about Twain's intentions
    (B) made the language of the river folk difficult to understand
    (C) convinced most readers that Twain's work was actually racist
    (D) provided detractors with valid reason to condemn *Pudd'nhead Wilson*
    (E) appeased Twain's critics about the author's feelings regarding slavery

21. The term *centennial celebration* in the first sentence is used to indicate
    (A) a party held in Mark Twain's honor
    (B) an anniversary of Twain's *Pudd'nhead Wilson*
    (C) the 100th anniversary of Mark Twain's birth
    (D) the 100th publication of the *Adventures of Huckleberry Finn*
    (E) the 100th anniversary of the publication of *The Adventures of Huckleberry Finn*

22. According to the passage, Pudd'nhead Wilson was
    (A) the student Twain befriended and financially assisted
    (B) a runaway slave in one of Twain's works
    (C) the dean of the Yale Law School
    (D) the runaway slave in *The Adventures of Huckleberry Finn*
    (E) a clever but somewhat bizarre fictional character

The fruits of modern technology have reduced the need for manpower, causing widespread unemployment. Therefore, modern technology is more of a curse than a blessing.

23. The argument above is based on which of the following assumptions?

    I. Modern technology does not create new jobs.
    II. Modern technology is a necessary evil.
    III. Widespread unemployment is bad.

    (A) I   (D) II
    (B) I and III   (E) III
    (C) I and II

Questions 24 through 28 refer to the following passage.

A painter with seven fingers sits at his easel, the Eiffel tower shining out the window, a Jewish village hovering in a cloud above his head.

This is how Marc Chagall painted himself in Paris in 1912. Three quarters of a century later the painting lives. But Chagall is dead, at 97.

Don't hang crepe, but strew flowers in his memory. A Jew from a Russian *shtetl* who revolutionized modern art by imposing his naive vision of beauty on a world that was consumed in the flames of the Holocaust, Chagall rescued images of a world that has largely vanished. There is life, not death, in his palate of bright colors; love, not bitterness in the paintings of cartwheeling lovers and rooftop fiddlers. And the enduring themes of Judaism glow in Chagall's stained glass windows in the Hadassah clinic in Jerusalem.

Chagall captures realism through the language of dream. A bearded peddler floats above the village of Vitebsk. A green violinist wearing a long purple coat plays an orange fiddle. Lovers astride a white horse embrace, while the horse holds a bouquet of flowers and a violin under its head. What do these paintings mean? That is like asking a bearded Hasid to explain the mysteries of the Kabala or asking history to explain why millions of simple Jews who dreamed of births and weddings and bar mitzvahs awoke to a nightmare of death in the concentration camps. Chagall left the interpretation to the art historians and critics. He painted the images that came to him, springing from his paintbrush to the canvas. But a closer look reveals a technical mastery and control of symbols that belies the primitive.

Chagall left his native Russian village of Vitebsk for Paris, then returned to Russia after the Bolshevik revolution. He joined other artists in trying to paint the new vision, but the Russian revolution was not interested in the revolution of modern art. The Kremlin wanted socialist realism not visionary painting. Chagall left, disillusioned, and returned to France. There he gained fame and wealth, only to be threatened as a Jew by the Nazis, and fled to New York. He returned to France after the war, oettling in Cute d'Azur. Though he remained sequestered, he left his imprint on the Paris Opera, Lincoln Center in New York, and other public buildings.

Chagall painted a Jewish village cemetery in 1917. Hebrew inscriptions mark the peeling plaster gate. Crooked tombstones carved with the Star of David retreat up a green hill. The sky is alive with color.

The Nazis expanded the graveyard to include all of Europe. Now the artist who evoked the village Jews' lives has joined them in death.

Through Chagall's paintings, their dreams survive the Holocaust—alive as the melody of a green violinist.

24. According to the passage, Chagall's paintings were
    (A) not meant to be interpreted
    (B) unfathomable, even by the painter
    (C) primitive in style and technical mastery
    (D) optimistic and uplifting
    (E) disillusioned and embittered

25. All of the following are true about the *village cemetery* mentioned in the passage except
    (A) Chagall is now buried there
    (B) it contains tombstones with Jewish markings
    (C) Hebrew inscriptions are on the entranceway
    (D) the sky above it is colored brightly
    (E) it exists in a painting by Chagall

26. Which of the following is implied by the passage?
    (A) The Russians should never have exiled Chagall to France.
    (B) Chagall's paintings are now more popular and valuable than ever before.
    (C) Chagall's brilliant and enduring paintings will live long after his death.
    (D) Artists, like Chagall, should paint only the uplifting experiences of life.
    (E) Chagall's dreamlike paintings have never received a popular acceptance.

27. According to the passage, Chagall's self-portrait suggests that Chagall
    (A) had only one hand
    (B) was a bearded peddler
    (C) also played the violin
    (D) once lived in France
    (E) could paint only Jewish themes

28. The phrase *don't hang crepe* in the passage is used to
    (A) urge others not to attend Chagall's funeral
    (B) remind mourners that flowers were requested by the family
    (C) emphasize Chagall's focus on life, not death
    (D) commemorate the death of a great painter
    (E) admonish those who caused a great painter to suffer

Questions 29 and 30 refer to the following graph.

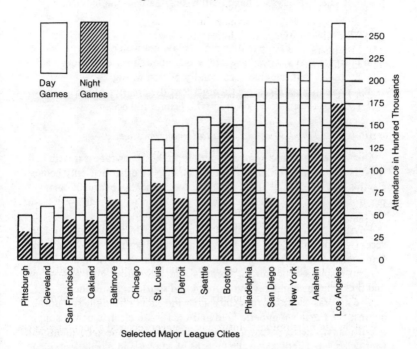

ATTENDANCE: SELECTED MAJOR LEAGUE BALL PARKS

Highest Annual, 1948–1985

Selected Major League Cities

29. According to the graph, which of the following cities had the highest
    night game attendance as compared with its day game attendance?
    (A) Los Angeles   (D) Chicago
    (B) New York   (E) Boston
    (C) Cleveland

30. According to the graph, which of the following pairs of cities had the
    highest combined day game attendance?
    (A) Boston/Los Angeles   (D) Seattle/Philadelphia
    (B) St. Louis/New York   (E) Baltimore/Detroit
    (C) Chicago/San Diego

We all know life originated in the ocean. Science tells us so. Perhaps a bolt of lightning struck through the ammonia and methane gases of a volcanic planet, igniting some form of life in the primordial soup of the storm-tormented sea. But no scientific theory is sacrosanct. And now a group of scientists says we have it all wrong: Life originated in clay.

31. The passage above
    (A) suggests that the earth began as clay, not water
    (B) argues that science has been wrong about a certain theory
    (C) implies that scientists are usually proven wrong
    (D) presents an alternative theory about the creation of life
    (E) denies the existence of life in the primordial ocean

Questions 32, 33, and 34 refer to the following passage.

Our planet Earth has a tail and, although the appendage is invisible, it must be somewhat similar to those of comets and other heavenly bodies. Earth's tail is an egg-shaped zone of electrically charged particles positioned about 400,000 miles from us—always on the side away from the sun.

Physicist Lou Frank, of the University of Iowa, says researchers recently calculated the tail's existence and position by examining Explorer 1 satellite photos of the northern and southern lights. These natural displays—the aurora borealis and the aurora australis—glow and flicker in the night sky of northern and southern hemispheres.

The auroras occur because the solar wind racing from the sun pushes against the Earth's magnetic field and creates an electric power supply in our planet's newly discovered tail. The displays are seen frequently at times of sunspot activity, in the months of March and April, September and October. Their colors are mostly green, sometimes red. They have been observed in the continental United States and in Mexico.

32. According to the passage, which of the following can be inferred about the aurora borealis and aurora australis?
    (A) They are unnatural phenomena caused by solar wind.
    (B) They are caused by sunspot activity in March, April, September, and October.
    (C) They are electrical phenomena caused by solar wind and magnetism.
    (D) They are egg-shaped and occur about 400,000 miles away.
    (E) They were first photographed by Lou Frank of the University of Iowa.

33. All of the following are true about Earth's tail except that
    (A) it is egg shaped
    (B) it contains charged particles
    (C) it remains on the side always away from the sun
    (D) it is invisible
    (E) it occurs during March, April, September, and October

34. It can be inferred from the passage that probably
    (A) aurora borealis and aurora australis occur at the equator
    (B) the Earth's magnetic field will someday transform this planet into a comet
    (C) astronomers will now be observing Earth's tail through high-power telescopes
    (D) the tails of comets are composed of electrically charged particles
    (E) the auroras race from the sun and push against the Earth's magnetic field

What history teaches is this: that people and governments have never learned anything from history.

35. The statement above may be best described as a(n)
    (A) ironic contradiction   (D) derisive condemnation
    (B) historical truism   (E) pragmatic condolence
    (C) effective anagram

Questions 36, 37, and 38 refer to the following passage.

No matter what we think of Warren Beatty or his film *Reds,* we cheer his victory for artistic purity in preventing ABC-TV from editing his movie for television. An arbitrator ruled that Mr. Beatty's contractual right of "final-cut" authority, which forbids editing he doesn't approve, prevented Paramount Pictures from granting that authority to ABC-TV. The network planned to cut six minutes from *Reds,* a 196-minute film, and air the truncated version next week.

Most theatrical films (movies made for theaters) ultimately appear on network television, usually preceded by the brief message "Edited for Television." The popular perception, argues Mr. Beatty, is that this editing removes obscenity. Often it does. Yet, some editing is done purely in the interests of commercial and local programming. Advertisements traditionally hover near hourly and half-hourly intervals. And local affiliate stations zealously protect their 11 p.m. time slot because it is commercially lucrative.

Mr. Beatty's case illustrates why studios contracting with directors for films rarely grant the coveted right of final cut. Televised theatrical movies receive wide exposure and are lucrative; Paramount had a $6.5 million contract with ABC-TV for *Reds*. True artistic control in filmmaking will come only when all directors receive final-cut guarantees, a right the Directors Guild of America hopes to obtain in future talks with movie producers. Mr. Beatty's victory is a step in the direction of protection for film.

36. Which of the following best supports the argument presented in the passage?
    (A) It would be artistically impermissible to delete 64 bars from a Beethoven symphony or to skip Act II from *Hamlet*.
    (B) Warren Beatty would be well served if he planned his theatrical features with television commercials in mind.
    (C) The Directors Guild of America will have a difficult time acquiring artistic control for film directors.
    (D) *Edited for Television* refers only to the removal of obscenities.
    (E) The best time to run commercials for television stations is at 11 p.m.

37. Which of the following is implied by the passage?
    (A) Artists should not yield to the pressures of a commercial industry.
    (B) The enormous amount of money involved in commercial television should temper an artist's ideals.
    (C) Film editing should be performed with commercial as well as artistic goals in mind.
    (D) Lucrative contracts demand compromise by all film collaborators.
    (E) Film studios should never allow artists to control final-cut rights on feature films.

38. Which of the following is the best title for the passage?
    (A) Warren Beatty and *Reds*
    (B) The Final Cut: Beatty vs. ABC
    (C) Edited for TV: Removing Obscenity
    (D) How Films Get Cut for Television
    (E) Directors Guild of America: A New Battle

Judgment is given to men that they may use it. Because it may be used erroneously, are men to be told that they ought not to use it at all?

39. The central idea of the passage may be summarized as follows:
    (A) Suspended judgment is better than no judgment at all.
    (B) Do not impose your judgment upon another.
    (C) Those who judge wisely are the only judges we need.
    (D) Those who judge are likely to judge wrongly.
    (E) The possibility of judging wrongly should not keep us from judging at all.

Questions 40 and 41 refer to the following passage.

California once prided itself on being the state with the finest roads in the nation. That is no longer true. Our gas taxes of 9 cents a gallon took care of California's highway needs for years, but they no longer are adequate. One reason the present tax no longer covers the bill is that modern cars are using less fuel. The main factor, though, is that the cost of building and maintaining highways has gone way up while the tax has remained fixed since 1963.

Certainly, California streets, roads, and highways need help. Two-thirds of city streets and 77 percent of country roads are substandard. Ruts and potholes can be found almost everywhere, and the longer they go without repair the more they will cost.

40. Which of the following best summarizes the passage?
    (A) Deterioration of California's roads has resulted from increased costs and decreased funds.
    (B) The quality of California roads is now second in the nation.
    (C) Fuel-efficient cars cause more wear and tear on the roads than did cars of the past.
    (D) Every road in the state is marred with potholes.
    (E) Over three-quarters of California's roads are substandard.

41. Which of the following is not a problem stated by the passage?
    (A) inadequate tax revenue
    (B) ruts and potholes
    (C) increased cost of building highways
    (D) a fixed gas-tax rate
    (E) demand for new highways

Adam Smith, the founder of political economy, treated economic existence as the true human life, money-making as the meaning of history, and was wont to describe statesmen as dangerous animals; yet this very England became what it became—the foremost country, economically speaking, in the world.

42. The meaning of *wont* in this passage is
    (A) desired   (D) unlikely
    (B) did not   (E) unable
    (C) accustomed

Questions 43 and 44 refer to the following passage.

The $5 million in state funds earmarked for advertising California's attractiveness as a tourist destination is an investment well worth making. Perhaps because California has long taken it for granted that everyone wanted to come here, and maybe because for many years Hollywood was California's most powerful publicist, the state has never spent a dime promoting itself to potential visitors. And that may be at least partly responsible for the decline in tourism here over the past five years, including a 10 percent drop in spending in 1983 alone. Since tourism is a $28 billion industry employing 1.6 million Californians, perhaps this new advertising was too long in coming.

43. Which of the following is an assumption of the passage?
    (A) California will never spend funds to promote tourism.
    (B) A proposed advertising campaign will decrease the competition from other states.
    (C) California tax revenues are only a result of tourism.
    (D) Increased tourism will result in higher state and local tax revenues as well as added state income.
    (E) More Californians are visiting other states than ever before.

44. Which of the following is implied by the passage?
    (A) If the advertising campaign works, the $5 million price tag will be a bargain.
    (B) Advertising campaigns should be carefully and slowly monitored.
    (C) Few Californians oppose the proposed advertising campaign.
    (D) Hollywood should not continue to be a drawing card to attract tourists.
    (E) The $28 billion is not enough to employ 1.6 million Californians.

It would be splendid if the states were willing to subscribe to treaties agreeing to submit all their disputes to arbitration. But even though great advances have been made in persuading nations to submit disputes to judicial determination, governments have always made an exception of matters which they deemed of major importance.

45. In the passage above, the terms *states* and *nations* are probably
    (A) without a judiciary
    (B) without decisive government
    (C) analogies
    (D) metaphors
    (E) synonyms

Questions 46 through 50 refer to the following passage.

Before one begins to read an unfamiliar work of literature, it is often helpful to know what kind of work it is—that is, what genre it belongs to. If we know what expectations we should have, we are less likely to misunderstand what the author is trying to accomplish. *The Lord of the Rings* is a work of fiction written in the middle of this century about a world that greatly resembles medieval times in Europe. It is unmistakably a novel, yet the real significance of the events and the characters will be clearer to readers who know something about the literary tradition, or genre, called the epic, and who have read, for example, *The Odyssey* or *Beowulf*. Moreover, there is a special kind of pleasure in the recognition of familiar patterns of events and characterization which are varied and even deliberately reversed. The skillful interplay of the familiar and the surprising is one of the marks of a great storyteller like Tolkien.

No one, of course, knows exactly what the Middle Ages were really like, but readers get an illusion in *The Lord of the Rings* of being in an ancient world which is in some mysterious way part of the history of our own world. Then, after the fashion of the epic tradition, they will expect that the story will follow the movements of a particular person who is of heroic stature (physically and mentally) and who embodies the ideals and values of a particular people. Readers feel sure that the hero will, like the heroes in *The Odyssey* and *Beowulf*, go on a journey and experience a variety of adventures, which he will survive after many hardships and will then return to his own home and people.

46. Which of the following is probably the intended audience for this passage?
    (A) students of the Middle Ages
    (B) those preparing to read the *Odyssey*
    (C) those who have never enjoyed *The Lord of the Rings*
    (D) those preparing to read *The Lord of the Rings*
    (E) those preparing to read *Beowulf*

47. The central point of the passage is best summarized as follows:
    (A) The heroes in Tolkien's story are identical to those in the *Odyssey* or *Beowulf.*
    (B) One should read familiar works of literature before reading an unfamiliar one.
    (C) The history of the ancient world is related to the history of our own world.
    (D) *The Lord of the Rings* is not only a novel.
    (E) Fully appreciating *The Lord of the Rings* involves familiarity with the epic tradition.

48. The author implies which of the following about the conclusion of *The Lord of the Rings?*
    (A) It is a happy one.
    (B) It is a unique one.
    (C) It has been plagiarized.
    (D) It is very much like the opening of the novel.
    (E) It contains explicit references to the *Odyssey* and *Beowulf.*

49. Which of the following is a basic assumption about the readers of this passage?
    (A) They find Tolkien's heroes especially fascinating.
    (B) They know very little about the Middle Ages.
    (C) They will find *The Lord of the Rings* surprising.
    (D) They will be reading *The Lord of the Rings.*
    (E) They like to create illusions.

50. We may infer that readers who expect *The Lord of the Rings* to contain elements of the epic tradition will
    (A) have a background that the author of this passage does not share
    (B) have ignored this passage
    (C) have misread this passage
    (D) have their expectations fulfilled
    (E) have their expectations disappointed

STOP: IF YOU FINISH BEFORE TIME IS CALLED, CHECK YOUR WORK ON THIS SECTION ONLY. DO NOT WORK ON ANY OTHER SECTION IN THE TEST.

SECTION II: MATHEMATICS

Time: 70 Minutes
50 Questions

DIRECTIONS

In the questions or incomplete statements below, select the one *best* answer or completion of the five choices given.

1. If 10 km equal 6.2 miles, then how many miles are in 45 km?
   - (A) 4.5
   - (B) 7.25
   - (C) 27.9
   - (D) 29.7
   - (E) 62

2. What is the temperature in centigrade (C) if the temperature in Fahrenheit degrees (F) is 140? Formula: $F = \frac{9}{5}C + 32$
   - (A) 14°
   - (B) 36°
   - (C) 60°
   - (D) 144°
   - (E) 284°

BILL FOR PURCHASES	
Science Textbooks	$840
Lab Equipment	$460
Formaldehyde	$320
Teacher's Manuals	$120
TOTAL	$2,220

3. Scholastic Supplies, Inc., sends the bill above to Zither Junior High School. Although the bill includes the cost of science lab workbooks, Scholastic Supplies forgot to list them on the bill. How much did the science lab workbooks cost Zither Junior High School?
   - (A) $480
   - (B) $500
   - (C) $520
   - (D) $560
   - (E) $620

4. Solve for q: $2/9 = 3/q$
   - (A) 3
   - (B) $\frac{7}{2}$
   - (C) $21\frac{1}{2}$
   - (D) $\frac{27}{2}$
   - (E) 18

267

5. Springfield High School's average SAT scores over a five-year period were:

	MATH	VERBAL
1979	520	540
1980	515	532
1981	518	528
1982	510	525
1983	507	510

What was the mean (average) of the verbal SAT scores for the five-year period 1979 through 1983?

(A) 512   (D) 527
(B) 514   (E) 528
(C) 521

6. $4y^3 - y^3 =$
  (A) y^3 (B) $4y$ (C) $3y^2$ (D) $3y^3$ (E) 4

7. $q + 6 - (q - 4) =$
  (A) 10   (D) $2q + 2$
  (B) 2   (E) -2
  (C) $q - 2$

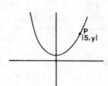

(Note: Figure not drawn to scale)

8. In the graph above, if at point P coordinates are (5, y), find y. Equation of curve is $y = x^2 + 1$
  (A) 1   (B) 5   (C) 25   (D) 26   (E) 36

9. In the equation $(y + 9)/(x + 2) = x^2 - 4$, x *cannot* equal
  (A) -2 (B) 0   (C) 2   (D) 4   (E) 9

> Rossanna knows that a geometric figure is a
> rectangle and that it has sides of 18 and 22.

10. How can Rossanna compute the area of a square that has the same *perimeter* as the rectangle above?
    (A) Add 18 and 22, double this sum, divide by 4, then multiply by 2.
    (B) Add 18 and 22, double this sum, divide by 4, then multiply by 4.
    (C) Add 18 and 22, double this sum, divide by 4, then square the quotient.
    (D) Add 18 and 22, double this sum, then multiply by 4.
    (E) Add twice 18 to twice 22, divide by 2, then square the quotient.

11. Arnold purchases one pair of slacks, a dress shirt, a tie, and a sports coat. The shirt and slacks each cost three times what the tie cost. The sports coat cost twice what the shirt cost. If Arnold paid a total of $156 for all four items, what was the price of the pair of slacks?
    (A) $12   (B) $36   (C) $48   (D) $78   (E) $84

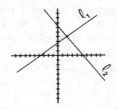

12. In the graph above, what is the solution of the equations of the two lines ℓ_1 and ℓ_2?
    (A) x = 4; y = 2   (D) x = 2; y = 4
    (B) x = 0; y = 2   (E) undetermined
    (C) x = 2; y = 0

13. Solve for x: x − 6 = y + 3
    (A) 3   (B) y + 3   (C) y + 6   (D) y + 9   (E) 9y

14. Tom is just 4 years older than Fran. The total of their ages is 24. What is the equation for finding Fran's age?
    (A) x + 4x = 24   (D) x + (x + 4) = 24
    (B) x + 4 = 24   (E) 4x + 1 = 24
    (C) 4x + x = 24

15. How can Sal compute 20 percent of 90?
    (A) 20 × 90   (D) 90 × 1/5
    (B) 90 ÷ 20   (E) 90 ÷ .20
    (C) 90 ÷ 1/5

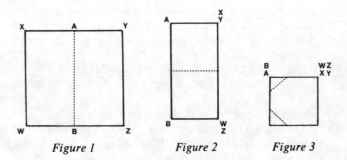

Figure 1   *Figure 2*   *Figure 3*

16. In Figure 1 above, a square piece of paper is folded along dotted line AB so that X is on top of Y and W is on top of Z (Figure 2). The paper is then folded again so that B is on top of A and WZ is on top of XY (Figure 3). Two small corners are cut out of the folded paper as shown in Figure 3. If the paper is unfolded, which of the following could be the result?

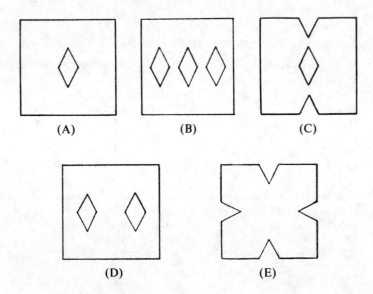

(A)   (B)   (C)

(D)   (E)

17. If cassette tapes cost $2.98 for a package of two tapes, how much change will Roy receive from a twenty dollar bill if he purchases twelve tapes?
    (A) $2.02   (B) $2.12   (C) $2.18   (D) $2.22   (E) $3.02

18. All of the following are equal to the equation $2x + 4 = 3x + 3$ *except*
    (A) $4 = x + 3$ (D) $x = -1$
    (B) $-x + 4 = 3$ (E) $2x = 3x - 1$
    (C) $2x + 1 = 3x$

19. Which of the following is the smallest?
    (A) ⅗   (B) 4/9   (C) 7/13   (D) 23/44   (E) ⅔

20. 210,000 equals
    (A) $(2 \times 10^4) + (1 \times 10^3)$ (D) $(2 \times 10^7) + (1 \times 10^6)$
    (B) $(2 \times 10^5) + (1 \times 10^4)$ (E) $(2 \times 10^8) + (1 \times 10^7)$
    (C) $(2 \times 10^6) + (1 \times 10^5)$

21. The product of two numbers is greater than 0 and equals one of the numbers. Which of the following *must* be one of the numbers?
    (A) -1 (D) a prime number
    (B) 0   (E) a reciprocal
    (C) 1

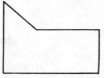

22. The best way to compute the area of the figure above would be to break it in which of the following ways?

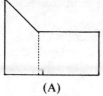 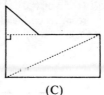

    (A)   (B)   (C)

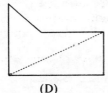

    (D)   (E)

> Holiday bouquets cost the Key Club $2.00
> each. The Key Club sells them for $4.75
> each.

23. Based on the above information, how could Clark determine how many
bouquets must be sold (Q) to make a profit of $82.50?
   (A) Q = $82.50 ÷ $2.00
   (B) Q = $82.50 − $2.00
   (C) Q = $4.75 − $2.00(Q)
   (D) Q = $82.50 ÷ $4.75 − $2.00
   (E) Q = $82.50 ÷ $2.75

24. Round off .14739 to the nearest thousandth.
   (A) .1473   (B) .1474   (C) .147   (D) .148   (E) .15

25. Reuben purchased 12 pounds of apples at 40¢ per pound. To compute the
total price he paid, Reuben used 12 × 40¢ = 480¢. Another simple
method to compute total price could have been
   (A) (6 × 40¢) + (4 × 40¢) + (1 × 40¢) + (1 × 40¢)
   (B) (12 × 10¢) + (12 × 20¢)
   (C) (6 × 20¢) + (6 × 20¢)
   (D) (10 × 40¢) + (2 × 40¢)
   (E) (12 × 50¢) − 10¢

26. Juan approximated 35 × 45 as 40 × 50, but the answer was much too
high. To get a better approximation he should multiply
   (A) 50 × 50   (D) 30 × 40
   (B) 45 × 50   (E) 20 × 30
   (C) 30 × 50

27. If 16 out of 400 dentists polled recommended Popsodint toothpaste, what
percent recommended Popsodint?
   (A) 4   (B) 8   (C) 16   (D) 25   (E) 40

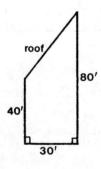

28. The cross-sectional diagram of a downtown office building shows dimensions as on p. 272. What is the length along the roof?
    (A) 30′   (B) 35′   (C) 40′   (D) 50′   (E) 65′

29. Teachers will be assigned special camp duty one day of the week during a seven-day camping trip. If all the days of the week (Monday through Sunday) are tossed into a cap and each teacher chooses one day of the week, what is the probability that the first teacher will randomly select a weekday (Monday through Friday)?
    (A) ¹/₇   (B) ²/₇   (C) ¹/₅   (D) ⁵/₇   (E) ⁵/₂

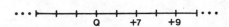

30. On the number line above, what is the point 15 units to the left of point Q?
    (A) 10   (B) 5   (C) 0   (D) −9   (E) −10

31. If the product of two numbers is five more than the sum of the two numbers, which of the following equations could represent the relationship?
    (A) AB + 5 = A + B   (D) A/B = 5 + A + B
    (B) 5AB = A + B   (E) A(B) + 5 = A + B + 5
    (C) AB = A + B + 5

32. Which of the following is determined by division?

    I. the price of car A if it costs six times the price of car B
    II. the difference in temperature between two cities
    III. the number of yards in 39 feet

    (A) I   (B) II   (C) III   (D) I and II   (E) I and III

STARS ON HOLLYWOOD AND VINE

** ** ** ** ** ** ** ** ** *
** ** ** ** ** ** ** ** ** *

33. According to the graph above, how many stars are on the pavements of Hollywood Boulevard and Vine Streets? (Key: each ** = 10 stars)
    (A) 45   (B) 47.5   (C) 90   (D) 92   (E) 95

34. A Spifmobile is selling at a 30% discount off its sticker price. Its sticker price is $8,000. What is its new selling price?
    (A) $2,400   (D) $7,970
    (B) $5,600   (E) $7,976
    (C) $6,600

35. Harmon's new sportscar averages 35 miles per each gallon of gasoline. Assuming Harmon is able to maintain his average miles per gallon, how far can he drive on 12 gallons of gas?
    (A) almost 3 miles   (D) 420 miles
    (B) 42 miles   (E) 700 miles
    (C) 350 miles

36. A parallelogram has two sides of dimensions 9 and 7. What would be the side of a square with the same perimeter?
    (A) 32   (B) 18   (C) 14   (D) 8   (E) 4

37. It is estimated that at a picnic each adult will drink ⅕ of a gallon of lemonade. How many gallons of lemonade should be brought to the picnic if 28 people, all adults, are expected to attend?
    (A) 3   (D) between 5 and 6
    (B) between 3 and 4   (E) more than 6
    (C) 5

38. If 150 family members attend the annual open house and there are more adults than children, which of the following could be the number of children?
    (A) 72.5   (B) 74   (C) 75   (D) 75.5   (E) 77

39. If it costs 82¢ to make a student chalk slate, how many such slates can be produced for $75?
    (A) 9   (B) 90   (C) 91   (D) 92   (E) 100

40. In a school of 280, only 35 students attend graduation. What percent of the school population attends graduation?
    (A) 12.5   (B) 18.5   (C) 22.5   (D) 25   (E) 32.5

41. If John can type twenty pages in four hours, how many hours will it take him to type fifty pages?
    (A) 5   (B) 6   (C) 8   (D) 9   (E) 10

42. Thomas purchased 20 goldfish at 85¢ each and then bought 8 bags of goldfish food, also at 85¢ each. What would be the simplest way to compute his total amount spent?
    (A) 20 × 85¢ + 4 × 85¢ + 2 × 85¢ + 2 × 85¢
    (B) 28 × 85¢
    (C) 8 × 20 × 85¢
    (D) 20 × 85¢
    (E) 850¢ × 2

43. In Hicksville's Little League, team A has twice as many victories as team B, team C has 5 fewer victories than team A, and team D has 4 more victories than team B. If total victories of all 4 teams equal 29, how many victories does team D have?
    (A) 5   (B) 9   (C) 10   (D) 12   (E) 14

44. Ernie cut a yardstick into two pieces, the larger piece being six inches more than the smaller. How could Ernie compute the size of the smaller piece, x?
    (A) $x + 6 = 36$ (D) $2x - 6 = 36$
    (B) $2x = 36$ (E) $2x + 6 = 30$
    (C) $x + x + 6 = 36$

45 Solve for p: $7p + 9 = 24$
    (A) $13/7$ (B) $15/7$ (C) $24/9$ (D) 6   (E) 8

$$\sqrt{(9 - y)^2} = 9 - y$$

46. In the equation above, which of the following *cannot* be the value of y?
    (A) -10 (B) -1 (C) 0   (D) 1   (E) 10

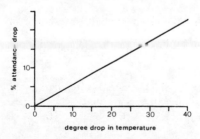

degree drop in temperature

47. According to the graph above, if temperature falls 35 degrees, what percentage will school attendance drop?
    (A) 10   (B) 20   (C) 30   (D) 40   (E) 50

48. George scored an average of 80% on three tests. What score must he get on the fourth test to bring his average to 85%?

    (A) 85%   (B) 88%   (C) 90%   (D) 95%   (E) 100%

49. Maria needed to compute 30% of 50. To get a correct answer, all of the following will work *except*

    (A) .30 × 50   (D) 50 ÷ 10/3
    (B) .50 × 30   (E) 50 ÷ 3/10
    (C) 3/10 × 50

50. 750 times 45 equals P. Therefore 750 times 44 equals

    (A) P − 45   (D) 44P
    (B) P − 750   (E) 750P
    (C) P − 1

STOP: IF YOU FINISH BEFORE TIME IS CALLED, CHECK YOUR WORK ON THIS SECTION ONLY. DO NOT WORK ON ANY OTHER SECTION IN THE TEST.

SECTION III: ESSAY WRITING

Time: 60 Minutes
2 Essays

DIRECTIONS

In this section, you will have 60 minutes to plan and write two essays, one for each topic given. You may use the bottom of this and the following page to organize and plan your essay before you begin writing. You should plan your time wisely. Read each topic carefully to make sure that you are properly addressing the issue or situation. YOU MUST WRITE ON THE SPECIFIED TOPIC. AN ESSAY ON ANOTHER TOPIC WILL NOT BE ACCEPTABLE.

The two essay questions included in this section are designed to give you an opportunity to write clearly and effectively. Use specific examples whenever appropriate to aid in supporting your ideas. Keep in mind that the quality of your writing is much more important than the quantity.

Your essays are to be written on the special answer sheets provided. No other paper may be used. Your writing should be neat and legible. Because you have only a limited amount of space in which to write, please do NOT skip lines, do NOT write excessively large, and do NOT leave wide margins.

Remember, use the bottom of this and the following page for any organizational notes you may wish to make.

Topic 1

Institutions can often play a major role in individuals' lives. Choose one such institution that has been a major influence in your life and describe its impact on you.

FOR EACH ESSAY, USE TWO SIDES OF AN 8½″ BY 11″ LINED SHEET OF PAPER.

Topic 2

Some people believe that the United States places more importance on the sight and sound media (film, television, radio, etc.) than on the printed word.

Present your views, either agreeing or disagreeing that reading has become less significant to Americans.

FOR EACH ESSAY, USE TWO SIDES OF AN 8½″ BY 11″ LINED SHEET OF PAPER.

ANSWER KEY FOR PRACTICE TEST 3

SECTION I READING COMPREHENSION			SECTION II MATHEMATICS		
1. D	18. B	35. A	1. C	18. D	35. D
2. A	19. C	36. A	2. C	19. B	36. D
3. D	20. A	37. A	3. A	20. B	37. D
4. D	21. E	38. B	4. D	21. C	38. B
5. D	22. E	39. E	5. D	22. E	39. C
6. C	23. E	40. A	6. D	23. E	40. A
7. B	24. D	41. E	7. A	24. C	41. E
8. C	25. A	42. C	8. D	25. D	42. B
9. C	26. C	43. D	9. A	26. C	43. B
10. D	27. D	44. A	10. C	27. A	44. C
11. B	28. C	45. E	11. B	28. D	45. B
12. D	29. E	46. D	12. D	29. D	46. E
13. C	30. C	47. E	13. D	30. E	47. B
14. D	31. D	48. A	14. D	31. C	48. E
15. E	32. C	49. D	15. D	32. C	49. E
16. B	33. E	50. D	16. C	33. E	50. B
17. C	34. D		17. B	34. B	

SCORING YOUR CBEST PRACTICE TEST 3

To score your CBEST Practice Test 3, total the number of correct responses for each section of the test separately. Do not subtract any points for questions attempted but missed, as there is no penalty for guessing. The score for each section is then scaled from 20 to 80. (About 70% right is a passing score.)

ANALYZING YOUR TEST RESULTS

The charts on the following page should be used to carefully analyze your results and spot your strengths and weaknesses. The complete process of analyzing each subject area and each individual question should be completed for this Practice Test. These results should be reexamined for trends in types of error (repeated errors) or poor results in specific subject areas. THIS REEXAMINATION AND ANALYSIS IS OF TREMENDOUS IMPORTANCE FOR EFFECTIVE TEST PREPARATION.

PRACTICE TEST 3: SUBJECT AREA ANALYSIS SHEET

	Possible	Completed	Right	Wrong
Reading Comprehension	50			
Mathematics	50			
TOTAL	100			

ANALYSIS—TALLY SHEET FOR QUESTIONS MISSED

One of the most important parts of test preparation is analyzing WHY you missed a question so that you can reduce the number of mistakes. Now that you have taken Practice Test 3 and corrected your answers, carefully tally your mistakes by marking them in the proper column.

	REASON FOR MISTAKE			
	Total Missed	Simple Mistake	Misread Problem	Lack of Knowledge
Reading Comprehension				
Mathematics				
TOTAL				

Reviewing the above data should help you determine WHY you are missing certain questions. Now that you have pinpointed the type of error, focus on avoiding your most common type.

ESSAY TOPIC 1 CHECKLIST

Use this checklist to evaluate your Topic 1 essay.

Diagnosis/Prescription for Timed Writing Exercise

A good essay will:

_____	address the assignment
	be well focused
_____	be well organized
	smooth transitions between paragraphs
	coherent, unified
_____	be well developed
	points adequately covered and supported
_____	be grammatically sound (only minor flaws)
	correct sentence structure
	correct punctuation
	use of standard written English
_____	use language skillfully
	variety of sentence types
	variety of words
_____	be legible
	clear handwriting
	neat

ESSAY TOPIC 2 CHECKLIST

Use this checklist to evaluate your Topic 2 essay.

Diagnosis/Prescription for Timed Writing Exercise

A good essay will:

_____ address the assignment
           be well focused
_____ be well organized
           smooth transitions between paragraphs
           coherent, unified
_____ be well developed
           points adequately covered and supported
_____ be grammatically sound (only minor flaws)
           correct sentence structure
           correct punctuation
           use of standard written English
_____ use language skillfully
           variety of sentence types
           variety of words
_____ be legible
           clear handwriting
           neat

ANSWERS AND COMPLETE EXPLANATIONS
FOR PRACTICE TEST 3

SECTION I: READING COMPREHENSION

1. (D) The author's entire argument is based on the recent studies indicating a downward trend in aptitude test scores. By extension, the author must assume that such studies are accurate.

2. (A) The term *bowl of oatmeal* is used sarcastically to condemn the actions of the City Council. Choice (B) is not correct as the situation is certainly not *tragic*.

3. (D) Trends showing that within two years a single-family dwelling will be unaffordable by the average family indicate that not only must housing costs be going up, but average family income will not meet the increased cost of housing.

4. (D) Both statements I and III weaken the author's argument. Statement I, if true, suggests that, in fact, there will be affordable single-family homes for the average family. Statement III suggests that average families may find it difficult to afford renting an apartment, thus weakening the author's final sentence.

5. (D) Both statements I and II are assumed by the author. First, the present trend (rise in housing cost) will continue, and second, families will turn to renting apartments (instead of, say, buying mobile homes or condominiums).

6. (C) In both the introductory and final paragraphs the writer is concerned with attacks on the First Amendment, and throughout the article emphasizes this with a detailed look at what he or she thinks is an attack on a particular group, the press, that is guaranteed a certain amount of freedom by that amendment. Because of this, choices (A) and (B) are much too broad, and choices (D) and (E) are supporting ideas rather than principal ideas; *slander and libel laws* and *Big Brother in government* are mentioned only briefly.

7. (B) The second paragraph says a *6–3 ruling*. So if two justices change their minds we would have a 4–5 ruling for the other side.

8. (C) The last sentence of the second paragraph says that reporters *now face a challenge to the privacy of their minds,* and the last sentence in the passage is a statement against *mind-control.* All other choices are not explicitly supported by material in the passage.

9. (C) As is stated in the fourth paragraph, actual malice is *with knowledge that the statements were false, or with reckless disregard of whether they were true or not.*

10. (D) As is often the case, the first sentence states the main idea of the passage. Choice (A) is incorrect, both because it is too narrow and because the passage tells the reader only that Kitty Litter is made from clay and does not tell how it is produced. Choice (B) is also too narrow. Choice (C) is incorrect because only one sentence mentions this fact. Choice (E) is incorrect because the article does not describe a method for preventing fires.

11. (B) The *they* in this sentence refers to *cats* in the first sentence of the paragraph. That first sentence describes cats watching the *hustle and bustle* with a sense of *superiority*. Given this information, we may infer that the grin described in the last sentence comes from watching the *hustle and bustle* of human antics, in this case the antics of the U.S. government making itself a nuisance. Notice that all choices except (B) may be eliminated, if only because each describes cats *laughing* instead of grinning.

12. (D) The tone of the author concerning Vieira is certainly positive but not so much as to be idolatrous or spiritual. *Admiring* is the best choice.

13. (C) Since the fewer number of accidents has not resulted in lower premiums, one suggestion of the passage is that the insurance companies are pocketing the savings rather than passing them on to the consumer. Thus the author implies that insurance companies are taking advantage of drivers.

14. (D) The statement initially assumes that *it is true there are two sides to every question,* or every question may be interpreted in more than one way.

15. (E) Both statements I and II are true. Using the example of flypaper is an analogy; that it makes a big difference which side the fly chooses indicates the importance of choice. The statement does not, however, point out the ways of getting stuck on a question.

16. (B) According to the chart, the largest *bonus discount* for Extra Firm mattresses is 75.00.

17. (C) According to the chart, the *sale price* of both the Regal, King, and the Royal Satin, Queen, is 699.00.

18. (B) "On this 150th anniversary of his birth, Twain . . ."

19. (C) "We have ground the manhood out of them and the shame is ours, not theirs; and we should pay for it."

20. (A) The irony and vernacular in *The Adventures of Huckleberry Finn* may have confused some readers and led to a *misunderstanding* of Twain's feelings about slavery and issues of race.

21. (E) Choice (C) is incorrect because this is the 150th anniversary of his birth according to the passage.

22. (E) According to the passage, Pudd'nhead Wilson was *eccentric but clever.*

23. (E) If the author concludes that technology is a curse because it results in widespread unemployment, then necessarily the author assumes that widespread unemployment is bad.

24. (D) "There is life, not death . . . love, not bitterness in the paintings."

25. (A) The next-to-last paragraph states all of the choices except (A).

26. (C) "Enduring themes" in his paintings and "through Chagall's paintings . . . dreams survive" indicate choice (C).

27. (D) The Eiffel tower in the painting indicates that the artist once lived in Paris.

28. (C) *Don't hang crepe, but strew flowers* means *don't mourn, but celebrate his life.*

29. (E) According to the graph, Boston had almost all night game attendance (about 90%) compared with very small day game attendance (about 10%).

30. (C) Chicago and San Diego had the largest combined day game attendance.

31. (D) The brief passage introduces the possibility that life may have begun in clay instead of in water as scientists have believed. Choices (B), (C), and (E) are much too strong to be supported by the passage, and choice (A) refers to the earth instead of to life.

32. (C) According to the passage, the auroras occur because of solar wind pushing against the Earth's magnetic field, causing an electric power supply. In choice (B), *caused by* makes the choice incorrect.

33. (E) The auroras occur during these months; Earth's tail is always present.

34. (D) Since Earth's tail is *similar to those of comets*, they are probably also composed of electrically charged particles.

35. (A) The first part of the quotation begins, *What history teaches is this* . . . , implying that we have something to learn from history. The second part goes on to state that we *never learned anything from history*. This is a contradiction using irony.

36. (A) Beatty argues that cutting even six minutes from his film destroys its artistic integrity. A similar and supporting line of argument would say that deleting parts of Beethoven's music or Shakespeare's plays would do the same.

37. (A) The final sentence of the passage indicates that the author supports Beatty's demands. Only choice (A) reflects this point of view.

38. (B) The thrust of the passage is the battle between Beatty and ABC for the final cut of the film *Reds*.

39. (E) Just because one may err does not mean one should not commit to a decision. That is best stated in choice (E).

40. (A) Choice (A) best summarizes the passage, citing two support points for the main idea—that California's roads have deteriorated. Choice (E) is incomplete and the *over three-quarters* is correct only in reference to the state's country roads.

41. (E) All the other choices are mentioned in the passage except the demand for new highways.

42. (C) The passage suggests that Adam Smith considered statesmen in a negative way; thus, you can determine from context that *wont* is probably used to mean *accustomed*.

43. (D) In promoting the spending of state funds to advertise California's tourist attractions, the author assumes such tourism will result in more income for the state. Choice (B) is incorrect because, while increased tourism may increase revenue, it cannot not be assumed that such an increase will decrease the competition from other states.

44. (A) Implied by the passage is the belief that the campaign, if effective, will bring in many times in tourist revenue what the advertising initially cost.

45. (E) *States* and *nations* are used in the passage synonymously as *countries* or independently governed territories.

46. (D) The passage is probably intended for those about to read *The Lord of the Rings*.

47. (E) To fully appreciate a work such as *The Lord of the Rings*, one should be familiar with its historical underpinnings and the *epic tradition*, a prescribed path which the story will follow.

48. (A) As does the hero in other epics, the hero in *The Lord of the Rings* will return home after surviving many hardships.

49. (D) As the passage is written for people about to read *The Lord of the Rings*, it is thus assumed that they will go on to read the epic.

50. (D) Since *The Lord of the Rings* satisfies the requirements of the epic tradition, a reader anticipating such elements will not be disappointed.

SECTION II: MATHEMATICS

1. (C) One way to solve this problem is to set up a ratio: 10 km is to 6.2 miles as 45 km is to how many miles? This is expressed in mathematical terms as:

$$\frac{10 \text{ km}}{6.2 \text{ m}} = \frac{45 \text{ km}}{x}$$

Cross multiplying gives

$$10x = 6.2 \times 45$$
$$10x = 279$$

Dividing both sides by 10 gives

$$\frac{10x}{10} = \frac{279}{10}$$

$$x = 27.9$$

Another method is to realize that 45 km is exactly 4½ times 10 km. Therefore, the number of miles in 45 km must be 4½ times the number of miles in 10 km, or 4½ times 6.2. Thus 4.5 × 6.2 = 27.9.

2. (C) One method of solving this problem is algebraically.

$$F = \tfrac{9}{5}C + 32$$
$$140 = \tfrac{9}{5}C + 32$$
$$140 - 32 = \tfrac{9}{5}C$$
$$108 = \tfrac{9}{5}C$$
$$(\tfrac{5}{9})108 = C$$
$$60 = C$$

Another, and perhaps simpler, method is to plug in answer choices and see which choice works in the equation. Answer choice (C) successfully completes the equation.

$$140 = \tfrac{9}{5}(60) + 32$$

3. (A) The four listed items total $1,740. Therefore, by subtracting from the listed total of $2,220, we can see that the missing item must have cost $480. $2,220 − $1,740 = $480.

290

4. (D) $2/9 = 3/q$. Cross multiplying gives $2q = 27$. Dividing both sides by 2 gives

$$\frac{2q}{2} = \frac{27}{2}$$

$$q = 27/2$$

Remember to check for this answer (in improper fraction form) in the answer choices before automatically changing to a mixed number ($13\frac{1}{2}$).

5. (D) The total of the five verbal SAT scores is 2,635. Dividing that total by 5 (the number of scores) gives 527 as the average.

6. (D) Remember that y^3 actually means $1y^3$.

$$4y^3 - y^3 = 4y^3 - 1y^3 = 3y^3$$

7. (A)
$$\begin{array}{r} q + 6 \\ -\quad q - 4 \\ \hline \end{array}$$

Note that q minus q will yield a remainder of 0. That leaves the operation

$$\begin{array}{r} +6 \\ -\quad -4 \\ \hline \end{array}$$

Remember that subtracting a negative number is equivalent to adding a positive number.

$$\begin{array}{r} +6 \\ -\quad -4 \\ \hline \end{array} = \begin{array}{r} + \\ \\ \end{array}\begin{array}{r} +\ 6 \\ +\ 4 \\ \hline +10 \end{array}$$

8. (D) Note that one point on the curve is $(5, y)$. Therefore at that point P, the x coordinate equals 5. By plugging the value for x, 5, into the equation of that curve, we can find y.

$$y = x^2 + 1$$
$$y = (5)^2 + 1$$
$$y = 25 + 1 = 26$$

9. (A) The denominator of a fraction can never equal zero or the fraction is undefined. Therefore $x + 2 \neq 0$. Subtracting 2 from both sides of the equation

$$x + 2 - 2 \neq 0 - 2$$
$$x \neq -2$$

x cannot equal -2.

10. (C) Since the figure is a rectangle, its opposite sides are equal. To find its perimeter, first add the two sides, then double the sum (or double each of the sides and add the results).

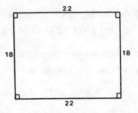

Now to determine the side of a square with the same perimeter, simply divide by 4, since the side of a square is ¼ its perimeter. Finally, to find the area of the square, multiply its side times itself (square it).

11. (B) If we call the price of the tie x, then the price of the shirt is 3x, the price of the slacks is 3x, and the price of the coat is twice the shirt, or 6x. Totaling the x's we get 13x. Since the total spent was $156, 13x = $156. Dividing both sides by 13 gives

$$\frac{13x}{13} = \frac{\$156}{13}$$

$$x = \$12$$

Therefore the price of the pair of slacks, 3x, is 3($12) = $36.

12. (D) The solution of two lines can be determined by the coordinates of the point at which the lines intersect. Lines ℓ_1 and ℓ_2 intersect at (2, 4). Therefore, x = 2 and y = 4.

13. (D) $x - 6 = y + 3$. Adding 6 to both sides gives

$$x - 6 + 6 = y + 3 + 6$$
$$x = y + 9$$

14. (D) If Tom is 4 years older than Fran, if we call Fran's age x, Tom's age must be 4 years more, or x + 4. Therefore, since the total of their ages is 24, Fran's age + Tom's age = 24.

$$x + (x + 4) = 24$$

15. (D) Twenty percent of 90 may be written as .20 × 90 or 20/100 × 90. Note that 20/100 is reduced to 1/5, which is answer choice (D).

16. (C) Take some scissors and a piece of paper and try it.

17. (B) To purchase twelve tapes, Roy must buy six packages. At $2.98 per package, he spends $17.88. His change from a twenty dollar bill will be $20.00 − $17.88 = $2.12.

18. (D) Solving the equation 2x + 4 = 3x + 3, first subtract 2x from each side.

$$2x + 4 - 2x = 3x + 3 - 2x$$
$$4 = x + 3$$

Now subtract 3 from both sides.

$$4 - 3 = x + 3 - 3$$
$$1 = x$$

By plugging in the above value of x (that is, 1) for each of the answer choices, we find that 1 satisfies all the equations *except* choice (D).

$$\text{Does } x = -1? \text{ No.}$$
$$1 \neq -1$$

Therefore (D) is the correct answer.

19. (B) Note that all choices except (B) are larger than $\frac{1}{2}$. Choice (B), $\frac{4}{9}$, is smaller than $\frac{1}{2}$.

20. (B) 210,000 is equivalent to $(2 \times 10^5) + (1 \times 10^4)$. A fast way of figuring this is to count the number of places to the right of each digit that is not zero. For instance,

2̲10,000	Note that there are 5 places to the right of the 2, thus 2×10^5.
21̲0,000	There are 4 places to the right of the 1, thus 1×10^4.

So 210,000 may also be written $(2 \times 10^5) + (1 \times 10^4)$.

21. (C) If the product of two numbers equals one of the numbers, then $(x)(y) = x$. If this product is more than 0, neither of the numbers may be zero. Therefore y must be 1: $(x)(1) = x$.

22. (E) The best way to compute the area of the figure is to divide it into as few parts as possible, making each part a simple shape whose area is easily calculated (for instance, a triangle, rectangle, or square). Choice (E) divides the shape into a rectangle and a triangle.

23. (E) The sale of each bouquet yields a profit of $2.75 (since each costs $2.00 and is sold for $4.75). Therefore the number of bouquets necessary to be sold to yield a total of $82.50 can be determined by dividing $82.50 by the profit from each sale, $2.75. Answer (D) is incorrect because in the order of operations division takes precedence over subtraction (is performed first).

24. (C) Rounding .14739 to the nearest thousandth means first looking at the digit one place to the right of the thousandths place: .14739. Since that digit is 4 or less, simply drop it. (There is no need to replace with zeros because they are not needed to the right of a decimal point.)

25. (D) Noting that 12 can be expressed as $(10 + 2)$, another way to easily compute 12×40 is $(10 \times 40) + (2 \times 40)$.

26. (C) Note that only choice (C) raises one of the numbers by five while it lowers the other number by five. This will give the best approximation of the five choices.

27. (A) Sixteen out of 400 may be expressed as a percent as 16/400. Dividing 16 by 400 gives us .04, or 4%.

28. (D) By drawing a line which divides the diagram into two parts—a rectangle and a right triangle—the length of the roof can be determined.

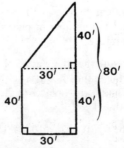

The upper triangular section has a base of 30′ and a height of 40′. Using the Pythagorean theorem for right triangles we get:

$$30^2 + 40^2 = (\text{length along roof})^2$$
$$900 + 1{,}600 = (\text{length along roof})^2$$
$$2{,}500 = (\text{length along roof})^2$$

Taking the square roots of both sides gives

$$50 = \text{length along roof}$$

(You may also recognize the sides of the right triangle as being in a 3–4–5 ratio, which is commonly found in right triangles.)

29. (D) Using the probability formula

$$\text{probability} = \frac{\text{number of "lucky" chances}}{\text{total number of chances}}$$

The chance of choosing a weekday = 5 weekdays/7 total days = 5/7

30. (E) Note that since there is a mark between $+7$ and $+9$, that mark must equal $+8$. Thus each mark equals 1. Counting back, point Q is at $+5$. Therefore fifteen units to the left of $+5$ would be $+5 - 15 = -10$.

31. (C) The *product of two numbers* indicates the numbers must be multiplied together. Their *sum* means "add." Therefore,

$$\underbrace{\text{the product of two numbers}}_{(A)(B)} \underbrace{\text{equals}}_{=} \underbrace{\text{five more than their sum.}}_{A + B + 5}$$

32. (C) Only III is determined by division ($39 \div 3$). The others are determined by multiplication ($6 \times B$) and subtraction, respectively.

33. (E) Since each cluster of symbols represents 10 stars, $9\frac{1}{2}$ clusters must equal 95 stars.

34. (B) Thirty percent off the original price equals a discount of $(.30)(\$8{,}000) = \$2{,}400$. Therefore, the new selling price is $\$8{,}000 - \$2{,}400 = \$5{,}600$.

35. (D) Since Harmon's sportscar averages 35 miles for each gallon of gas, on 12 gallons he'll be able to drive 12×35, or 420 miles.

36. (D) Remember that a parallelogram has equal opposite sides. Therefore its sides are 9, 7, 9, and 7. Its perimeter then is 32. If a square has the

same perimeter, one of its sides must be 1/4 its perimeter (since the four sides of a square are equal). One-fourth of 32 is 8.

37. (D) If each adult drinks 1/5 of a gallon of lemonade, one gallon is consumed by each 5 adults. Since 28 adults attend the picnic, 28/5 = slightly over 5 gallons.

38. (B) Note that if there were an equal number of adults and children, there would be 75 of each. Since there are more adults than children, the number of children must be lower than 75. Since (A), a mixed number, is a ridiculous answer, of the choices given only (B) could be the number of children.

39. (C) To determine the number of slates costing 82¢ each that can be purchased for $75, simply divide: $75.00 \div .82 = 91.4+$. Note that since slates cannot be a fractional answer, 91 is the answer.

40. (A) To determine the percent of the school population that attends graduation

$$\frac{\text{part}}{\text{total}} = \frac{35}{280}$$

Dividing 35 by 280 gives .125, or 12.5%.

41. (E) There are several quick methods of solving this problem. As in question 1 a ratio can be set up.

$$\frac{20 \text{ pgs}}{4 \text{ hrs}} = \frac{50 \text{ pgs}}{x}$$

Cross multiplying will give 10 hours for the answer. Or determining John's hourly rate (5 pages per hour) tells us he will need 10 hours to type 50 pages.

42. (B) Note that a total of 28 items were purchased, each costing 85¢. Therefore the simplest way to compute the total amount spent would be $28 \times 85¢$.

43. (B) If team B's victories are called x, then team A must have 2x victories, team C must have $(2x - 5)$ victories, and team D must have $(x + 4)$ victories. All together these total $6x - 1$. We are told that the total equals 29 victories. Thus,

$$6x - 1 = 29$$
$$6x = 30$$
$$x = 5$$

Therefore team D has $(x + 4)$ victories, or $(5 + 4) = 9$.

44. **(C)** If we call the smaller piece x, then the larger piece (6 inches bigger) must be $x + 6$. Since the two pieces together equal a yardstick,

$$x + (x + 6) = 36$$
$$x + x + 6 = 36$$

45. **(B)** Solving for p, first subtract 9 from both sides.

$$7p + 9 = 24$$
$$7p + 9 - 9 = 24 - 9$$
$$7p = 15$$

Now divide both sides by 7.

$$\frac{7p}{7} = \frac{15}{7}$$

$$p = 15/7$$

46. **(E)** Since we are dealing only with *real* numbers, *imaginary* numbers (negative square roots) are not permitted. Using 10 for a value of y will give a negative square root.

$$\sqrt{(9 - 10)^2} = 9 - 10$$
$$\sqrt{(-1)^2} = -1$$

Since such negative square roots are not allowed, y may *not* equal 10.

47. **(B)** Note that on the graph a 35 degree drop in temperature on the line correlates with a 20% attendance drop (the fourth slash up the graph).

48. **(E)** So far George has averaged 80% on each of three tests. Therefore his *total* points scored equals three times 80, or 240 points. In order to average 85% for four tests, George needs a total point score of four times 85, or 340 points. Since George presently is 100 points short of 340, he needs to get 100 points, or 100%, on the fourth test.

49. **(E)** Note that 30% of 50 may be expressed several ways: $.30 \times 50$; $3/10 \times 50$. Whichever way it is expressed, it will still total 15. The only answer choice that does not total 15 is choice (E), which totals $166\frac{2}{3}$.

50. (B) Drawing a picture may be helpful.

750 times 45 equals P.

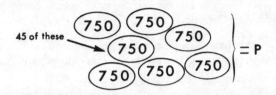

Note that 750 times 44 is the same as above but with one less circle. Therefore, it equals P − 750. If this is still difficult to understand, think in terms of dollars. You are paid $750 each week for 45 weeks. Therefore your total pay (P) is $750 times 45. But suppose that you work only 44 weeks. Then your total pay will be P − one week's pay, or P − $750.

FINAL PREPARATION: "The Final Touches"

1. Make sure that you are familiar with the testing center location and nearby parking facilities.
2. The last week of preparation should be spent on a general review of key concepts, test-taking strategies, and techniques.
3. Don't cram the night before the exam. It is a waste of time!
4. Arrive in plenty of time at the testing center.
5. Remember to bring the proper materials: identification, admission ticket, three or four sharpened Number 2 pencils, an eraser, several ballpoint pens, and a watch.
6. Start off crisply, working the questions you know first, and then coming back and trying to answer the others.
7. Try to eliminate one or more choices before you guess, but make sure you fill in all of the answers. There is no penalty for guessing.
8. Mark in reading passages, underline key words, write out important information, and make notations on diagrams. Take advantage of being permitted to write in the test booklet.
9. Make sure that you are answering "what is being asked" and that your answer is reasonable.
10. Cross out incorrect choices immediately, this will keep you from reconsidering a choice that you have already eliminated.
11. Using the TWO SUCCESSFUL OVERALL APPROACHES (p. 7) is the key to getting the questions right that you should get right—resulting in a good score on the CBEST exam.